Human Well-Being Research

C000040254

Series Editors

Richard J. Estes, School of Social Policy & Practice, University of Pennsylvania, Philadelphia, PA, USA

M. Joseph Sirgy , Department of Marketing, Virginia Polytechnic Institute & State University, Blacksburg, VA, USA

This series includes policy-focused books on the role of the public and private sectors in advancing quality of life and well-being. It creates a dialogue between well-being scholars and public policy makers. Well-being theory, research and practice are essentially interdisciplinary in nature and embrace contributions from all disciplines within the social sciences. With the exception of leading economists, the policy relevant contributions of social scientists are widely scattered and lack the coherence and integration needed to more effectively inform the actions of policy makers. Contributions in the series focus on one more of the following four aspects of well-being and public policy:

- Discussions of the public policy and well-being focused on particular nations and worldwide regions
- Discussions of the public policy and well-being in specialized sectors of policy making such as health, education, work, social welfare, housing, transportation, use of leisure time
- Discussions of public policy and well-being associated with particular population groups such as women, children and youth, the aged, persons with disabilities and vulnerable populations
- Special topics in well-being and public policy such as technology and well-being, terrorism and well-being, infrastructure and well-being.

This series was initiated, in part, through funds provided by the Halloran Philanthropies of West Conshohocken, Pennsylvania, USA. The commitment of the Halloran Philanthropies is to "inspire, innovate and accelerate sustainable social interventions that promote human well-being." The series editors and Springer acknowledge Harry Halloran, Tony Carr and Audrey Selian for their contributions in helping to make the series a reality.

More information about this series at http://www.springer.com/series/15692

Isidro Maya Jariego

Community Prevention of Child Labor

Evidence-based Practices to Promote the Psychological Well-being of Minors

 Springer

Isidro Maya Jariego
Departamento de Psicología Social
Universidad de Sevilla
Sevilla, Spain

ISSN 2522-5367   ISSN 2522-5375   (electronic)
Human Well-Being Research and Policy Making
ISBN 978-3-030-70812-2   ISBN 978-3-030-70810-8   (eBook)
https://doi.org/10.1007/978-3-030-70810-8

© The Editor(s) (if applicable) and The Author(s), under exclusive license to Springer Nature Switzerland AG 2021
This work is subject to copyright. All rights are solely and exclusively licensed by the Publisher, whether the whole or part of the material is concerned, specifically the rights of translation, reprinting, reuse of illustrations, recitation, broadcasting, reproduction on microfilms or in any other physical way, and transmission or information storage and retrieval, electronic adaptation, computer software, or by similar or dissimilar methodology now known or hereafter developed.
The use of general descriptive names, registered names, trademarks, service marks, etc. in this publication does not imply, even in the absence of a specific statement, that such names are exempt from the relevant protective laws and regulations and therefore free for general use.
The publisher, the authors, and the editors are safe to assume that the advice and information in this book are believed to be true and accurate at the date of publication. Neither the publisher nor the authors or the editors give a warranty, expressed or implied, with respect to the material contained herein or for any errors or omissions that may have been made. The publisher remains neutral with regard to jurisdictional claims in published maps and institutional affiliations.

This Springer imprint is published by the registered company Springer Nature Switzerland AG.
The registered company address is: Gewerbestrasse 11, 6330 Cham, Switzerland

This book is dedicated to Sandra, Sara, and José Antonio, who are always my company, no matter if it is times of closeness, times of physical distance, or times of "social distance." With them I also shared the lives of working children.

Preface

In May 2016, we celebrated the completion of the "Edúcame Primero Perú" (Educate Me First Peru) program with the delivery of a set of children's books to those schools that had participated in the intervention. Accompanied by Jorge Palacio, professor at the Universidad del Norte in Barranquilla (Colombia), and by Esperanza Márquez, coordinator of the cooperation project in the field, we followed the route of the Pan-American Highway, as it passes through Lima, to cross the extensive metropolitan region from north to south. On the same day, we visited schools in the Jicamarca highlands, in Villa El Salvador, and in the vicinity of Pachacámac.

This approach to the city is an eye-opening experience in itself. Tourists who visit the colonial heritage of the Cercado de Lima or who enjoy the comforts of the modern city in the districts of Barranco, San Isidro, and Miraflores acquire only a partial view of the capital of Peru. On the other hand, visiting the "slums" and human settlements that surround Lima brings you closer to the true nature of one of the largest cities in Latin America. When you get to know the periphery, you become aware that it is a city located in the middle of the desert, which continues to grow with alluviums of the population that occupy urban space in a disorganized manner, and which is crossed, from north to south and from east to west, by inequality.

We had started planning the book delivery about 2 months before. First, we contacted a Spanish publisher with distribution in Latin America, so that the purchase of books could be made directly in Lima. Then we organized reading workshops, taking advantage of the fact that the participating schools had just joined the "Plan Lector en la Escuela Peruana" (reading plan in the Peruvian school), and we agreed with the directors that the books would be deposited in the library of each school. Some school that did not have a library prepared a reading room for the occasion. The fact of concluding with a delivery of books to the children was an enormously symbolic act (although in practice in some cases it meant providing the centers with resources that they lacked). With this, we wanted to provide an adequate closure to a psycho-educational intervention for the prevention of child labor in which the schools had been participating for 2 academic years.

Article 32 of the Convention on the Rights of the Child, ratified by the United Nations in 1989, establishes "the right of the child to be protected from economic exploitation and from performing any work that is likely to be hazardous or to interfere with the child's education, or to be harmful to the child's health or physical, mental, spiritual, moral or social development." When we began to open the boxes of books with Jorge and Esperanza, surrounded by excited children who literally ripped them out of our hands, we felt that this was a concrete representation of abstract ideas about the value of education and child protection. The "Edúcame Primero" program consisted precisely of empowering the social-emotional capacities of children and implementing actions to promote academic performance and prevent school drop-out. There is no doubt that promoting access to quality education is a powerful alternative to child labor.

Since 2010 the Laboratory of Personal Networks and Communities (LRPC) of the University of Seville has participated in the implementation of child labor prevention programs in Colombia, Peru, and Honduras. This has allowed us to accumulate some experience on the adaptation of preventive programs in different sociocultural contexts. As we will try to demonstrate throughout this book, institutional and community factors are decisive in obtaining positive results. As the case of the "Edúcame Primero" program shows, in addition to having evidence-based practices, effective prevention depends on the families, local communities, and political context in which the intervention is developed.

Children, parents, and teachers are the real protagonists of this book. The fight against child labor means having time reserved for education and learning, which contributes to the balanced development of children. As we will see in the following pages, a large part of these experiences takes place in schools and families, as well as in the interaction between the two. We hope that readers of this book will find the information useful in designing and implementing child labor prevention policies and programs.

Seville, Spain   Isidro Maya Jariego
May 8, 2020

Acknowledgments

Over a decade we have participated in a collective effort that has involved, along with our Personal Networks and Communities Lab team, international volunteers, local practitioners, and colleagues from Latin American universities. At different times and with different intensity, we have had the collaboration of Jorge Palacio and Vanessa Romero in Colombia; Rosa Cueto, Agustín Espinosa, and Javier Ávila in Peru; and Jerson Cárcamo, Andrea Cecilia Castillo, and Amílcar Valladares in Honduras. Daniel Holgado, Esperanza Márquez, Ignacio Ramos, and Fran Santolaya participated in the field coordination. Francisco José Medina, Graciela Tonón, José Antonio Francés, Guillermo d'Onofrio, and José Orihuela contributed to the promotion and dissemination of the program. As volunteers from the University of Seville, we had the collaboration of Irene Aceituno, Raquel Bosque, Elena Chapa, Raisa Charlín, Verónica Cortés, Pablo Delgado, Carmen Fernández, Antonio Gallardo, Carmen García, Marta Jiménez, Carmen Molina, Paloma Navarro, Rocío Periago, Natalia Rodríguez, and Blanca Treviño. Sergio Granados Chahín collaborated in the preparation of the manuscript. My sincere thanks to all of them for their contribution to an initiative in which we have tried to combine research and intervention with working children and children at risk of child labor. Part of that experience is reflected in this book.

The editors of the *Human Well-Being Research and Policy Making* series, Richard J. Estes and M. Joseph Sirgy, provided suggestions and revisions that contributed significantly to improve the final product. I am also grateful to the Springer editorial team for their support throughout the process. We cannot forget the participation of children and their families in our own experience of program implementation in Colombia, Honduras, and Peru. We thank them for the time they dedicated to us and the kindness with which they always received us.

The photographs in Annexes A and B correspond to the implementation of the "Edúcame Primero" program in Colombia and Peru. The families participating in the program signed informed consent specifying the scientific uses and disclosure of the minors' personal information. We are in debt to all the volunteers who participated in the dissemination of the program with the ultimate aim of benefiting the minors. This book is an academic product that shares the same goal.

It is quite common to conclude the acknowledgments pages by apologizing to the family for the time that writing has stolen from the author. In this case, however, I have written these pages during the spring confinement of 2020, under special circumstances. In those days of quarantine and writing, I was not separated from the family but continuously surrounded by them. If my memory does not betray me, this is the first time that during lunch or dinner I have commented with them about what I was writing. We even had some discussion about child labor. In those harsh and strange times, that combination of family and writing was my best antidote to the evils of confinement.

About This Book

This book is divided into two parts. The first six chapters define the concept of child labor, examine the causes and consequences of the problem, and systematically review programs that are effective in preventing and reducing its prevalence. The second part, Chaps. 7–11, provides a practical guide to improve the implementation of policies and programs against child labor.

The first chapter (*What is child labor*) is focused on the definition of child labor. For this, we begin to show how the development of determined work activities can have some positive repercussions on minors, because these activities offer them opportunities to collaborate with their families, to develop personal autonomy, and to enhance their knowledge about the environment in which they operate. In contrast to these experiences, the International Labor Organization (ILO) considers child labor as "all that activity that deprives children of their childhood, their potential, and their dignity, and that is harmful to physical and mental development." Most of the working children around the world are involved in agriculture, fishing, and cattle raising. However, there are also minors engaging in the family business, working on domestic tasks, or involved in peddling, among other activities. Both the type of work activity and the working conditions can be determinants of the impact of child labor on the quality of life of minors. In this regard, the interruption of compulsory primary education and the health risk arise as two relevant elements in the definition of the concept. Finally, we review the worst forms of child labor in a continuum of vulnerability covering from the realization of activities that exceeds their physical capacity to homeless children. In this context, the critical analysis of the "working children's movements" allows us to present the debate between "abolitionist" and "reformist" approaches in the prevention of child labor.

Chapter 2 (*Causes and consequences of child labor*) summarizes, first, which are the social, economic, and educative factors predicting the involvement of minors in labor activities. Child labor usually emerges in contexts of poverty, either in families who need their children to work to supplement the household income or when the parents count on the collaboration of the minors as additional labor in the family's means of subsistence. The latter is common in commerce, agriculture, fishing, and cattle raising. Other risk factors for child labor have to do with the low quality of the education system or with family background, such as having parents with no education or who also worked during their childhood. Second, we assess the impact of child labor on health, psychological well-being, academic performance, completion of compulsory education, employability, and labor market insertion during adult life. Specifically, it has been shown that child labor not only reduces educational performance but can also adversely affect children's physical and mental health under certain circumstances. Furthermore, it also restricts employment opportunities during adulthood, helping to close the "vicious circle of poverty."

The third chapter (*What is effective in the prevention of child labor*) is a review of policies and programs that have shown a positive impact on the reduction of the problem prevalence. Over the last few decades, a very significant decrease in the number of working children in the world has been observed, demonstrating in part the effectiveness of preventive actions. Among other initiatives, coalitions of social agents, programs to promote compulsory education, and conditional cash transfer programs have had positive results. Both regulations of the minimum working age and systems of labor monitoring and inspection seem to be a requirement for the proper functioning of these policies. Besides, interventions to strengthen the quality of the education system are essential to ensure access to compulsory education and to prevent early school leaving. Finally, conditional cash benefits have become an evidence-based practice with exceptional results in some cases.

The fourth chapter (*How to improve the implementation of child labor prevention programs*) focuses on organizational and community factors influencing the implementation of preventive interventions. In doing so, we rely especially on our own experience in implementing a psycho-educational program for the prevention of child labor in Latin America. Among the different institutional contexts, primary schools play a central role in the community life of disadvantaged neighborhoods. That is why parent schools contribute to the development of informal relationships and promote a psychological sense of community. Both the convergence of expectations between families and schools and the reinforcement of simultaneous intervention in different microsystems enhance the effectiveness of preventive actions. It is also shown that the articulation of relationships between families in the neighborhood has a direct effect on social control mechanisms. The relationships between families facilitate the supervision of minors and result in the prevention of child labor.

Finally, in Chap. 5 (*Child labor, psychological well-being, and public policies*), we summarize the principal lessons learned in child labor prevention. As a conclusion, we gather the most meaningful evidence-based practices. Based on the results from the last few decades, we propose preventive community-based strategies, with actions at multiple levels and intervention contexts. Chapter 6 is the epilogue to the first part.

In the second part, we review the dilemmas and key actors in the practice of effective interventions, and it is composed of three main chapters (Chapters 7–9) and two concluding sections (Chapters 10–11).

Chapter 7 is a summary of current debates on prevention policies: *Dilemmas in public policy against child labor*. On the one hand, both the international action against child labor and the campaigns of activists against the commercialization of manufactured products with the participation of child labor have drawn attention to the worst forms of child labor and have contributed to public awareness of the exploitation of children in different regions of the planet. On the other hand, programs promoted by international organizations have been particularly effective in reducing the prevalence of the problem. However, both the approach and the content of public policies have been subject to strong criticism. First of all, they have been attributed with a certain lack of sensitivity to local cultures, ignoring the traditions of labor socialization in some regions, in certain ethnic groups, and in rural contexts. Secondly, concrete proposals have been made to replace the goal of eradicating child labor with less ambitious actions to regulate the labor market, addressing the economic needs of low-income families. Thirdly, it is considered necessary to introduce participatory dynamics that incorporate the point of view of children and reflect the perceived needs of the child population. This set of criticisms has served to review and improve preventive actions. In any case, as far as the content and nature of the programs are concerned, a series of central components of the intervention have been maintained, which over the last 20 years have proven to be consistently effective in practice.

With the title *From science to practice on child labor prevention,* Chap. 8 describes the process of implementing preventive policies, following the sequence by which scientific knowledge is transferred to concrete community contexts. First, it is interpreted as a process of diffusion of innovation, in which available evidence on what kind of actions are effective in reducing child labor should be disseminated among social, educational, and health service professionals. Secondly, it is analyzed as a process of community preparation, assuming that the presence of adequate levels of local participation and organization predisposes for a positive impact of child labor reduction policies. The last part of the chapter highlights the multitude of actors involved in the development of preventive policies and analyzes the role of each of them in the implementation process. In each case, it is completed with practical recommendations for each of the stakeholders involved in child labor prevention.

In Chap. 9, which is *A practical guide to improve the results of prevention actions against child labor*, we describe in detail the implementation process of two types of child labor interventions: psychosocial programs and political-legal actions. The former is based on behavior-based strategies to reduce risk factors and enhance protective factors in child labor. The latter follow a normative approach: they introduce changes in the regulatory framework of labor relations, promote political consensus, and attempt to transform social norms. The first part of the chapter shows how the adequate implementation of preventive programs depends on both the transfer of scientific knowledge and the technical assistance received by the intervention facilitators. The second part describes the ten basic components of any child labor program, following the "Getting to Outcomes"® (GTO) model. In conclusion, it reflects on how, in addition to evidence-based practices, positive outcomes depend on organizational capacities and efforts to adapt the intervention to local contexts. All of the above sections follow a practical orientation and provide concrete recommendations for improving the intervention.

Contents

About the Author

Isidro Maya Jariego is Associate Professor of Psychology at the University of Seville, and Principal Researcher of the Personal Networks and Communities Laboratory (HUM-059). Over the last decade, he has led the implementation of the "Educate Me First" program for the prevention of child labor in Colombia, Honduras, and Peru. This has allowed the Networks Laboratory to accumulate experience on psycho-educational intervention in communities at risk in Latin America, with the participation of international volunteer teams in development cooperation programs. Isidro Maya Jariego has published studies on typologies of personal networks, acculturation and psychological adaptation of immigrants, social cohesion in fishing communities, and implementation of programs to prevent child labor. He was the founder and coordinator of the master's degree in Psychology of Social and Community Intervention (2010–2013), and coordinator of the Doctoral Program "Social Intervention with the Community" (2007–2013). He has directed and participated in research projects funded by the European Commission and by national research agencies in Spain, Colombia, Chile, and Mexico, among others. He is currently a member of the Society for Community Research and Action (SCRA) and the International Network for Social Network Analysis (INSNA). Since 2002, he has been the editor of REDES: *Hispanic Journal for Social Network Analysis*. In his research, he combines social network analysis with community psychology.

List of Figures

List of Tables

Part I
Causes, Consequences, and Effective Programs Against Child Labor: Key Factors and Evidence-Based Practices

Chapter 1
What Is Child Labor

Abstract In this chapter, we define the concept of child labor according to the International Labor Organization (ILO), which refers to those work activities carried out by children that interfere with their physical and psychological development. We first review some cases where early initiation into work contributes to the development of personal skills and the acquisition of local ecological knowledge. This leads us to consider two factors that are fundamental in the definition of the concept: (a) the conditions under which the work activity takes place and (b) the impact of the work on the continuation of compulsory education. Finally, we refer to the "worst forms of child labor", as well as to the groups that suffer a situation of greater vulnerability, such as street children.

Keywords Child labor · International Labor Organization · Ecological local knowledge · Movements of working children · Working conditions · Worst forms of child labor · Street children · Types of child labor

1.1 Introduction

When the winter months are over, Orlando gets up at four in the morning and accompanies his uncle to the mangrove. Although he remembers making incursions into the wetlands since he was about 5 years old, it was not until he was nine that he started going several times a week, to help the family. Because he moves nimbly through the muddy areas, he can pick up a basket of seashells in one morning. Once the workday is over, they move to the market square of San Lorenzo to sell the clams. Even though many fishers try to sell them directly to the restaurants for tourists, his uncle knows a Salvadoran buyer who buys all the goods "at a good price".

Orlando is happy to be able to contribute at home and help his parents. He doesn't even think he can do anything else. Besides, since he has been doing "marisqueo" (collecting seafood on foot) he has learned to move among the tree roots and the bushes at low tide. He enjoys that kind of direct contact with the natural environment. His uncle has shown him some of the best places to extract seashells and now

© The Author(s), under exclusive license to Springer Nature Switzerland AG 2021
I. Maya Jariego, *Community Prevention of Child Labor*, Human Well-Being
Research and Policy Making, https://doi.org/10.1007/978-3-030-70810-8_1

he knows that about a month later he can return to the same location, "when the pups have grown up". He knows the tidal flats like the back of his hand. However, he has stopped going to school. Although at first, he tried to attend once or twice a week, he has lost contact lately and his parents do not remind him of his obligation to study either.

Collection of "curiles" (a type of bivalve mollusk from the *Arcidae* family) is widespread among children living near the San Lorenzo wetlands in the Gulf of Fonseca, Honduras. Fishing in the mangroves is carried out by poor families, who sometimes resort to catching crabs and clams as their only means of subsistence. This is a type of work that can harm the health of the children. That is why it is classified by the International Labor Organization (ILO) as "dangerous work". In this area of the Pacific, children work long hours until they have completed a basket and often begin to "mariscar" (peddling seafood) without having eaten breakfast, or with a poor diet. Routine movements in the mangroves cause cuts and small injuries to hands and feet. Skin diseases from contact with mud and permanent exposure to a humid environment are also very common. Also, it is customary for children to smoke. Tobacco smoke keeps insects away and is used to prevent the spread of dengue fever from mosquito bites. As a result, there is a high prevalence of acute respiratory diseases in the child population segment.

In this chapter, we introduce the concept of child labor. As we have illustrated with the case of Orlando, initiation into the world of work is part of a general process of socialization that allows the development of personal skills and the acquisition of relevant knowledge about the immediate environment. However, it can also result in early truancy and consequently negatively interfere with personal development. Although Orlando acquires valuable ecological knowledge from an early age, his involvement in the family's livelihood may reduce his employment opportunities in adulthood. In practice, not having expectations of social mobility could even be a decisive factor in maintaining poverty in the long term.

Next, we successively analyze both sides of the coin of the early start in work activities. This will allow us to reach an operational definition of child labor.

1.2   Initiation into the World of Work

Early work experiences influence attitudes and knowledge about the world of work and may, therefore, affect later occupational development (Steinberg et al., 1981). They can also be an opportunity to acquire positive work habits, discover personal vocation, or explore possible careers (Yuen et al., 2010). The International Labour Organization (ILO) itself recognizes that some early experiences of child labor socialization "contribute to the development of children and the well-being of their families; they provide them with skills and experience and help prepare them to be productive members of society in their adult life" (ILO, 2004, p. 16).

As we will see below, children's engagement in work activities can connect with the personal growth process (or maturation), the development of responsible behavior with the family, and the acquisition of knowledge about the environmental context.

1.2.1   The Development of Individual Responsibility and Autonomy

Some children perceive that working offers them opportunities they would not otherwise have. Perhaps counterintuitively, studies that have tried to incorporate the children's point of view find that for some children work increases their perception of control, as they feel more able to express their interests and feel they have gained some independence (Bessell, 2009; Invernizzi, 2003). It has also been found that children aged thirteen or fourteen show some autonomy in their economic behavior and even in their decision to migrate (Iversen, 2002).

In the case of girls, when they contribute financially to the family unit they experience an improvement in their relative status and acquire greater control over their day-to-day lives (Bessell, 2009). For example, they may be more independent in organizing their free time, or in their relationships with boys, in a context where they are usually more exposed to control by the family.

1.2.2   Respect for Parents and Commitment to the Family

For many children, working is simply a way of fulfilling their family obligations (Bessell, 2009). In some cases, they do not consider any other alternative, because from an early age they have learned to respect their parents and follow their instructions. It is a process that begins at home and then extends to life outside the family. For example, children who help at home are often more responsible and obedient, which is also a great help in performing well at school (Kandel & Post, 2003). Among children who work as street vendors, longer hours spent doing commercial work on the street seem to be associated with a kind of "economic empathy" for the precarious situation of their parents (Estrada, 2016). When they work in the family business they perceive that in some way they are reducing the burden on their parents. These experiences may also be reflected in the development of their ability to establish mutually dependent relationships with other adults.

1.2.3   Learning and the Acquiring of Local Ecological Knowledge

When children help with fishing, livestock grazing, and farming, they come into contact with adults who pass on traditional ecological knowledge. Both the direct relationship with the environment and the intergenerational transfer of knowledge based on experience become an excellent learning opportunity. As a result, children's participation in such practices contributes indirectly to the conservation of such informal knowledge, as in the case of ethnobotany, for example (Tian, 2017; Quinlan et al., 2016). Accordingly, in a wide range of socio-ecological contexts, attempts have been made to demonstrate that formal education does not necessarily lead to a loss of indigenous knowledge. Nor does the opposite have to be the case, but under certain conditions, the two can become complementary. This has been proven, for example, in the case of pastoralists (Oteros-Rozas et al., 2013; Tian, 2016), horticulturists (Reyes-García et al., 2010), and honey collectors (Demps et al., 2012).

> **Box 1.1: Recreational Work in the Himalayan Mountains**
> In a remote village in the high Himalayas, children start helping their parents with household chores when they are 7 or 8 years old. Soon after that, they begin to participate in grazing. It is a type of activity that allows them to play and interact with their peers while coming into contact with animals, plants, and the land. Other tasks include collecting leaf litter for the cattle stables or collecting lichen from trees. It is a form of "playful work", which involves active exploration of the environment. The children come into direct contact with nature and learn how to climb trees, which parts of the lowland forest are most productive or which bushes provide edible wild fruit. Any activity becomes an opportunity for play, so that "the groves were hiding places … and the ice in the stream could be collected to make 'mountain cookies'". This intimate relationship with the ecosystem is inseparable from children's sense of humor and sociability with their peers. Through these experiences, they develop a strong emotional attachment to their surroundings.
> Based on: Dyson, J. (2014). *Working childhoods: Youth, agency, and the environment in India.* Cambridge University Press.
> [India]

1.2.4   The Movements of Working Children

The evidence that children can combine school and work in their daily lives in a balanced way (Dyson, 2014), together with the verification of the eventually positive impact that we have just glossed over, has led some authors to question the very concept of child labor. While the International Labour Organisation (ILO), which is the world's reference body in this field, has led the design and implementation of actions to eradicate child labor, voices have emerged that question the relevance of such a policy. The paradigmatic case is probably that of the working children's movements in Latin America.

In Bolivia, Ecuador, and Peru, associations of working children have emerged to defend "the right of children to work" (sic). On the one hand, they draw on the norms and traditions of the Andean region to affirm that child labor is part of the process of socialization so that it takes place within the framework of a relationship of respect for parents and fulfillment of family obligations. On the other hand, they express an ideological approach that emphasizes children's ability to make their own decisions. In line with this, they emphasize individual "agency", oppose the treatment of children as mere victims or as dependent persons, and advocate a participatory approach that takes into account the children's point of view.

In practice, however, children's decisions are strongly constrained by a context that limits their options (Bessell, 2011; Lieten & Strehl, 2014; Maya Jariego, 2017). In addition, it is common for them to carry out work activities that pose a significant risk to their health and development. That is why it is important to establish a clear differentiation of the modalities of child labor and to examine in each case the potential impact that they can have on the development of children. This is what we intend to do in the rest of the chapter.

1.3   The International Labor Organization (ILO) Definition

Normally, the following definition from the International Labour Organization is taken as a reference for defining what child labor is:

> The term "child labor" is often defined as work that deprives children of their childhood, their potential, and their dignity, and that is harmful to physical and mental development. It refers to work that: is mentally, physically, socially or morally dangerous and harmful to children; and interferes with their schooling: by depriving them of the opportunity to attend school; by obliging them to leave school prematurely; or by requiring them to attempt to combine school attendance with excessively long and heavy work. In its most extreme forms, child labor involves children being enslaved, separated from their families, exposed to serious hazards and illnesses and/or left to fend for themselves on the streets of large cities—often at a very early age (International Labor Organization & Inter-parliamentary Union, 2002, pp. 15–16).

According to this definition, child labor is that which (a) adversely affects a child's development, (b) jeopardizes the child's physical health or psychological well-being, and (c) interferes with compulsory schooling. This means that not all work done by children is a form of child labor. For example, helping parents in the family business, or engaging in some activity outside of school hours that allow them to earn some money for their expenses, can be positive for their personal development and does not have to interfere negatively with their studies. Furthermore, it follows that there is a gradation in the severity of the conditions under which the work activity is carried out and, therefore, in the potential consequences on the child.

This definition is consistent with the establishment of international standards for "decent work" that this United Nations agency has been promoting since its foundation (Estacio & Marks, 2005). In 1919, the minimum age for employment in the industry was established at 14 years (Convention 5). In 1973, it was prohibited to employ children under the age set for compulsory schooling, and the minimum age for "hazardous work" was set at 18 (Convention 138). In 1999, the "worst forms of child labor" were prohibited (Convention 182). These regulations have been generating a de facto consensus on what is meant by child labor.

However, this is not a scientific definition. It is, in any case, a normative definition, or a minimum agreement on which to establish common policies. When used as an operational guide in empirical research, the problems of circular definitions can arise. For example, "studying the negative psychological consequences of child labor" may be a contradiction in terms, as long as we have defined child labor precisely as that which, among other possibilities, has negative psychological consequences. Taking a pragmatic view, we could instead explore how different forms of involvement in work activities, at different ages, or under certain conditions, impact on those psychological aspects that are of interest to us.

This shifts the focus to working conditions and patterns of work activity. Ultimately, the label of 'child labor' applies equally to children selling sweets at traffic lights, children helping their parents with agricultural work, girls working in domestic service, children engaged in forced labor in mining, or girls engaged in prostitution, to name but a few. However, the potential impact of each of these activities is truly diverse, just as it often affects the continuation of studies in quite different ways, for example. Moreover, it is clear that some of these activities are particularly harmful and require special attention.

In the following section, we review different types of labor activity and describe which are the "worst forms of child labor".

1.4   Types of Child Labor

According to the most recent estimates, 152 million children are engaged in child labor, of which 73 million are in hazardous work (ILO, 2017). Since 2000 there has been a net decrease of 94 million, which is a reduction of approximately 38% in child labor worldwide (ILO, 2018).

Of the total number of child workers, 58% are boys and 42% girls.[1] The regions with the highest prevalence of the problem are Africa (19.6%), Asia (7.4%), and the Americas (5.3%). Most work in the agricultural sector (71%), doing unpaid work

---

[1]The performance of household chores, in which girls are in the majority, is not counted as child labor.

within their family unit (69%). However, as we will explain below, the conditions, schedules, and risks to which they are exposed can be very variable.

1.4.1 Agriculture, Family Businesses, and Other Working Sectors

Most child labor in the world is concentrated in agriculture, fishing, and cattle raising. In this sector, it is relatively common for them to be involved in subsistence activities or to collaborate on family farms, under the supervision of their parents. In both rural areas and urban agriculture, parents expect their children to contribute economically, while a sense of obligation to their parents is deeply rooted among children (Mlozi, 1995). In practice, the exploitation of child labor is a means of ensuring the economic sustainability of the smallholdings cultivated by the family unit (Beegle et al., 2006; Wyer, 1986). Although in some cases they may perform low-risk tasks, appropriate for their age, or that do not interfere with their studies, intensive work in tilling, planting, or harvesting fields is usually reflected in a reduction of their educational and work opportunities in the medium and long term (Beyer, 2012; Hurst, 2007).

The relationship with employers is more common in the industrial sector, although it is usually informal employment (Bequele & Boyden, 1988). Children work in activities as varied as brick-making, garment making, leather tanning, construction, mineral extraction, carpet making, artisanal mining, and so on. Compared to agriculture, they have worse working conditions: they are more exposed to heat, dust, noise, and toxic substances (Tiwari, 2005; Pollack et al., 1990); in mechanized tasks, they come into contact with machinery and dangerous objects (Brown et al., 1992; McKechnie et al., 1998); and they are more often required to work fast and under pressure (Gani & Shah, 1998).

In the service sector, children work in peddling, domestic service, or a variety of support tasks in hotels and restaurants. These are usually jobs that involve many hours of continuous activity, and sometimes involve collaboration with family businesses (Webbink et al., 2012). Domestic service is predominantly performed by girls (Thorsen, 2012), sometimes through their parents' agreement with a relative, or even as a form of informal debt repayment (Bourdillon & Chinodya, 2006). On the other hand, the realization of activities in the street is an additional risk factor (Hernandez et al., 1996; Ruchirawat et al., 2005), on which we will return later.

1.4.2 Conditions, Working Hours, and Risks

The modalities we have mentioned in the previous section not only vary in the sector of activity but also working conditions, schedules, and associated risks. Although the content of the work activity is an aspect of the information on the type of child labor, it can sometimes mask other equally relevant aspects of the conditions in which the activity is carried out. In other words, focusing on what children do may result in not paying enough attention to how they do it. For example, working at night, spending long hours on the streets until they are profitable, or working around school hours can have a significant impact on their own, sometimes regardless of the sector of work in which they are engaged. Similarly, the level of physical demand can lead to frequent absences from school or to fatigue affecting educational performance. Different tasks may have the same result depending on the conditions under which the work is performed.

The use of time seems to be directly related to the acquisition of traditional ecological knowledge (Ruiz-Mallén et al., 2013). How time is distributed between play, work activities, and (where appropriate) school conditions learning opportunities. As we develop in the following section, problems can arise when time devoted to education and work compete with each other.

1.4.3   The Competition Between Child Labor and School Attendance

One of the strongest evidences that early entry into the world of work has potentially negative consequences for children is the impact on their educational outcomes. It is estimated that approximately one-third of working children do not attend school. The other two-thirds have little time to spend on study outside of class or are too tired to complete the day with homework and other school activities (ILO, 2017). The result is that, in addition to being more likely to drop out of compulsory education, they often perform less well academically than their non-working peers. They are also more likely to repeat a grade and take longer to complete their studies.

There seems to be an inverse relationship between time spent on child labor and time spent in school. These are two competing alternatives. The number of hours per week devoted to a work activity reduces educational involvement and performance. Similarly, when work schedules coincide with school hours, the most significant impact on educational outcomes is observed (Holgado et al., 2014). Conversely, when work activity is carried out after school, the same type of negative impact on children is not observed (Kandel & Post, 2003).

1.4.4   The Worst Form of Child Labor

The category of "worst forms of child labor" includes a range of work activities that are considered intolerable because they are particularly harmful and are performed by the most vulnerable children. Specifically, ILO Convention 182 explicitly prohibits four types of activities: (a) slavery, trafficking, servitude, forced labor or recruitment for armed conflict, (b) sex work, prostitution, and pornography, (c) illegal activities such as drug trafficking, and (d) "hazardous work", which can harm the health, safety or morality of children.[2]

The latter are those performed in a work environment that can cause injury or illness, and in general, those that put health or life at risk. A wide variety of activities correspond to this profile. For example, working in mines and quarries typically involves carrying heavy loads, sometimes beyond the physical capacity of children (Hilson, 2008; Woolf, 2002), and providing services on the street often involves a higher risk of exposure to violence, crime, and drug abuse (Black, 1995; Celik, 2009; Pinzon-Rondon et al., 2010), while sorting and trading trash is associated with infectious diseases and all kinds of injuries or skin diseases (Batool & Anjum, 2016; Cuadra et al., 2009; Ostos & Gunn, 1993).

Many other activities can have negative health consequences, cause permanent disability, produce psychological damage, or affect the social-emotional develop-ment of children. These include working underground or in confined spaces, oper-ating dangerous machinery, or working long hours or at night.

Given the seriousness of the consequences associated with such working condi-tions, it has been comparatively easier to generate some international consensus in trying to eradicate this form of child labor. This is especially so given that children are generally more vulnerable to difficult working conditions than adults. Against this background, the most recent ILO regulations have aimed at eradicating the "worst forms of child labor". At the national level, this convention has been translated into the elaboration of lists of "hazardous work" in the local context, which have proved particularly effective in the work of inspecting and monitoring child labor. We will return to this topic in Chap. 3.

Box 1.2: Life in the Dumpster

The city's waste is deposited in the municipal crematorium in Tegucigalpa. An informal economy based on waste recovery has been created around the landfill. Some 400 people scavenge through the garbage every day to recover items they can sell or recycle. The families who work at the crematorium live in self-built houses, with wooden planks taken from the rubbish dump itself. Criminal gangs control the entrance to the crematorium, set the hours, and force families to pay a fee to have access to garbage collection. In the case of children, this is one of the "worst forms of child labor". In addition to working long hours scavenging in unhealthy conditions, they are exposed to extortion and coercive control by the "maras". Children working in the landfill often show weight and height indicators below their age, as well as a high incidence of symptoms of respiratory diseases. Moreover, it is a group at social risk, with

(continued)

---

[2]ILO Convention 182, Article 3.

Box 1.2 (continued)
poor development of social-emotional skills. They are often victims of youth
gang violence or resort to aggressive behavior themselves in their relationship
with their immediate environment.
    [Honduras]

1.4.5   Children on the Street and Children of the Street

Living on the street means being exposed to all kinds of risks. In addition to the lack
of hygiene or insufficient protection from the weather, life on the streets is associated
with a certain disruption of schedules (or in general of behavioral habits), as well as a
greater likelihood of drug use and abuse (Forster et al., 1996). Children living on the
street often have a previous history of violence and neglect. They are generally more
vulnerable to abuse of power by adults and are also more susceptible to joining
criminal gangs. As some working children are (to varying degrees) active on the
street, they may experience some of the circumstances described above.

UNICEF introduced the distinction between children on the street and children of
the street. The former maintains regular contact with their families while the latter
lives on the street. However, the boundaries between the two groups are blurred and
a gradual process has been described whereby children who work on the street end
up living on the street (Lieten & Strehl, 2014). Normally, they go through different
stages in which their contacts with their families decrease and they begin to spend
more and more time on the street until in some cases they replace the home with the
street more or less definitively. Once this lifestyle has been adopted, it is particularly
difficult to leave it. In the initial stages, they turn around and play in the street, which
gives them a sense of freedom and independence. Later on, cohesive groups of
homeless children are formed, where peer pressure to maintain certain patterns of
behavior is very high.

1.5   Towards a Typology of Labor Activities Performed by Minors

We have reviewed in the previous sections the great diversity of situations that tend
to be encompassed under the same term of "child labor". Furthermore, we have
followed a sequence that has led us from relatively unharmful forms of work
involvement to those that restrict individual freedom or that seriously condition
the balanced emotional growth of children. Research has devoted little time to
examine the different forms, conditions, and effects of child labor. However, efforts
to systematize the different work activities performed by children can help to better
understand the phenomenon. To take some first exploratory steps in that direction, in

Table 1.1 Three categories of child labor

Modality	Description	Most common contexts
Subsistence economy	Unpaid activities within the family unit	• Agriculture, fishing, cattle raising • Family businesses
Wage work in the informal economy, with different degrees of risk	Salaried activities that condition the development and affect the continuity of studies	• Working as an employee in hotels and restaurants
	Wage-earning activities with risk to health and psychological well-being	• Jobs in the industry with a strong physical component • Working on the street
Forced labor and work that affects the morality of minors	Child prostitution Child soldiers Illicit activities Slavery and servitude	• Immigrants and displaced persons • Abuse of adult power • Political conflict • Authoritarian regimes

Table 1.1 we have proposed three categories of child labor, ordered from least to the greatest potential impact on child development. In each case, we describe the type of activity and illustrate it with some of the most common work contexts in which it takes place.

First, we have found that the most common type of participation of children in the world of work is in unpaid activities within the family unit, as part of a subsistence economy. Very often, children help their parents with farm work in rural environments or help with fishing in coastal communities. It can also occur in urban contexts, where children support the family business, usually in commercial activities or in the provision of services. On paper, this is one of the least risky forms of child labor, not least because it is carried out under family supervision with the expectation of facilitating learning. However, when children are involved in survival activities from a very early age, they are unlikely to aspire to occupations different from those performed by their parents. As a result, their opportunities for social mobility are reduced. Sometimes they simply do not consider that their lives can be otherwise.

Secondly, some children are engaged in wage-earning activities for employers in the informal economy. This category includes several jobs that represent a wide range of risks to health, psychological well-being, and educational performance. For example, we assume that it is less dangerous to work in a restaurant, even if it involves many hours of dedication than to do extractive work in an underground mine. A separate chapter can also be made for those who work on the street (or those who live on the street) since this is a collective in which individual deterioration, the destructuring of relationships, and uprooting are more frequent. Nevertheless, even in this last case, the normal thing is to find a great diversity of circumstances:

> Children working on the streets but living at home, children helping family members on the street, children working at markets, children living with family on the street, children

sleeping in night shelters, children without any family contact, children sleeping temporarily or permanently on the streets, children in youth gangs, etc. (Lieten & Strehl, 2014, position 231–233).

Finally, the most extreme cases concern forced labor, which affects the morality of minors or involves the carrying out of illegal activities. As we have already indicated, this includes the recruitment of children in armed conflicts, the commercial sexual exploitation of children, forced labor to compensate for the indebtedness of parents, or the use of children in drug trafficking. These are modalities that "deprive children of their childhood", represent an abuse of adult power, and have a far-reaching impact on the lives of the victims.

These three modalities of child labor set the framework for designing relevant and potentially effective interventions. When children are involved in their parents' livelihood activities, there may be a need to influence the culture of work and the family's livelihood alternatives. In contrast, in "dangerous work" for employers, labor monitoring and inspection actions, coalitions between social agents, initiatives that promote community control, or social dialogue tables on working conditions may be more relevant. Forced labor and illegal activities, on the other hand, may require police intervention, along with other actions to ensure compliance with the law. In Chap. 3, we will review in more detail which strategies have proven effective in preventing child labor.

Furthermore, it should be noted that different profiles can also be observed within the same activity sector. In a study with minor motorcycle taxi drivers in Lima, Ballet and Bhukuth (2019) found that many of them had been pushed to work for the family. However, there was also a large group of adolescents who had decided to carry out this activity on their own initiative, with which they obtained income that they could spend with their friends on tobacco, alcohol, and nights out.

1.6 Conclusion

Not all work done by children is child labor. As we have seen, early experiences in the world of work can even have a positive impact on labor socialization, allowing the development of skills that contribute to greater employability during adult life. It all depends to a great extent on the conditions under which the activity is carried out. In particular, when participation in the world of work involves early school leaving, when it exceeds the physical capacity of children, or when it negatively affects their development and psychological well-being, we speak of child labor.

This has led us to conceive the different forms of participation in the world of work as a gradation of the health, psychological, or educational risks to which children are exposed. Firstly, the most frequent type of child labor consists of helping in the fields or going out fishing with the parents, as part of the family unit's subsistence activities. Second, much less common, but considerably more negative, are the so-called "hazardous jobs", which correspond to a wide variety of activities, ranging from shoe shining in the street to stone-cutting in a quarry. Finally, the most extreme cases include forced labor, child soldiers, involvement in illicit activities, and child prostitution.

On the other hand, a corollary of the above grading is the possibility of assessing the deterioration in living and working conditions to which some children are exposed. In some cases, it is common to observe a progressive worsening of their situation. This has been empirically demonstrated, clearly and consistently, in the case of the transition from working on the streets to living on the streets. But it can be extended to the individual journey between the different forms of child labor.

In the second part of the book, we will analyze the strategies for the prevention of child labor. However, this first chapter of the definition has already allowed us to extract some interesting observations from a practical point of view. First, the intervention strategies could be modulated according to the type of child labor we want to influence. Second, both because of the associated risk and the level of community preparedness, it may be appropriate to prioritize the worst forms of child labor. Third, preventive actions could also halt the progression towards forms of child labor that carry a higher risk or more serious impact on children. In any case, before focusing on intervention strategies, in the next chapter, we will examine the background and consequences of child labor.

References

Ballet, J., & Bhukuth, A. (2019). Adolescent work: Freedom of choice or family obligation? The case of young mototaxi drivers in Lima, Peru. In *Child exploitation in the Global South* (pp. 51–64). Cham: Palgrave Macmillan.

Batool, Z., & Anjum, F. (2016). A sociological study of trash picker children in Faisalabad City, Punjab, Pakistan. *Pakistan Journal Life of Social Sciences, 14*(1), 33–37.

Beegle, K., Dehejia, R. H., & Gatti, R. (2006). Child labor and agricultural shocks. *Journal of Development Economics, 81*(1), 80–96.

Bequele, A., & Boyden, J. (Eds.). (1988). *Combating child labor.* Geneva: International Labour Organization.

Bessell, S. (2009). Indonesian Children's views and experiences of work and poverty. *Social Policy and Society, 8*(4), 527–540.

Bessell, S. (2011). Influencing international child labor policy: The potential and limits of children-centered research. *Children and Youth Services Review, 33*(4), 564–568.

Beyer, D. (2012). Child labor in agriculture: Some new developments to an ancient problem. *Journal of Agromedicine, 17*(2), 197–207.

Black, M. (1995). *In the Twilight Zone: Child workers in the hotel, tourism, and catering industry.* Geneva: International Labour Organization.

Bourdillon, M. F., & Chinodya, J. (2006). *Child domestic workers in Zimbabwe.* Harare: Weaber Press.

Brown, M., Christiansen, J., & Philips, P. (1992). The Decline of Child Labor in the US fruit and vegetable canning industry: Law or Economics? *The Business History Review, 66*(4), 723–770.

Celik, S. S. (2009). Verbal, physical, and sexual abuse among children working on the street. *The Australian Journal of Advanced Nursing, 26*(4), 14–22.

Cuadra, S., Lundh, T., & Jakobsson, K. (2009). Exposure to heavy metals in children working at a waste disposal site, and in reference children from Managua, Nicaragua. *Epidemiology, 20*(6), S95.

Demps, K., Zorondo-Rodriguez, F., Garcia, C., & Reyes-Garcia, V. (2012). The selective persistence of local ecological knowledge: Honey collecting with the Jenu Kuruba in South India. *Human Ecology, 40*(3), 427–434.

Dyson, J. (2014). *Working childhoods: Youth, agency, and the environment in India*. London: Cambridge University Press.

Estacio, E. V., & Marks, D. F. (2005). Child labor and the International Labour Organization's Convention 182: A critical perspective. *Journal of Health Psychology, 10*(3), 475–484.

Estrada, E. (2016). Economic empathy in family entrepreneurship: Mexican-origin street vendor children and their parents. *Ethnic and Racial Studies, 39*(9), 1657–1675.

Forster, L. M., Tannhauser, M., & Barros, H. M. (1996). Drug use among street children in southern Brazil. *Drug and Alcohol Dependence, 43*(1-2), 57–62.

Gani, A., & Shah, M. A. (1998). Child Labour in Carpet Industry of Kashmir. *Indian Journal of Industrial Relations, 33*(3), 349–366.

Hernandez, P., Zettna, A., Tapia, M., Ortiz, C., & Soto, I. C. (1996). Childcare needs of female street vendors in Mexico City. *Health Policy and Planning, 11*(2), 169–178.

Hilson, G. (2008). 'A load too heavy': Critical reflections on the child labor problem in Africa's small-scale mining sector. *Children and Youth Services Review, 30*(11), 1233–1245.

Holgado, D., Maya-Jariego, I., Ramos, I., Palacio, J., Oviedo-Trespalacios, O., Romero-Mendoza, V., & Amar, J. (2014). Impact of child labor on academic performance: Evidence from the program "Edúcame Primero Colombia". *International Journal of Educational Development, 34*, 58–66.

Hurst, P. (2007). Health and child labor in agriculture. *Food and Nutrition Bulletin, 28*(2), 364–371.

International Labour Organization. (2004). *Child labour. A textbook for University Students*. Geneva: ILO.

International Labour Organization. (2017). *Global estimates of child labor: Results and trends, 2012–2016*. Geneva: ILO.

International Labour Organization. (2018). *Ending child labor by 2025: A review of policies and programs*. Geneva: ILO.

International Labor Organization & Inter-parliamentary Union. (2002). *Eliminating the worst forms of child labour: A practical guide to ILO convention (No. 182)*. Geneva: ILO, Inter-Parliamentary Union.

Invernizzi, A. (2003). Street-working children and adolescents in Lima: Work as an agent of socialization. *Childhood, 10*(3), 319–341.

Iversen, V. (2002). Autonomy in child labor migrants. *World Development, 30*(5), 817–834.

Kandel, W., & Post, D. (2003). After school work in Mexico: Competing for children's time success. *International Journal of Educational Development, 23*(3), 299–314.

Lieten, G. K., & Strehl, T. (2014). *Child street life: An inside view of hazards and expectations of street children in Peru*. New York: Springer.

Maya Jariego, I. (2017). "But we want to work": The movement of child workers in Peru and the actions for reducing child labor. *American Journal of Community Psychology, 60*(3–4), 430–438.

McKechnie, J., Hobbs, S., Lindsay, S., & Lynch, M. (1998). Working children: The health and safety issue. *Children & Society, 12*(1), 38–47.

Mlozi, M. R. (1995). Child labor in urban agriculture: The case of Dar es Salaam, Tanzania. *Children's Environments, 12*(2), 197–208.

Ostos, Z., & Gunn, S. E. (1993). Los niños basureros de Filipinas y los dilemas inherentes al trabajo infantil. *Revista Internacional del Trabajo, 112*(3), 461–480.

Oteros-Rozas, E., Ontillera-Sánchez, R., Sanosa, P., Gómez-Baggethun, E., Reyes-García, V., & González, J. A. (2013). Traditional ecological knowledge among transhumant pastoralists in Mediterranean Spain. *Ecology and Society, 18*, 3.

Pinzon-Rondon, A. M., Botero, J. C., Benson, L., Briceno-Ayala, L., & Kanamori, M. (2010). Workplace abuse and economic exploitation of children working in the streets of Latin American cities. *International Journal of Occupational and Environmental Health, 16*(2), 150–157.

Pollack, S. H., Landrigan, P. J., & Mallino, D. L. (1990). Child labor in 1990: Prevalence and health hazards. *Annual Review of Public Health, 11*(1), 359–375.

Quinlan, M. B., Quinlan, R. J., Council, S. K., & Roulette, J. W. (2016). Children's acquisition of ethnobotanical knowledge in a Caribbean horticultural village. *Journal of Ethnobiology, 36*(2), 433–456.

Reyes-García, V., Kightley, E., Ruiz-Mallén, I., Fuentes-Peláez, N., Demps, K., Huanca, T., & Martínez-Rodríguez, M. R. (2010). Schooling and local environmental knowledge: Do they complement or substitute each other? *International Journal of Educational Development, 30*(3), 305–313.

Ruchirawat, M., Navasumrit, P., Settachan, D., Tuntaviroon, J., Buthbumrung, N., & Sharma, S. (2005). Measurement of genotoxic air pollutant exposures in street vendors and school children in and near Bangkok. *Toxicology and Applied Pharmacology, 206*(2), 207–214.

Ruiz-Mallén, I., Morsello, C., Reyes-García, V., & De Faria, R. B. M. (2013). Children's use of time and traditional ecological learning. A case study in two Amazonian indigenous societies. *Learning and Individual Differences, 27*, 213–222.

Steinberg, L. D., Greenberger, E., Vaux, A., & Ruggiero, M. (1981). Early work experience: Effects on adolescent occupational socialization. *Youth & Society, 12*(4), 403–422.

Thorsen, D. (2012). *Child domestic workers: Evidence from West and Central Africa*. Discussion Paper. UNICEF WCAR, Dakar.

Tian, X. (2016). Day-to-day accumulation of indigenous ecological knowledge: A case study of pastoral Maasai children in southern Kenya. *African Study Monographs, 37*(2), 75–102.

Tian, X. (2017). Ethnobotanical knowledge acquisition during daily chores: The firewood collection of pastoral Maasai girls in Southern Kenya. *Journal of Ethnobiology and Ethnomedicine, 13*(1), 2.

Tiwari, R. R. (2005). Child labor in the footwear industry: Possible occupational health hazards. *Indian Journal of Occupational and Environmental Medicine, 9*(1), 7–9.

Webbink, E., Smits, J., & De Jong, E. (2012). Hidden child labor: Determinants of housework and family business work of children in 16 developing countries. *World Development, 40*(3), 631–642.

Woolf, A. D. (2002). Health hazards for children at work. *Journal of Toxicology. Clinical Toxicology, 40*(4), 477–482.

Wyer, J. (1986). Child labor in Brazilian agriculture. *Critique of Anthropology, 6*(2), 63–80.

Yuen, M., Gysbers, N. C., Chan, R. M., Lau, P. S., & Shea, P. M. (2010). Talent development, work habits, and career exploration of Chinese middle-school adolescents: Development of the career and talent development self-efficacy scale. *High Ability Studies, 21*(1), 47–62.

Chapter 2
Causes and Consequences of Child Labor

Abstract In this chapter, we examine the causes and consequences of child labor. Working children usually come from low-income families and, among other possible outcomes, there is a high risk that they will drop out of compulsory education. The most relevant and contrasting background factor is poverty. Other empirically documented causes are family size, immigration, family history of child labor, and public attitudes. Among the consequences is the educational impact. It is generally assumed that child labor also has an impact on the health and psychological well-being of children, and in the long term, on employability and working conditions during adulthood. However, empirical research on these negative effects is significantly less developed.

Keywords Child labor · Causes · Consequences · Poverty · Family background · Truancy · School dropout

2.1 Introduction

The official from the Colombian Institute of Family Welfare asked the agent to stop at the corner of Carrera 51 and Calle 85, to make the routine inspection of the mobile stands that are usually installed in the area. Every week they find some cases to report to the Childhood and Adolescence Police of the Barranquilla City Hall. On this occasion, a child of about 9 years old is in charge of a humble stand with paper handkerchiefs, mineral water, soursop juice, and "lulo" candies.

Jairo was a little scared when the police started questioning him, so he answered all his questions frankly, one by one. That morning he woke up early in the house in Pinar del Rio. His mother's cousin picked him up and brought him in a mule cart to the north of the city. He says he lives with his mother and stepfather. He explains that the situation changed drastically when his father abandoned them a few years ago. "My mother doesn't pay attention to me and sends me out on the streets to sell with her cousin. On a normal day, I stay at the stand and sell until late afternoon, when they come to pick me up on their way home. Many times I have been left alone on

© The Author(s), under exclusive license to Springer Nature Switzerland AG 2021   19
I. Maya Jariego, *Community Prevention of Child Labor*, Human Well-Being
Research and Policy Making, https://doi.org/10.1007/978-3-030-70810-8_2

Table 2.1 Background and consequent factors of child labor

Antecedents	Consequences
• Low family income • Parents with no education or who worked as children • Large families, immigration, and forced displacement • Poor quality of the education system • Favorable values and attitudes towards child labor in the general population	• It affects the quality of life and mental health of children • They are more vulnerable to the physical impact of work and suffer more accidents at work • It reduces their academic performance and worsens their school experience • They have lower wages as adults • It reduces job opportunities and affects their employability profile in adulthood • It appears to have an indirect effect in terms of maintaining poverty

Source: own elaboration, Maya Jariego (2017)

the street for several days. The man my mother lives with hits me and I prefer to stay outside until things calm down a bit".

Many children work on the streets under the supervision of an adult relative, to whom they can turn if they have a problem. These children give most of their income to their families. However, several of Jairo's neighbors have already moved onto the streets on their own, attracted by the possibility of earning an income of their own, or seduced by the drugs and entertainment opportunities the city has to offer. To earn a living, they sell mobile phone cards, clean car windows at traffic lights, sell drinks and sweets, or play the role of informal shoe polishers. Pinar del Río is a settlement formed by people displaced by political violence, where mostly poor families live. For many children, there is no great difference between sleeping on the street and sleeping on the floor of their house, in a house without electricity or water.

In this chapter, we look at the causes and consequences of child labor. As Jairo's case reveals, children who work on the street are highly likely to come from dysfunctional families, have experienced geographic displacement, or live in poverty. Even so, this is a very heterogeneous group: some live permanently on the street; others live at home, even if they work on the street; and many are in a constant flow between the street and the home. Among other factors, domestic violence, low family income, father's alcoholism, neglect, and abuse are among the antecedents of this form of child labor.

We then describe the most common causes of different types of child labor and examine some of the most relevant consequences, paying particular attention to the educational impact and the repercussions on employability during adult life. In Table 2.1 we have summarized the set of factors that we are going to review in the following pages.

2.2 Social, Economic, and Educational Antecedent Factors to Child Labor

Child labor is considered both a cause and a consequence of the lack of economic development (Edmonds, 2016). On the one hand, the rate of child labor is directly related to the gross domestic product. On the other hand, there is evidence that a country's economic development reduces the rate of child labor. At the macroeconomic level, this process runs parallel to the reduction of the relative weight of the primary sector in the economy[1] (and is also partly associated with technological development).

At the microeconomic level, increased family income improves living standards and, in the long term, reduces child labor. The change is more significant in the poorest households (Edmonds, 2005). In the short term, however, there may be a temporary upturn, when households involve their children in work activities to take advantage of new opportunities (Kambhampati & Rajan, 2006). It is therefore advisable to adopt a perspective that transcends economic cycles.

In this context, a widespread type of study consists of an econometric analysis of the determinants of child labor. In the first part of this chapter, we review in some detail some of the most relevant background factors. In the second part, although it has had comparatively less weight in research on the topic, we summarize some of the existing evidence on the impact on health, educational experience, and future work.

2.2.1 Poverty and Child Labor

Family poverty is the first direct antecedent that pushes children to work. It is usually assumed that adults only send their children to work when their own income falls to very low levels (Basu & Van, 1998; Fan, 2011). Consequently, household poverty is positively related to the likelihood of children working and negatively related to schooling (Amin et al., 2004; Ray, 2000; Triningsih & Ichihashi, 2010; Verner & Blunch, 1999). Keeping children away from work is a luxury that poorer families cannot afford.

Nonetheless, the evidence for this is not always consistent and the size of the effect may be small (Fan, 2011; Wahba, 2000). This has led to some efforts to demonstrate the "transmission of poverty", with the understanding that child labor contributes to the intergenerational perpetuation of poverty. Also, there may be other family, educational, or social variables that modulate the relationship between household income and child labor (Holgado et al., 2016).

---

[1]Let us remember that the bulk of child labor is in agriculture, where children do unpaid work in the family unit.

Box 2.1: The Axiom of Luxury, the Substitution of Adult Labor and the Paradox of Wealth

Research has connected household income with the likelihood that children will work in at least two different ways: (1) poverty as a cause of child labor: low household income increases the likelihood that children will work, (2) transmission of poverty: children are more likely to work if their parents worked as children. Basu and Van (1998) theorized about this, assuming that parents do not take advantage of it for selfish interests but are forced to have their children work for survival needs. On paper, the prevalence of child labor could have a negative impact on the working conditions of adults. Based on these previous approaches, they introduced two operating principles:

- The axiom of luxury: "a family will send children into the labor market only if the family income from non-child labor sources falls very low".
- The axiom of substitution: "from a company's point of view, child labor and adult labor are substitutes".

However, in the rural contexts of developing countries, it has been found that sometimes a better relative position of the family is associated with the fact that their children work. This is particularly the case in the agricultural sector where a subsistence economy predominates, so an alternative operating principle can be introduced (Bhalotra & Heady, 2003):

- The paradox of wealth: "children from land-rich households are often more likely to work than those from land-poor households".

This has led to the idea that the substitutability of adult work for child labor is more important as an explanatory factor than the absolute income of the parents.

Based on: Fan, C. S. (2011). The luxury axiom, the wealth paradox, and child labor. *Journal of Economic Development*, 36(3), 25–45.

2.2.2 Family Background

The educational level of the parents and the fact that the parents worked as children are also predictive factors to take into consideration. A study in Egypt found that having a parent who worked as a child doubled the likelihood of a child entering the labor market. Moreover, the influence was much greater when it was the mother who had worked during her childhood (Wahba, 2000). Consistent with this, data from India showed that the higher the mother's educational level, the less likely her children are to work (Mukherjee & Das, 2008). Being educated seems to influence parents to place more importance on children's schooling.

The intergenerational transmission of the educational level can be reflected in a limitation of the opportunities available in the labor market. It not only generically reduces social mobility, for women it is one of the factors influencing the gender gap (Van Putten et al., 2008).

2.2.3   The Characteristics of the Families

Econometric models have controlled for the effect of household income by incorporating other household characteristics that may have an impact, such as the number of siblings, the number of people in the household, and the order of birth. The size of the family group facilitates the specialization of its members so that some children work while others study (Patrinos & Psacharopoulos, 1997). In particular, it is more common for first-born children to be involved in work activities and to contribute to the family income so that younger siblings can devote themselves to study (Emerson & Souza, 2008).

On the other hand, both exposures to an armed conflict and forced displacement of the family are risk factors for school dropouts and early incorporation into the labor market (Holgado et al., 2016; Rodriguez & Sanchez, 2012). Similarly, rural-urban migration results in the resettlement of large segments of the population on the outskirts of urban centers, where they encounter problems of access to basic resources and live in conditions of poverty and social exclusion (Plummer et al., 2007; Siddiqi & Patrinos, 1996). The risk is greater for unaccompanied minors.

In contrast, the international migration of parents can have a protective effect on the child labor of children left behind (Antman, 2012; Mansuri, 2006), especially in the case of mothers (Acosta, 2011a). Remittances sent by immigrants make it possible to invest in children's human capital (Acosta, 2011b; Alcaraz et al., 2012).

2.2.4   The Quality of the Education System

Shortcomings in the education system may be a precursor to child labor. This refers to the quality of teaching, teacher training, accessibility for high-risk groups, institutional capacity to guarantee compulsory education, teaching conditions, and, where appropriate, the overcrowding of classes or the lack of adequate infrastructure. A fairly informative fact in this regard is usually the salary of primary and secondary school teachers, as well as their working conditions. When the education system functions poorly, a higher proportion of working children is often found (Canagarajah & Coulombe, 1999; Canagarajah & Nielsen, 1999). In contrast, programs to improve the quality of education not only increase school attendance but indirectly discourage the involvement of children in work activities, especially at the secondary level (Rossi & Rosati, 2007).

2.2.5   The Culture of Work and the Attitudes of the Population

Finally, several cultural factors should be mentioned among the determinants, such as prevailing population values, parental beliefs, and social perception of child labor. In many families, girls are still expected to engage in domestic activities, just as boys are expected to help on the family farm in the countryside. Parents have different degrees of concern about the safety of their children (Runyan et al., 2009); and they also differ in their expectations about the role that boys and girls should play (Buchmann, 2000), or in the impact that work may have on their learning for life (Bahar, 2014). The degree of society's tolerance for children's work may also vary considerably between countries (Bahar, 2014; Maya Jariego, 2017).

> **Box 2.2: Two Profiles of Child Labor**
> Child labor takes different forms depending on the social and community context in which it occurs. In a survey of 3259 families in the Colombian Caribbean, two profiles were identified based on background factors for child labor involvement. First, in families living in urban areas, child labor was significantly related to family income and the socio-labor characteristics of the mothers. Specifically, children were more likely to work when their mothers were unemployed, they had no education or they had worked as children. In any case, family income was the best predictor of child labor. Therefore, the background of this profile corresponds to some of the key factors identified in the previous literature on the subject.
>
> However, in families living in a rural or peri-urban environment (on the outskirts of large cities) the most relevant predictor was having experienced forced displacement in the last 5 years. Migration to the city is a situation of risk of child labor, which generates special needs. This risk profile can be enhanced when symptoms of post-traumatic stress occur among those who have been victims of political violence. Colombia is one of the countries with the largest number of internally displaced persons in the world, so child labor is necessarily connected to this phenomenon in a significant part of the population.
>
> Based on Holgado, D., Maya-Jariego, I., Palacio, J. & Oviedo-Trespalacios, O. (2016). Two profiles of child labor in the Colombian Caribbean Coast: relocated children to suburban areas compared to the key role of social and labor characteristics of mothers in urban settings. In Tonón, G (Ed.). Indicators of Quality of Life in Latin America, pp. 251–273. *Social Indicators Research Series, Vol. 62*. New York: Springer.
> [Colombia]

2.3   The Impact on Health, Educational Experience, and Future Employment

The existence of a large pool of child workers can have a negative impact on economic development, either by indirectly reducing the wages of unskilled labor or by discouraging the adoption of knowledge- or skills-intensive technology (Edmonds, 2016). By definition, child labor generates an impact on the human capital of the younger generation. In turn, the impact on children's training, development, and capabilities is reflected in the long term in a reduced take-up of opportunities for economic growth.

In this section, we will pay special attention to the impact on the educational field, where most evidence has been accumulated. Complementarily, we gather the available information on the consequences on health, welfare, and employability.

2.3.1   Risk, Health, and Mortality

Child labor can be associated with both short-term and long-term health problems. Much of the research has focused on assessing the impact of performing hazardous work, along with the combined effect of dropping out of studies. The risks are highly variable depending on the activity, ranging from exposure to pesticides in agricultural work, or inhalation of toxic substances during shoemaking, to broken bones during fruit picking on trees, or injuries caused by machinery.[2] Although there are no reliable statistics and many incidents are simply not reported, occupational accidents and child mortality rates appear to be at least comparable to those of adults. In turn, delaying entry into the workforce reduces the likelihood of the early onset of back pain, arthritis, or reduced physical strength (Lee & Orazem, 2010). With data aggregated by country, evidence has been found of the relationship between child labor and adolescent mortality, the level of nutrition of the population, and the presence of infectious diseases (Roggero et al., 2007).

Two recent systematic reviews link child labor with growth problems, malnutrition, a higher incidence of infectious diseases, a high prevalence of injuries, behavior problems, and a lower coping capacity (Batomen Kuimi et al., 2018; Ibrahim et al., 2019).

---

[2]For a detailed report of the risks by sector of activity, it is recommended to consult International Labor Office (2011). *Children in hazardous work: what we know, what we need to do.* Geneva: International Labour Office.

2.3.2 Psychological Well-Being and Quality of Life

There are comparatively few studies analyzing the consequences of child labor on children's mental health. Some epidemiological studies have documented a higher relative prevalence of mood problems and separation anxiety (Benjet, 2010; Doocy et al., 2007; Fekadu et al., 2006), and for girls a higher likelihood of family violence (Catani et al., 2009). Engaging in risky activities and long hours can generate feelings of frustration, so many children become withdrawn and uncommunicative (Uddin et al., 2009). In the case of child soldiers, ex-combatants experience symptoms of post-traumatic stress, are more vulnerable to drug abuse, and may have more difficulties with social interaction and community integration (Schauer & Elbert, 2010).

2.3.3 Academic Performance and School Dropout

In the educational field, the two most contrasting results are school dropouts and deteriorating academic performance. In the first place, working time seems to displace the time dedicated to studies (Fernandez & Abocejo, 2014) and can reduce the period of schooling by up to 2 years (Psacharopoulos, 1997). Dropout rates may increase when local labor market opportunities improve (Duryea & Arends-Kuenning, 2003; Kruger, 2007), and are generally higher in rural contexts (Canagarajah & Coulombe, 1999). In urban areas, they are concentrated in disadvantaged neighborhoods with higher levels of social risk (Crane, 1991).

Second, working children perform worse in language and mathematics (Gunnarsson et al., 2006), and are more likely to repeat grades (Psacharopoulos, 1997). The negative impact in terms of learning may be due to fatigue and "the diversion of their interests away from academic concerns" (Heady, 2003). In addition, it is directly related to the number of hours dedicated to work and the performance of work activities in a schedule that coincides with that of the school (Holgado et al., 2016). Jobs that are more intense or require more dedication may also have a more pronounced impact on academic performance.

Results may also depend in part on family characteristics. In large families, there is a greater likelihood of dropouts or poorer educational outcomes. There seems to be a kind of "specialization" in the household so that some children are dedicated to studying and others are not (Patrinos & Psacharopoulos, 1995). A study in Peru found that the number of siblings was associated with the probability of repeating a grade (Patrinos & Psacharopoulos, 1997).

In addition, when making decisions about their children's education, families often also consider educational facilities, the number of teachers, the percentage of female teachers, and the distance to school (Huisman & Smits, 2009). When there are more teachers in the district of residence, children are more likely to go to school. In the specific case of girls, parents also positively value the availability of female teachers. Finally, in many cases, geographical distance and lack of adequate transport infrastructure remain a barrier to access, especially for low-income families.

2.3.4   Employability, Job Opportunities, and Working Conditions

It is often suggested in this area that having worked during childhood may contribute to unemployment and low salaries among adults (Bequele & Boyden, 1988), although there is little empirical development to demonstrate this. In the short term, the work involvement of children increases household income and the probability of survival, but in the long term, it can contribute to the perpetuation of poverty to the extent that it reduces "human capital accumulation" (Galli, 2001). Early engagement in unskilled work (whether in agriculture or industry) reduces opportunities for skills development and later translates into lower-paid jobs during adulthood.

In a study with longitudinal data in Tanzania, working during childhood was found to be a significant predictor of staying in the agricultural sector 10 years later (Beegle et al., 2008). More specifically, when children worked between 10 and 20 h/week, they were more likely to be in vulnerable jobs as adults. Besides, working on the family farm had the most negative effects on girls (Burrone & Giannelli, 2019).

Recently, the "Global Report on Child Labour 2015" (ILO, 2015) has also attempted to document the connection between working during childhood and employment outcomes during youth. An extensive survey examining the transition from school to work found that individuals who had worked as children showed greater youth vulnerability, along with more difficulty in finding good jobs. Also, it revealed that adolescence is a high-risk profile, with a high prevalence of "hazardous work" between the ages of 15 and 17.

These types of studies that follow the trajectory of working children through the life cycle are likely to become more frequent in the coming years. Not only would they serve to analyze the long-term impact, but they are also useful for assessing the equation between protective factors and cumulative risk factors.

Box 2.3: At the Street School
Environmental psychology has studied individual differences in the representation of space, to then determine how it influences movements in complex urban environments. One of the most frequent case studies consists of analyzing the "cognitive maps" of taxi drivers since they accumulate experience of movement within the city that is clearly above that of the average citizen. It has been found that taxi drivers can estimate shorter travel distances than the general public, among other things because they know more shortcuts.

(continued)

Box 2.3 (continued)

Therefore, it seems that their professional experience allows them to develop enriched representations of the street map of the locality in which they work. It would be interesting to see whether the widespread use of GPS has in any way undermined their ability to navigate efficiently in the city.

What about working children? Do they learn anything in the "street school"? Some research seems to indicate this. A study with children in the Northeast of Brazil showed that those who sold sweets on the street acquired levels of mathematical understanding that in some dimensions were above the comparison group. Specifically, the vendors developed adequate strategies to solve arithmetic problems and were better able to handle large numerical values. In this case, cognitive development seems to be connected to participation in everyday buying and selling practices.

Adult traders often jokingly say that they have "graduated from the psychology of the street" because they are in constant contact with people of all kinds who test their communication skills. This is another area in which it would be of interest to explore the skills developed by children working on the street.

Based on Saxe, G. B. (1988). The mathematics of child street vendors. *Child Development*, 1415–1425.

[Brazil]

2.4   The Cycle of Poverty

Research on the causes and consequences of child labor allows us to draw a hypothetical cycle of poverty, as we have represented in Fig. 2.1. This sequence is based on some of the evidence we have found in our previous review of the literature. Families with low income are more likely to send their children to work. This can interfere with the continuation of compulsory education and therefore has a negative impact on the type of skills that allow upward labor mobility. As a result, children are highly likely to reproduce as adults the same kind of subsistence activities that their parents performed. This closes the intergenerational cycle that explains the persistence of poverty in certain segments of the population.

This is a cycle that is especially documented in children who carry out non-salaried activities in the family unit, collaborating in tasks generally in the primary sector. Especially in the case of subsistence agriculture. The "vicious circle

Fig. 2.1 The hypothetical cycle of poverty. *Source:* own elaboration

of poverty" is also widely documented in development economics. It has been shown that lack of income prevents the generation of savings and thus the accumulation of capital needed to increase income (Bauer, 1965). The result is that societies with higher levels of income inequality tend to have lower levels of intergenerational income mobility as a consequence (Sakamoto et al., 2014).

At the micro-level, something similar seems to be happening. To the extent that children from low-income households have to spend their time helping the family, they cannot free up the time needed to invest in the human capital that would improve their positioning in the labor market, and that would potentially allow them to reverse their situation. From a psychological point of view, both the accumulation of risk factors and continued exposure to stressors can result in some deterioration of cognitive abilities (Sakamoto et al., 2014). It also often results in the development of fatalistic attitudes and the generalization of feelings of learned helplessness.

2.5 Conclusion

Child labor has a higher incidence in low-income families, so it seems related to situations of poverty. However, this is a complex relationship. On the one hand, there does not seem to be a simple linear correlation between family income and the probability of children working, but rather it is modulated by family characteristics as well as other social and cultural factors. For example, parents' educational expectations, along with their own history of child labor, carry significant weight. On the other hand, econometric models have been specifically based on economic survival activities, rather than on forced or dangerous work, so it would be necessary to check to what extent they can be generalized to this type of situation as well.

Secondly, we have described some of the mechanisms that seem to underpin the intergenerational perpetuation of poverty through the impact of child labor on education. In the long term, one can follow the implications of educational interruption on adult salaries, incomes, and poverty (Ilahi et al., 2000, 2009). If in Chap. 1 we presented prevention as a strategy to avoid the aggravation among the various forms of child labor, in this chapter we discovered its potential to avoid the worsening or intergenerational permanence of child labor in certain segments of the population. As we shall see below, actions to ensure universal primary and secondary education are directly related to poverty reduction.

The consequences of child labor seem to be grouped around two types of effects: some related to health and well-being, while others are related to education and employability. Research on health risks has paid more attention to those considered "hazardous work", while assessment of the impact on education has been comparatively more frequent in primary sector livelihood activities. However, there is a need to systematically unravel what effects are associated with each form of child labor. The comparative study of modalities and effects can contribute to a better understanding of the phenomenon.

Finally, we have identified at least two topics for further research in the future. First, although negative consequences are part of the very definition of child labor, their empirical documentation has been relatively scarce, so it would be interesting to delve deeper into this aspect in the future. Second, as research in other areas has shown, protective factors contribute to the resilience of a significant proportion of those individuals who experience an accumulation of risks in their childhood. Consequently, it would be of interest to explore which elements specifically contribute to the resilience of working children.

References

Acosta, P. (2011a). Female migration and child occupation in rural El Salvador. *Population Research and Policy Review, 30*(4), 569–589.

Acosta, P. (2011b). School attendance, child labor, and remittances from international migration in El Salvador. *Journal of Development Studies, 47*(6), 913–936.

Alcaraz, C., Chiquiar, D., & Salcedo, A. (2012). Remittances, schooling, and child labor in Mexico. *Journal of Development Economics, 97*(1), 156–165.

Amin, S., Quayes, M. S., & Rives, J. M. (2004). Poverty and other determinants of child labor in Bangladesh. *Southern Economic Journal, 70*(4), 876–892.

Antman, F. M. (2012). Gender, educational attainment, and the impact of parental migration on children left behind. *Journal of Population Economics, 25*(4), 1187–1214.

Bahar, O. S. (2014). Should they work or should they not? Low-income Kurdish migrant mothers' beliefs and attitudes about child labor. *Global Social Welfare, 1*(1), 37–52.

Basu, K., & Van, P. H. (1998). The economics of child labor. *American Economic Review, 88*(3), 412–427.

Batomen Kuimi, B. L., Oppong-Nkrumah, O., Kaufman, J., Nazif-Munoz, J. I., & Nandi, A. (2018). Child labour and health: A systematic review. *International Journal of Public Health, 63*, 663–672.

Bauer, P. T. (1965). The vicious circle of poverty. *Weltwirtschaftliches Archiv, 95*, 4–20.

Beegle, K., Dehejia, R. H., Gatti, R., & Krutikova, S. (2008). *The consequences of child labor: Evidence from longitudinal data in rural Tanzania*. Washington, D.C.: The World Bank.

Benjet, C. (2010). Childhood adversities of populations living in low-income countries: Prevalence, characteristics, and mental health consequences. *Current Opinion in Psychiatry, 23*(4), 356–362.

Bequele, A., & Boyden, J. (Eds.). (1988). *Combating child labor*. Geneva: International Labour Organization.

Bhalotra, S., & Heady, C. (2003). Child farm labor: The wealth paradox. *The World Bank Economic Review, 17*(2), 197–227.

Buchmann, C. (2000). Family structure, parental perceptions, and child labor in Kenya: What factors determine who is enrolled in school? *Social Forces, 78*(4), 1349–1378.

Burrone, S., & Giannelli, G. (2019). *Does Child Labor Lead to Vulnerable Employment in Adulthood? Evidence for Tanzania*. IZA Discussion Paper No. 12162. Retrieved from SSRN: https://ssrn.com/abstract=3390149.

Canagarajah, S., & Coulombe, H. (1999). *Child labor and schooling in Ghana*. Washington, D.C.: The World Bank.

Canagarajah, S., & Nielsen, H. S. (1999). *Child labor and schooling in Africa: A comparative study*. Washington, D.C.: World Bank, Social Protection Team.

Catani, C., Schauer, E., Elbert, T., Missmahl, I., Bette, J. P., & Neuner, F. (2009). War trauma, child labor, and family violence: Life adversities and PTSD in a sample of school children in Kabul.

Journal of Traumatic Stress: Official Publication of the International Society for Traumatic Stress Studies, 22(3), 163–171.

Crane, J. (1991). The epidemic theory of ghettos and neighborhood effects on dropping out and teenage childbearing. *American Journal of Sociology, 96*(5), 1226–1259.

Doocy, S., Crawford, B., Boudreaux, C., & Wall, E. (2007). The risks and impacts of portering on the well-being of children in Nepal. *Journal of Tropical Pediatrics, 53*(3), 165–170.

Duryea, S., & Arends-Kuenning, M. (2003). School attendance, child labor, and local labor market fluctuations in urban Brazil. *World Development, 31*(7), 1165–1178.

Edmonds, E. V. (2005). Does child labor decline with improving economic status? *Journal of Human Resources, 40*(1), 77–99.

Edmonds, E. V. (2016). *Economic growth and child labor in low-income economies. A synthesis paper prepared for IZA/DFID.* Bonn: Institute for the Study of Labor.

Emerson, P. M., & Souza, A. P. (2008). Birth order, child labor, and school attendance in Brazil. *World Development, 36*(9), 1647–1664.

Fan, C. S. (2011). The luxury axiom, the wealth paradox, and child labor. *Journal of Economic Development, 36*(3), 25–45.

Fekadu, D., Alem, A., & Hägglöf, B. (2006). The prevalence of mental health problems in Ethiopian child laborers. *Journal of Child Psychology and Psychiatry, 47*(9), 954–959.

Fernandez, R. C. E., & Abocejo, F. T. (2014). Child labor, poverty, and school attendance: Evidence from the Philippines by region. *CNU Journal of Higher Education, 8*, 114–127.

Galli, R. (2001). *The economic impact of child labor.* Geneva: International Institute for Labour Studies.

Gunnarsson, V., Orazem, P. F., & Sánchez, M. A. (2006). Child labor and school achievement in Latin America. *The World Bank Economic Review, 20*(1), 31–54.

Heady, C. (2003). The effect of child labor on learning achievement. *World Development, 31*(2), 385–398.

Holgado, D., Maya-Jariego, I., Palacio, J., & Oviedo-Trespalacios, O. (2016). Two profiles of child labor in the Colombian Caribbean Coast: Relocated children to suburban areas compared to the key role of social and labor characteristics of mothers in urban settings. In G. Tonón (Ed.), *Indicators of quality of life in Latin America* (Social Indicators Research Series) (Vol. 62, pp. 251–273). New York: Springer.

Huisman, J., & Smits, J. (2009). Effects of household and district-level factors on primary school enrollment in 30 developing countries. *World Development, 37*(1), 179–193.

Ibrahim, A., Abdalla, S. M., Jafer, M., Jihad Abdelgadir, J., & de Vries, N. (2019). Child labor and health: A systematic literature review of the impacts of child labor on child's health in low- and middle-income countries. *Journal of Public Health, 41*(1), 18–26. https://doi.org/10.1093/pubmed/fdy018.

Ilahi, N., Orazem, P., & Sedlacek, G. (2000). *The implications of child labor for adult wages, income, and poverty: Retrospective evidence from Brazil.* Washington, D.C.: The World Bank.

Ilahi, N., Orazem, P. F., & Sedlacek, G. (2009). *How does working as a child affect wages, income, and poverty as an adult?. Child labor and education in Latin America* (pp. 87–101). New York: Palgrave Macmillan.

International Labor Office. (2011). *Children in hazardous work: What we know, what we need to do.* Geneva: International Labour Office.

International Labour Organization. (2015). *World report on child labor 2015: Paving the way to decent work for young people.* Geneva: International Labour Organization.

Kambhampati, U. S., & Rajan, R. (2006). Economic growth: A panacea for child labour? *World Development, 34*(3), 426–445. https://doi.org/10.1016/j.worlddev.2005.08.010.

Kruger, D. I. (2007). Coffee production effects on child labor and schooling in rural Brazil. *Journal of Development Economics, 82*(2), 448–463.

Lee, C., & Orazem, P. F. (2010). Lifetime health consequences of child labor in Brazil. In R. K. Q. Akee, E. V. Edmonds, & K. Tatsiramos (Eds.), *Child labor and the transition between school and work* (pp. 99–133). Bingley: Emerald Group Publishing.

Mansuri, G. (2006). *Migration, school attainment, and child labor: Evidence from rural Pakistan.* Washington: The World Bank.

Maya Jariego, I. (2017). "But we want to work": The movement of child workers in Peru and the actions for reducing child labor. *American Journal of Community Psychology, 60*(3–4), 430–438.

Mukherjee, D., & Das, S. (2008). Role of parental education in schooling and child labor decision: Urban India in the last decade. *Social Indicators Research, 89*(2), 305–322.

Patrinos, H. A., & Psacharopoulos, G. (1995). Educational performance and child labor in Paraguay. *International Journal of Educational Development, 15*(1), 47–60.

Patrinos, H. A., & Psacharopoulos, G. (1997). Family size, schooling, and child labor in Peru–An empirical analysis. *Journal of Population Economics, 10*(4), 387–405.

Plummer, M. L., Kudrati, M., & Yousif, N. D. H. (2007). Beginning street life: Factors contributing to children working and living on the streets of Khartoum, Sudan. *Children and Youth Services Review, 29*(12), 1520–1536.

Psacharopoulos, G. (1997). Child labor versus educational attainment. Some evidence from Latin America. *Journal of Population Economics, 10*(4), 377–386.

Ray, R. (2000). Child labor, child schooling, and their interaction with adult labor: Empirical evidence for Peru and Pakistan. *The World Bank Economic Review, 14*(2), 347–367.

Rodriguez, C., & Sanchez, F. (2012). Armed conflict exposure, human capital investments, and child labor: Evidence from Colombia. *Defense and Peace Economics, 23*(2), 161–184.

Roggero, P., Mangiaterra, V., Bustreo, F., & Rosati, F. (2007). The health impact of child labor in developing countries: Evidence from cross-country data. *American Journal of Public Health, 97* (2), 271–275.

Rossi, M., & Rosati, F. C. (2007). Impact of school quality on child labor and school attendance: The case of the CONAFE Compensatory Education Program in Mexico. *Understanding Children's Work Programme Working Paper, February 2007.* https://doi.org/10.2139/ssrn. 1780249.

Runyan, C. W., Schulman, M., Dal Santo, J., Bowling, J. M., & Agans, R. (2009). Attitudes and beliefs about adolescent work and workplace safety among parents of working adolescents. *Journal of Adolescent Health, 44*(4), 349–355.

Sakamoto, A., Rarick, J., Woo, H., & Wang, S. X. (2014). What underlies the Great Gatsby Curve? Psychological micro-foundations of the "vicious circle" of poverty. *Mind & Society, 13*(2), 195–211.

Saxe, G. B. (1988). The mathematics of child street vendors. *Child Development, 1998*, 1415–1425.

Schauer, E., & Elbert, T. (2010). The psychological impact of child soldiering. In E. Martz (Ed.), *Trauma rehabilitation after war and conflict* (pp. 311–360). New York, NY: Springer.

Siddiqi, F., & Patrinos, H. A. (1996). *Child labor: Issues, causes, and interventions. HCO Working Papers, 56.* Washington, DC: World Bank.

Triningsih, N., & Ichihashi, M. (2010). The Impact of poverty and educational policy on child labor in Indonesia. *IDEC Hiroshima University Discussion Paper.*

Uddin, M. N., Hamiduzzaman, M. & Gunter, B. G. (2009). Physical and psychological implications of risky child labor: A study in Sylhet City, Bangladesh (July 1, 2009). *Bangladesh Development Research Working Paper Series, 8.* https://doi.org/10.2139/ssrn.1428206.

Van Putten, A. E., Dykstra, P. A., & Schippers, J. J. (2008). Just like mom? The intergenerational reproduction of women's paid work. *European Sociological Review, 24*(4), 435–449.

Verner, D., & Blunch, N. H. (1999). *Revisiting the link between poverty and child labor: The Ghanaian experience.* Washington, D.C.: The World Bank.

Wahba, J. (2000). Child labor and poverty transmission: No room for dreams. *Economic Research Forum Working Papers Series, 108.* Cairo, Egypt.

Chapter 3
What Is Effective in Preventing Child Labor

Abstract Child labor indicators have shown a significant decline since registration began. This is an area where policies and programs have been relatively effective, and there are some evidence-based practices. Actions promoted by the International Labor Organization have followed an institutional approach, involving governments, trade unions, business associations and other social actors. The introduction of legal regulations and social dialogue policies have established the framework for changing sociocultural norms on child labor. In this context, the two types of specific interventions that have proved most effective are conditional cash transfers and programs to guarantee compulsory education.

Keywords Child labor · Policy · Programmes · Effectiveness · Social dialogue · Community coalitions · Conditional cash transfers · Compulsory education

3.1 Introduction

The town hall is not particularly functional, but it lets in a pleasant light. The wooden coffered ceiling and the gallery of the municipal presidents give the room a certain solemnity. It is an appropriate place to meet with the representatives of the employers' association. The "Procurador para la Protección de Niñas, Niños y Adolescentes" (Ombudsman for the Protection of Children and Adolescents) has called on the employers of Patzcuaro to explain the latest national agreements on the policy of "zero tolerance for child labor". The agenda of the day includes the presentation of the "action plan in the value chain of the sugar cane agroindustry in Mexico" and the "code of conduct for the protection of children from sexual exploitation in tourism and the travel industry". Hence, there is a large representation of the town's landowners and hotel owners among the attendees. Meetings such as this one have been repeated in other locations in Michoacán, to raise awareness and training business people in the region.

During the harvest season it is common to find (especially among migrant families) that the children of "jornaleros" (day laborers) are involved in cutting sugar cane, one of the activities considered "hazardous work" by the International

© The Author(s), under exclusive license to Springer Nature Switzerland AG 2021   33
I. Maya Jariego, *Community Prevention of Child Labor*, Human Well-Being
Research and Policy Making, https://doi.org/10.1007/978-3-030-70810-8_3

Labor Organization. The National Chamber of Sugar and Alcohol Industries approved a declaration against child labor, with the participation of unions and employers. Training and awareness-raising sessions were then held in all sugar mills. A census of cutters in each harvest was also taken and a clause on the eradication of child labor was introduced in the contracts that the mills sign with each supplier farm.

In the case of hotels, the code of conduct to combat the commercial sexual exploitation of children and adolescents is an international initiative to which tourism companies can commit themselves. Reception staff receives specific training to detect cases of abuse. After an accreditation process, participating hotels receive a badge that recognizes them as companies committed to the prevention of child exploitation and can be posted in access areas or rooms. During the meeting, the prosecutor announced that both the labor inspectorate and the social services would collaborate in detecting cases of violation of children's rights.

The work of raising awareness, training and recognition of employers is one of the institutional initiatives that have proved effective in preventing child labor. It is normally integrated into the social dialogue policies of each country, with the government negotiating with the social agents. Besides, it usually has a component of changing attitudes, modifying social norms, and implementing instruments of surveillance, monitoring and control. In this chapter we will review the approval of legal agreements and regulations, income transfer programs and actions to strengthen the education system. In each case, we will explain which components of the intervention are effective in preventing child labor.

Box 3.1: The Dilemma of Protecting or Giving Voice to Children

Non-governmental organizations working with children in Peru are divided between those who advocate for the regulation of child labor and those who want to abolish it. This polarization has been described by one side as a debate between "regulationists" and "abolitionists". The former defends the right of children to work, while the latter emphasizes the protection of children. In the first case, children are considered to be "small adults", capable of making decisions for themselves. In the second case, the emphasis is placed on disadvantaged contexts that force children to work and reduce their personal options. The confrontation has led to the entities on both sides not wanting to collaborate with each other.

Those who defend the right of children to work criticize the fact that minors are seen as victims or as dependent persons. Instead, they understand that they are active citizens, who can participate in decision-making and are even capable of transforming society. Furthermore, they think that in certain cultures the work of the youngest is part of the socialization process.

Advocates for child protection measures align themselves with the policies of the International Labor Organization and point out that behind the

(continued)

Box 3.1 (continued)

movements of working children there are adults who make ideological use of their situation. In this case, they emphasize the negative consequences of child labor.

In this context, researchers G. K. Lieten and Talinay Strehl argue in favor of traditional child protection policies and question the "agency" approach, even though the latter currently has a great influence on the literature on children's rights: "The argument of some of the academics on children's rights that the street child should not be considered a victim, but rather an agent of change, an active citizen, denies the basically unjustified context in which these children are growing up and which pushes them onto the streets".

Based on Lieten, G. K., & Strehl, T. (2014). *Child street life: an inside view of hazards and expectations of street children in Peru*. Springer.

[Peru]

3.2 Concerted Action by Governments and Social Partners

As the previous chapters have shown, the International Labor Organization (ILO) leads the way in policies to eradicate child labor at the global level. To this end, it has relied mainly on the establishment of international agreements, together with collaboration with governments through social dialogue policies in each country. On the one hand, this has introduced a marked institutional character into the design and implementation of programs, with the involvement of trade unions, business associations, and public administration units. On the other hand, an eminently normative approach has also been followed, through the approval of agreements, regulations, and all kinds of legal instruments. However, this impact on public policy also has an indirect effect on social control mechanisms. The establishment of agreements between key actors can contribute to changing social norms and, in practice, is a facilitator of child labor monitoring actions.

3.2.1 International Conventions and Agreements Against Child Labor

As we have just noted, through the commitment of countries, efforts have been directed preferably towards the creation of international standards. In addition to the establishment of common standards, this process involves the political commitment of governments, which they then have to translate into the functioning of the labor market in their countries. This means launching social consultation initiatives to catalyze socio-cultural change. In fact, the mere prohibition of child labor can have counterproductive effects (Bharadwaj et al., 2020), so it is necessary to influence those psychosocial factors that determine the practice of labor relations.

There are a large number of cases in the literature that illustrate the importance of political initiatives and legal regulation. For example, in the tobacco industry, the commitment of business associations to international treaties, monitoring by non-governmental organizations and direct litigation in cases involving children on tobacco farms have been proposed as strategies with preventive value (Ramos, 2018). The adoption of codes of conduct, social audits and other non-governmental regulatory systems have also shown their potential for improving industrial relations (O'Rourke, 2003). In the case of the United States, a clause on child labor standards has been suggested for inclusion in international trade agreements (Garg, 1998). However, there still seems to be a need to move towards a greater consensus on such standards (Moran, 2005).

3.2.2   The Regulation of the Minimum Age for Access to Employment

The legal working age is different in each country, with a minimum variable ranging, with some exceptions, between 14 and 16 years of age. The "Convention concerning Minimum Age for Admission to Employment" (ILO C138, 1973) requires signatory countries to commit themselves to the goal of eradicating child labor and is therefore a central element in all other preventive policies. It has been proven that raising the minimum age for work can increase school attendance in low- and middle-income countries (Oppong-Nkrumah et al., 2019), although it seems to explain only a small percentage of the variance in child labor (Edmonds & Shrestha, 2012). Conversely, from a developmental point of view, lowering the minimum working age may interfere negatively with schooling, reduce the time spent in family life, or even increase the consumption of tobacco, alcohol, and marijuana (Greenberger, 1983). During adolescence, and in general, when children are experiencing personal transitions, it can become an added risk factor.

3.2.3   Coalitions of Employers, Trade Unions, and Other Social Partners

Trade union representation and collective bargaining have a contrasting impact on industrial relations. Negotiating tables foster trust and cooperation among social agents, introduce strategies to improve productivity, and are an effective mechanism for wage regulation (Freeman & Medoff, 1981; Hübler & Jirjahn, 2003). In practice, they are a way of institutionalizing consensus in labor contexts. At the national level, policies for the eradication of child labor are based on such mechanisms of social dialogue and promote the establishment of alliances between the different social sectors involved. This not only allows for the representation of the interests of workers, employers, and other social actors but also facilitates the emergence of shared social standards. This is relevant insofar as they constitute a mechanism of social control that exerts informal pressure on impermissible labor practices; and in the long term, they can counteract the permissive attitudes of the population referred to in Chap. 2.

3.2.4 Labor Inspectors and Community Control Mechanisms

Although little systematic evaluation of results has been carried out, the labor inspectorate appears to be an effective mechanism in the fight against child labor. A pioneering study in this area found that a slight increase in labor inspections in Brazil was significantly related to a decrease in the proportion of working children and adolescents (De Almeida & Kassouf, 2016). In the Dominican Republic, those inspectors who carry out their work with special competence have proved to be an alternative with which to overcome the shortcomings of collective bargaining (Schrank, 2009). However, to be effective, inspectors must establish alliances with those social groups that are more favorable to the application of labor legislation, as shown by the case of preventing child labor in brick manufacturing companies in Argentina (Amengual, 2014).

3.3 Conditional Cash Transfer Programs

Bolsa Escola is a program that provides financial assistance to poor families in Brazil, conditional on their children continuing to attend school regularly. Its implementation in the second half of the 1990s and in the early 2000s showed that it was possible to link income transfer programs with the effective reduction of school dropout (Nascimiento & Aguiar, 2006). It subsequently gave rise to a broader program called *Bolsa Familia*, which gradually extended the geographical coverage and modalities of action. At the same time, other benefits and initiatives were created, such as the Program for the Eradication of Child Labor (PETI), which sought to achieve similar objectives at the federal level. However, its pioneering character, together with the good results obtained by Brazil in the implementation of preventive actions, have made the *Bolsa Escola* program an emblematic practice in the reduction of child labor. It has often been used as a reference model for the design of similar interventions.

Brazil is one of the countries that has experienced a more substantial change in the reduction of child labor and, in parallel, an increase in the coverage of compulsory education. In about a decade and a half, there was a reduction of more than half in the work activity of children between 7 and 15 years, along with an increase of more than 10% points in regular school attendance (Rosati et al., 2011). These results are not only attributable to the *Bolsa Escola* program (and others like it), but are part of a broad set of policies to improve the quality of the education system and reduce problems of access to school, which were implemented simultaneously with numerous other actions at the national, regional and local levels.

In their most basic form, conditional cash transfer programs provide financial support to disadvantaged families, as long as they can prove that their children are still in school. Other versions are not limited to education, but require medical follow-up of children, the participation of families in community activities or direct withdrawal of children from child labor. In some cases, priority is given to families whose children work, for example, in coal mining or agave cultivation, which are considered to be hard and high-risk jobs.[1] Table 3.1 lists the characteristics of a small selection of programs applied in Latin America. These are four of the best-known income transfer programs with an emphasis on education, corresponding to the cases of Brazil, Chile, Colombia, and Mexico.[2]

According to its theoretical design, this type of money transfer is not only an income redistribution policy, but also conditions incentives to the achievement of certain behavioral objectives by families. In other words, it combines a compensatory action for low family incomes with the strengthening of appropriate child-rearing patterns. It is therefore a behavioral program. This is reflected in the fact that participating families undertake medium- and long-term projects. Specifically, mothers are more interested in their children's studies, begin to save and in some cases incorporate family planning strategies.

However, to achieve these kinds of results it is essential to develop an appropriate implementation. Among other factors, both delays in payments to families and problems with the reliability of school attendance verification mechanisms can lead to the loss of control over the programs (Nascimiento & Aguiar, 2006). Conversely, both the participation of families in extracurricular activities and the implementation of education boards (also called "social councils") help to strengthen the intervention and can improve the program's impact. We will return to these community control strategies in Chap. 4.

This type of intervention integrates very well with maternal and perinatal health programs, since it promotes compliance with follow-up medical visits by pregnant women and nursing mothers (Bourguignon et al., 2004). They also reduce the risk of malnutrition (Paes-Sousa et al., 2011). In general, the introduction of specific health conditions can increase medical check-ups and improve access to preventive programs (Lopez-Arana et al., 2016).

---

[1] As in the case of the PETI program in Brazil.

[2] Among others, it may be of interest to consult the *Progresando con Solidaridad* program of the Dominican Republic (ILO, 2015), or the *Superémonos* program in Costa Rica (Duryea & Morrison, 2004). For a more extensive review of programs in Latin America, see the report by Sauma (2008).

Table 3.1 A selection of income conditional transfer programs

Program	Description	Results
Bolsa Escola (Brazil)	• It grants a scholarship to poor families and it is renewed as long as the children benefiting from the program maintain 90% school attendance • It reached coverage of five million families and eight million children	• Reduction of school dropouts • Reduction of the percentage of suspensions • Reduction in the number of cases of child labor • Improvement of housing, food and health conditions for families
Chile Solidario (Chile)	• A bonus is paid to families in extreme poverty • The payment is made to the woman of the household (either the head of the family or the couple) • It starts with home visits by social workers • The amount is gradually reduced in successive annual instalments	• Positive effect on psychosocial well-being • Facilitates the use of other social programs • Significantly associated with the employment of the head of household • It also has effects on the number of workers in the family
Familias en acción (Colombia)	• The health component requires child vaccination, medical follow-up of children, and participation of mothers in workshops on feeding, contraceptives, and hygiene • The education component requires children to attend school for 80% of the school year • The aids are delivered directly to the mothers	• Increase the use of preventive programs • Conducting medical check-ups • Increases diversity in diet
Oportunidades (México)	• The beneficiaries are chosen from among the most marginalized municipalities, selecting in each case families from a lower social stratum • Communities are involved in the selection process • The food voucher is conditional on participation in training sessions on nutrition and health • The scholarship is conditional on school attendance and medical check-ups • The amount of the scholarship is higher in the higher grades	• Reduction of income inequality • Increased school attendance • Reduces child labor

Source: Program data are based on the work of Lopez-Arana et al. (2016); Hoces de la Guardia et al. (2011); Nascimiento and Aguiar (2006); Sauma (2008); and Soares et al. (2009). The *"Oportunidades"* program was originally called *"Progresa"*. In Chile, cash transfers are called *"Programa de Protección a las Familias"*

3.4   Programs to Enhance Compulsory Education

In many of the preventive actions we have reviewed we find interventions that achieve an educational impact but are not sufficient to reduce the prevalence of child labor. They cannot be considered failed actions, insofar as we are aware that educational problems are often a direct antecedent to the involvement of children in work activities. However, they do help us to detect that the preventive value of educational interventions extends to child labor when the school functions as an alternative scenario that competes in time with the dedication to work activities. In this context, we will now review three types of interventions. First, institutional actions that seek to improve the quality standards of schools or to increase educational coverage. Secondly, psycho-educational interventions with minors at risk, which seek to prevent school drop-out or improve academic performance. Thirdly, initiatives aimed at informing, raising awareness, and training families on the value of education.

3.4.1   The Evaluation and Improvement of the Quality of Schools

Increased funding for primary education, the establishment of quality standards in schools, and the evaluation of the education system improve both coverage and performance. In its most basic form, the mere provision of adequate educational infrastructure in rural contexts encourages families to decide to send their children to school (Ersado, 2005). In terms of education management and teachers, programs to improve the quality of schools in Mexico have been shown to influence family decisions on investment in the human capital of their children, thus having a deterrent effect on child labor (Rossi & Rosati, 2007).

3.4.2   Accessibility to Education

Another approach is to remove barriers to access. For part of the population, going to school means traveling long distances, overcoming architectural barriers, or bearing the cost of transport and educational materials. In other cases, the required transport is simply not available. That is why the building of educational centers, the provision of transport infrastructure and urban redesign are among the strategies that can have a positive impact, especially among the highest risk groups. As population density being a key factor (Romanillos & García-Palomares, 2018) as well as the rural/urban dimension, the geographical location of public resources can be decisive in the emergence of possible spatial imbalances or social inequalities.

3.4.3 The Prevention of School Dropouts

"Edúcame Primero" is a psycho-educational program for the prevention of child labor. It is usually implemented through extracurricular sessions focused on the development of skills and, in some cases, participation in play activities. The social-emotional skills training modules can reverse the risk situations faced by participants and, consequently, prevent them from dropping out of school (Maya Jariego & Palacio Sañudo, 2014). They can also have a positive impact on academic performance (Holgado et al., 2014). On the other hand, free play sessions (in the safe context provided by the school) function as an alternative space to participate in work activities or in negative socialization contexts (Chapa et al., 2012).

The above case is an illustrative sample of psychoeducational interventions with preventive purposes. They can be carried out outside school hours, as in the example, or be integrated in a transversal way in the regulated subjects. Sometimes they are carried out in parallel with tutoring and academic support sessions for children at higher risk. In any case, the evidence is very consistent about the effectiveness of all kinds of preventive programs, both at school and in the community context (Wilson et al., 2011). Among other actions, the following may have a positive effect:

- Extracurricular support, with personalized or small group tutoring.
- Training in social-emotional skills.
- Peer mentoring programs.
- Recording and ongoing monitoring of attendance.
- Referral to vocational schools or alternative training contexts.
- Restructuring the school into smaller classes with lower teacher-student ratios.

3.4.4 Improving Educational Performance

The programs mentioned in the previous section also have an impact on educational outcomes. In fact, grade repetition, low grades, and academic engagement are among the best predictors of school dropout (Janosz et al., 1997). Consequently, actions to improve motivation and academic performance can be considered secondary prevention strategies for both school dropouts and child labor. Many of these practices relate to classroom management and vary from activities that involve students with strategies to increase high-performance expectations, correct inappropriate behaviors and provide individualized supervision (Simonsen et al., 2008). Complementarily, psycho-educational interventions are often designed to affect both performance and the risk of dropout, such as the "Edúcame Primero" program mentioned in the previous section.

3.4.5 Parent Training

In the analysis of the causes, in the previous chapter, we found that the higher the educational level of the parents, the greater the probability that the children will remain in school and, consequently, the lower the probability of child labor (Ersado, 2005). This leads us to think that educational actions on parents can have a preventive impact. More specifically, we have empirical evidence that parenting skills training programs prevent the emergence of behavioral and emotional problems in children (Sanders, 1999). In fact, parenting skills seem to be more decisive in the socialization of children than the distribution of parents' time between work and home (Greenberger & Goldberg, 1989). Hence, positive parenting programs not only reduce children's behavioral problems at school but also prevent the deterioration of the situation and the emergence of more far-reaching adjustment problems (Webster-Stratton et al., 2001).

Box 3.2: The Value of Education

"On the rough five-mile trail that separates Wikdi from his school, dozens of donkeys have broken their necks. There, the paramilitaries have also tortured and killed many people. However, Wikdi does not stop to think about how dangerous this path is, which is full of stones, dry mud, and weeds. If he did, he would die of fright and would not be able to study. He walks back and forth between his ranch, located in the indigenous reservation of Arquía, and his school, located in the municipality of Unguía, for 5 h a day. So, he always faces the journey with the same calm look he has now, while closing the zipper of his backpack" (Salcedo, 2016, p. 9).

This excerpt is part of Alberto Salcedo Ramos' chronicle of a Colombian boy who spends 5 h a day going to and from school. It is not fiction. Communities besieged by political violence in remote rural areas face serious problems in accessing the education system. There are contexts in which going to school is an odyssey, but at the same time one of the few places where a different future can be established. So much so that families see no alternative but to sacrifice in order to take advantage of the few existing opportunities.

Based on Salcedo, A. (2016). *Viaje al Macondo real y otras crónicas*. Logroño: Pepitas de Calabaza Editorial.

[Colombia]

3.5 Effective Practices in Preventing Child Labor

In the review we have carried out in the three previous sections we have verified the positive impact (mostly consistent) of three types of preventive actions. If we focus on the psychosocial processes they trigger, we can define them respectively in the following terms:

Table 3.2   Three effective practices in community-based prevention of child labor

Programs type	Intervention challenges	Some results
Community coalitions	• To raise awareness of the work that children do in rural environments, in the informal sector and in domestic service • Legal regulation has to be applied in practice	• Compliance with labor legislation • Improvement of working conditions in the sector • Reduction of child labor
Conditional cash transfers	• To have a sufficient economic endowment (per family and at the aggregate level) • Ensure effective control of family obligations • Check that the beneficiaries belong to families in need • Integrate the program with other actions to generate employment for adults	• Increased school attendance • Improved nutrition and medical follow-up • Increased family cohesion • Improvements in academic performance • A decrease in child labor • Reduction in the number of children living on the street
Promotion of compulsory education	• To have the necessary infrastructure • Involve the teaching staff in the processes of institutional change	• Reduction of school dropouts • Improvement of academic performance • Increase in educational coverage • A decrease in child labor

Source: own elaboration. In the results column we have highlighted those where there is more consistent evidence

1. The establishment of agreed social standards, with the participation of some of the key community actors, or with the representation of workers and employers.
2. The strengthening of appropriate child-rearing behaviors, with special attention to school attendance, balanced nutrition, and regular medical check-ups.
3. The reduction of barriers to access to the education system, as an alternative scenario that competes directly with time spent at work.

Table 3.2 summarizes some of the contrasting results of these three types of preventive actions, and also lists some of the most significant challenges faced during the implementation process. Below, we compare the preventive contributions of these three types of actions.

Community coalitions. The establishment of international standards, collective bargaining and labor inspections contribute to compliance with labor legislation. Indirectly, they can also improve working conditions for adult employment in the sectors concerned. The effectiveness of such actions is underpinned by mechanisms of monitoring, social control and the setting-up of shared standards. This is what allows legal regulations to be implemented and ultimately to be effective. In any case, the concentration of child labor in the informal economy makes it particularly difficult to obtain results. In addition, girls working as domestic servants or children working in remote rural areas generally have a less social visibility. Coupled with the involvement of children in illicit businesses, bringing all existing child labor to the surface becomes a challenge in itself.

Conditional cash transfers. The social benefits known as *"Bolsa Escola"* in Brazil and *"Oportunidades"* in Mexico are the oldest, best known and most financially endowed programs. The PETI program, also in Brazil, is the first to introduce the withdrawal of children from child labor as a condition.[3] Although there may be some inconsistency in the empirical evidence, it is generally assumed that conditional cash transfers reduce the prevalence of child labor (Edmonds & Schady, 2012), decrease the number of hours worked per week (De Hoop & Rosati, 2014; Tagliati, 2019), and improve school attendance or academic performance (Cardoso & Portela-Souza, 2004). Complementarily, they also appear to have a direct impact on the eating patterns and health status of family members, among other outcomes (Bourguignon et al., 2003; Duryea & Morrison, 2004; Ferro et al., 2010; Hoces de la Guardia et al., 2011; Maluccio, 2009; Yap et al., 2009).

To this end, the design of conditional cash transfers is based on two fundamental elements, which consist of establishing (a) a maximum amount of income below which families are eligible for the program, and (b) a behavioral requirement to obtain the cash incentive. This second element, i.e., the contingencies of reinforcement, could be a determinant of the program's impact. In fact, the ex-ante evaluation has shown a "surprisingly strong" effect of the conditionality of the economic benefit on school attendance (Bourguignon et al., 2004, p. 225).

However, not all increases in school attendance necessarily translate into reductions in child labor (Rosati, 2016). Moreover, the positive impact of transfer programs may depend in part on the context in which they are applied (as is the case when integrated with other interventions). Sometimes it is not so much the effect associated with the implementation of a single program, but rather the accumulation of interventions that can generate an aggregate effect. Furthermore, the generalization of these types of programs has coincided in part with a period of relative economic growth in Latin America (Maurizio, 2016).

In practice, there is a dialectic tension between the two program objectives: immediate poverty alleviation and long-term human capital accumulation (Soares et al., 2010). The first objective involves implementing appropriate household selection strategies to ensure that the highest risk groups are reached. The second objective involves monitoring compliance with family obligations, which implies applying high standards to people living in extreme need. To complicate matters further, we know that it is practical to combine actions to eradicate child labor with a series of other measures to promote adult employment. Ultimately, we cannot lose sight of the impact on families of withdrawing children from child labor.

Compulsory education. Educational actions have been used to raise community awareness, defend the interests of minors at risk, prevent school dropouts and

---

[3]The other intervention of this type that explicitly mentions child labor among its objectives is the *"Avancemos"* programme in Costa Rica.

improve academic performance. Interventions can be directed at educational institutions, families, or minors. In order to be effective, they must be sufficiently intense, sustained over time, and have institutional support. Furthermore, both the provision of adequate infrastructure and the levels of training and recognition of teachers are key factors in the functioning of the education system. De-motivation and school failure are some of the indicators that can be used for the early detection of the risk of dropping out of school. Psychoeducational intervention on these factors is a form of secondary prevention of child labor. In China, exposure to free compulsory education has significantly proved to reduce the incidence of child labor in the case of boys (Tang et al., 2020).

Box 3.3: A Psychologist Against Increasing Teenage Working Hours

In 1982, the U.S. Department of Labor formulated a proposal to "increase work opportunities" for 14- and 15-year-old children by increasing the number of hours per week allowed during the school period. Ellen Greenberger testified in Parliament presenting the results of her research on the psychological impact of work on adolescents. Studies by her team at the University of California, Irvine, had shown that adolescents who worked generally experienced a reduction in their involvement in school and that the impact clearly depended on the number of hours worked per week. Their statement in Washington was to explain the negative consequences that working hours among teenagers could have on their family life, their educational performance, and their drug use. She, therefore, proposed instead to concentrate efforts on fighting unemployment among young people and adults.

Professor Greenberger acknowledges that after participating in the parliamentary hearing, she increased her commitment to advocating for adolescent welfare. In addition, she reinforced her participation in the media to disseminate the arguments she had presented in the parliamentary commission. In her opinion, "it is desirable that there be more psychologists in the discussions relevant to public policy."

Based on Greenberger, E. (1983). A researcher in the policy arena: The case of child labor. *American Psychologist, 38*(1), 104–111.

[United States]

3.6 Conclusion

The effective prevention of child labor is based on the promotion of standards of social control by the community, the development of appropriate parenting patterns by families and the inclusion of children in the education system until they complete their compulsory education.

At the community level, the prevention of child labor is a process of sociocultural change. Over the last few decades, international bodies have led a process of political transformation, involving governments in the protection of children's rights and in the promotion of preventive initiatives. The adoption of a perspective of consensus and social dialogue has enabled the establishment of shared social standards, adapted to each specific national context. The result has been less tolerance for different forms of child labor, which has facilitated the implementation of monitoring and control measures. Overall, the policy initiative appears to have increased levels of community readiness, paving the way for the effective functioning of cash transfers to poor families and the development of psycho-educational programs.

The conditionality of financial benefits for low-income families is one of the practices that has proved particularly effective in developing countries. On the one hand, it takes into consideration the poverty contexts to which child labor is inextricably linked. On the other hand, it introduces an element of behavioral basis that requires certain patterns of parenting and supervision by parents, which in turn are conducive to the well-being of children. According to available evidence, these programs increase school attendance and improve medical follow-up. With this background, in those more selective interventions, it seems advisable to incorporate the withdrawal of child labor among the behavioral requirements to obtain the monetary incentive. This is the case, for example (with encouraging results), in the Program for the Eradication of Child Labor (PETI), which focuses on hazardous work performed by children in Brazil.

On the other hand, psycho-educational interventions to promote academic performance and avoid dropping out of school seem to work as a strategy for secondary prevention of child labor. The effect is enhanced when study hours compete with children's working hours so that the educational context acts as an alternative protective setting. Positive role models, instrumental support in schoolwork and training of individual skills can be used to make this happen. By promoting achievement motivation and academic performance, children are less likely to leave the school context and the risk of their involvement in work activities is reduced.

Two other elements that stand out among effective strategies are the emphasis on the role of women and the accumulation of preventive measures of various kinds. On the one hand, cash transfer programs make the money available preferably to mothers. As in the case of microcredit in development cooperation contexts, establishing responsibility in women improves household outcomes: they are usually responsible for the education and feeding of their children and are comparatively more likely to invest the resources obtained in the well-being of the family. On the other hand, we have seen how programs sometimes work not only because of the content of individual actions but also because of the accumulation of initiatives that generate an aggregate effect at the community level. When many social agents agree on their goals and a great diversity of programs have shared objectives, it is more viable to raise awareness among the population and it is more likely that community organization will make it possible to obtain the desired changes.

References

Amengual, M. (2014). Pathways to enforcement: Labor inspectors leveraging linkages with society in Argentina. *ILR Review, 67*(1), 3–33.

Bharadwaj, P., Lakdawala, L. K., & Li, N. (2020). Perverse consequences of well intentioned regulation: Evidence from India's child labor ban. *Journal of the European Economic Association, 18*(3), 1158–1195.

Bourguignon, F., Ferreira, F. H., & Leite, P. G. (2003). Conditional cash transfers, schooling, and child labor: Micro-simulating Brazil's Bolsa Escola program. *The World Bank Economic Review, 17*(2), 229–254.

Bourguignon, F., Ferreira, F. H., & Leite, P. G. (2004). Ex ante evaluation of conditional cash transfer programs: The case of Bolsa Escola. In F. H. Ferreira, C. E. Velez, & R. Paes de Barros (Eds.), *Inequality and Economic Development in Brazil* (pp. 225–248). Washington: The World Bank.

Cardoso, E. & Portela-Souza, A. (2004). The Impact of Cash Transfers on Child Labor and School Attendance in Brazil. *Vanderbilt University Department of Economics Working Papers 0407*, Vanderbilt University Department of Economics.

Chapa, E. D., Ramos, I., & Maya-Jariego, I. (2012). "Baúl de Juegos": Una iniciativa lúdica para reducir la incidencia y los efectos del trabajo infantil en menores de Barranquilla. In I. Maya-Jariego & J. E. Palacio (Eds.), *Edúcame Primero Colombia. Un espacio de colaboración entre la Universidad de Sevilla y la Universidad del Norte*. Sevilla: Oficina de Cooperación al Desarrollo de la Universidad de Sevilla.

De Almeida, R. B., & Kassouf, A. L. (2016, July). The effect of labor inspections on reducing child labor in Brazil. In *Anais do XLIII Encontro Nacional de Economia* [Proceedings of the 43rd Brazilian Economics Meeting] (No. 238). Brazilian Association of Graduate Programs in Economics.

De Hoop, J., & Rosati, F. C. (2014). Cash transfers and child labor. *The World Bank Research Observer, 29*(2), 202–234.

Duryea, S. & Morrison, A. R. (2004). The effect of conditional transfers on school performance and child labor: Evidence from an ex-post impact evaluation in Costa Rica. *Inter-American Development Bank Working Paper, No. 418.* https://doi.org/10.2139/ssrn.1818707.

Edmonds, E. V., & Schady, N. (2012). Poverty alleviation and child labor. *American Economic Journal: Economic Policy, 4*(4), 100–124.

Edmonds, E. V., & Shrestha, M. (2012). The impact of minimum age of employment regulation on child labor and schooling. *IZA Journal of Labor Policy, 1*(1), 14.

Ersado, L. (2005). Child labor and schooling decisions in urban and rural areas: Comparative evidence from Nepal, Peru, and Zimbabwe. *World Development, 33*(3), 455–480.

Ferro, A. R., Kassouf, A. L., & Levison, D. (2010). The impact of conditional cash transfer programs on household work decisions in Brazil. *Research in Labor Economics, 31*, 193–218.

Freeman, R. B., & Medoff, J. L. (1981). *The impact of collective bargaining: Illusion or reality? National Bureau of Economic Research Working Paper Series, n° w0735.* Massachusetts: Cambridge.

Garg, A. (1998). A child labor social clause: Analysis and proposal for action. *NYU Journal of International Law and Politics, 31*, 473.

Greenberger, E. (1983). A researcher in the policy arena: The case of child labor. *American Psychologist, 38*(1), 104–111.

Greenberger, E., & Goldberg, W. A. (1989). Work, parenting, and the socialization of children. *Developmental Psychology, 25*(1), 22–35. https://doi.org/10.1037/0012-1649.25.1.22.

Hoces de la Guardia, F., Hojman, A., & Larranaga, O. (2011). Evaluating the Chile Solidario program: Results using the Chile Solidario panel and the administrative databases. *Estudios de Economia, 38*(1), 129. June 2011. Retrieved from SSRN: https://ssrn.com/abstract=1876589.

Holgado, D., Maya-Jariego, I., Ramos, I., Palacio, J., Oviedo-Trespalacios, O., Romero-Mendoza, V., & Amar, J. (2014). Impact of child labor on academic performance: Evidence from the program "Edúcame Primero Colombia". *International Journal of Educational Development, 34,* 58–66.

Hübler, O., & Jirjahn, U. (2003). Works councils and collective bargaining in Germany: The impact on productivity and wages. *Scottish Journal of Political Economy, 50*(4), 471–491.

ILO. (1973). Convention C138: Minimum Age Convention (Convention concerning Minimum Age for Admission to Employment). 58th Conference Session Geneva 1973, 1015 United Nations Treaty Series, p. 297.

Janosz, M., LeBlanc, M., Boulerice, B., & Tremblay, R. E. (1997). Disentangling the weight of school dropout predictors: A test on two longitudinal samples. *Journal of Youth and Adolescence, 26*(6), 733–762.

Lieten, G. K., & Strehl, T. (2014). *Child street life: An inside view of hazards and expectations of street children in Peru.* Springer.

Lopez-Arana, S., Avendano, M., van Lenthe, F. J., & Burdorf, A. (2016). The impact of a conditional cash transfer programme on determinants of child health: Evidence from Colombia. *Public Health Nutrition, 19*(14), 2629–2642.

Maluccio, J. A. (2009). Education and child labor: Experimental evidence from a Nicaraguan conditional cash transfer program. In *Child Labor and Education in Latin America* (pp. 187–204). New York: Palgrave Macmillan.

Maurizio, R. (2016, May). Conditional cash transfers and poverty eradication in Latin America. In *Inter-agency Expert Group Meeting on "Employment and Decent Work for Poverty Eradication in Support of the Second UN Decade for the Eradication of Poverty (2008–2017).* Bangkok, Thailand.

Maya Jariego, I., & Palacio Sañudo, J. E. (2014). La red de facilitadores de los "Espacios para Crecer" en Barranquilla (Colombia): Estrategias de continuidad, ajuste comunitario y mejora de la implementación en los programas de prevención del trabajo infantil. *Journal de Ciencias Sociales, 2*(2), 73–85.

Moran, T. H. (2005). Monitoring compliance with international labor standards: How can the process be improved, and what are the implications for inserting labor standards into the WTO? *Journal of Business Ethics, 59*(1–2), 147–153.

Nascimiento, E. P., & Aguiar, M. (2006). Bolsa Escola: Historia y evolución. In *Cuadernos de Investigación del Instituto Internacional de Planeamiento de la Educación (IIPE).* Paris: UNESCO.

Oppong-Nkrumah, O., Kaufman, J. S., Heymann, J., Frank, J., & Nandi, A. (2019). The impact of increasing the minimum legal age for work on school attendance in low-and middle-income countries. *SSM—Population Health, 8,* 100426.

Organización Internacional del Trabajo. (2015). *Erradicando el trabajo infantil desde los programas sociales: El caso del programa progresando con solidaridad de la República Dominicana.* Geneva: OIT.

O'Rourke, D. (2003). Outsourcing regulation: Analyzing nongovernmental systems of labor standards and monitoring. *Policy Studies Journal, 31*(1), 1–29.

Paes-Sousa, R., Santos, L. M. P., & Miazaki, É. S. (2011). Effects of a conditional cash transfer programme on child nutrition in Brazil. *Bulletin of the World Health Organization, 89,* 496–503.

Ramos, A. K. (2018). Child labor in global tobacco production: A human rights approach to an enduring dilemma. *Health and Human Rights, 20*(2), 235.

Romanillos, G., & García-Palomares, J. C. (2018). Accessibility to schools: Spatial and social imbalances and the impact of population density in four European cities. *Journal of Urban Planning and Development, 144*(4), 04018044.

Rosati, F. C. (2016). Can cash transfers reduce child labor? *IZA World of Labor Conference 2016.*

Rosati, F. C., Manacorda, M., Kovrova, I., Koseleci, N., & Lyon, S. (2011). Understanding the Brazilian success in reducing child labour: Empirical evidence and policy lessons. In *Understanding Children's Work Report.* Geneva: ILO.

Rossi, M., & Rosati, F. C. (2007). Impact of school quality on child labor and school attendance: The case of CONAFE Compensatory Education Program in Mexico. *Understanding Children's Work Programme Working Paper, February 2007*. https://doi.org/10.2139/ssrn.1780249.

Salcedo, A. (2016). *Viaje al Macondo real y otras crónicas*. Logroño: Pepitas de Calabaza Editorial.

Sanders, M. R. (1999). Triple P-Positive Parenting Program: Towards an empirically validated multilevel parenting and family support strategy for the prevention of behavior and emotional problems in children. *Clinical Child and Family Psychology Review, 2*(2), 71–90.

Sauma, P. (2008). *Child labour and conditional cash transfer programmes in Latin America*. Geneva: ILO.

Schrank, A. (2009). Professionalization and probity in a patrimonial state: Labor inspectors in the Dominican Republic. *Latin American Politics and Society, 51*(2), 91–115.

Simonsen, B., Fairbanks, S., Briesch, A., Myers, D., & Sugai, G. (2008). Evidence-based practices in classroom management: Considerations for research to practice. *Education and Treatment of Children, 31*(3), 351–380.

Soares, S., Osório, R. G., Soares, F. V., Medeiros, M., & Zepeda, E. (2009). Conditional cash transfers in Brazil, Chile and Mexico: Impacts upon inequality. *Estudios Económicos*, 207–224.

Soares, F. V., Ribas, R. P., & Osório, R. G. (2010). Evaluating the impact of Brazil's Bolsa Familia: Cash transfer programs in comparative perspective. *Latin American Research Review, 2010*, 173–190.

Tagliati, F. (2019). Child labor under cash and in-kind transfers: Evidence from rural Mexico. *Banco de España Working Paper No. 1935*. https://doi.org/10.2139/ssrn.3472904.

Tang, C., Zhao, L., & Zhao, Z. (2020). Does free education help combat child labor? The effect of a free compulsory education reform in rural China. *Journal of Population Economics, 33*(2), 601–631.

Webster-Stratton, C., Reid, M. J., & Hammond, M. (2001). Preventing conduct problems, promoting social competence: A parent and teacher training partnership in Head Start. *Journal of Clinical Child Psychology, 30*(3), 283–302.

Wilson, S. J., Tanner-Smith, E. E., Lipsey, M. W., Steinka-Fry, K., & Morrison, J. (2011). Dropout prevention and intervention programs: Effects on school completion and dropout among school-aged children and youth. *Campbell Systematic Reviews, 7*(1), 1–61.

Yap, Y. T., Sedlacek, G., & Orazem, P. F. (2009). Limiting child labor through behavior-based income transfers: An experimental evaluation of the PETI program in rural Brazil. In *Child labor and education in Latin America* (pp. 147–165). New York: Palgrave Macmillan.

Chapter 4
How to Improve the Implementation of Child Labor Prevention Programs

Abstract The implementation of psychoeducational programs depends on a complex interaction between the organizational factors of the educational institutions and the characteristics of the community. Primary schools relate to the community environment in a way that is critical to the quality and intensity of interventions. In this chapter, we successively review the role of schools, families, and the wider community in the practical implementation of preventive programs. First, schools are hubs of community life, facilitating the establishment of relationships between neighbors and the development of a psychological sense of community. Second, the relationship of families with the school reinforces consistency between microsystems and enhances the results of the intervention. Thirdly, relations between families in the community have a preventive value, insofar as they affect the mechanisms of social control and monitoring of child labor. In general, community empowerment actions prove to be an effective way of improving program implementation.

Keywords Child labor · Schools · Educational institutions · Family-school relationship · Community readiness · Participation · Empowerment

4.1 Introduction

Every time she sees the school sign at the end of the street, Maria Elena rejoices a little. It is the only colorful note at the top of Jicamarca. Some mothers say it is "a flower in the desert" because it is literally surrounded by sandy streets. On the slope, an endless succession of self-built houses made of wooden planks and waste materials have been concentrated, with a certain amount of disorder. The school is very small, but it is built with cement, and the entrance has been painted in bright colors, with children's drawings and a huge sign where you can read "welcome".

When she leaves her son with the teacher, Maria Elena hurries down the slope to the lot where the water trucks are parked. As the "aguaderos" (water carriers) come up today, she has prepared with her bucket to collect water. Since she arrived from Huancavelica, and even more so since her son was born, she has learned to care for

© The Author(s), under exclusive license to Springer Nature Switzerland AG 2021
I. Maya Jariego, *Community Prevention of Child Labor*, Human Well-Being
Research and Policy Making, https://doi.org/10.1007/978-3-030-70810-8_4

and recycle every drop. Besides, she does not mind admitting that she likes to do this walk in the mornings when the Pacific fog mixes with the dust of the Lima desert. Before she starts queuing up in front of the water trucks, she goes into the little grocery store and buys some lemon cookies for when her child gets out of school. The shopkeeper has obtained a portable electric generator and has just placed a seemingly extemporaneous advertisement at the entrance: "Fax, mobile cards, Internet".

On the outskirts of Lima "human settlements" have been formed in which people from the Andes or the Amazon rainforest have been building their own residential environment. These slums are formed through land invasions, in which communities occupy areas without urban infrastructure, without electricity or water, and build their own homes. In cases such as the Jicamarca hills, these environments are exposed to flooding and landslides, among other environmental risks. Neighbors often set up a community center and become self-organizing, while they begin to request services from the municipalities. There are cases such as that of Villa El Salvador, in the south of Lima, which are recognized precisely because they are self-managed towns, where even urban planning has been designed by the inhabitants.

In these contexts, primary schools can become a center of reference for the community. It is a place where families meet, exchange impressions, and, in the long term, develop relationships of social support. Many mothers participate in the activities planned by the school, follow up on their children's education, attend parties organized to raise funds, and sometimes meet at "parents' schools". For this reason, it is one of the settings from which one can contribute to community development and to meeting the needs of the neighbors. Especially when there are not many alternative scenarios in which neighbors can relate to each other.

To develop this idea, in this chapter we outline the link between schools, families, and the community. In the final section, we will explain how the interaction between organizational factors (of the school) and community factors (of the neighborhood) are decisive in the implementation of psychoeducational programs.

4.2 Schools as Community Hubs

Schools are, to varying degrees, a central axis of community life. First of all, they are a focus of activity for families, where they establish mutual relations and access valuable information or resources. Schools also develop community activities, which contribute to local cohesion. In recent years schools have strengthened their links with social services and health services, thus integrating learning with service provision in the same context. In some neighborhoods, the school is the only public building where neighbors can meet. In fact, in the most extreme situations, as we have just shown in the introduction, it is the only physical environment that allows residents to meet.

Therefore, several levels can be recognized in the degree to which each school is open and integrated with the community environment: that is, in the functions it

Table 4.1 A continuum in the community use of schools

Levels	Description
• Community use of schools	Outside school hours, social groups can reserve the school's space for activities.
• Parallel use and shared use of schools	A program is implemented, a course is taught, or a service is provided on a continuous basis on the school premises.
• Co-location of community services	The municipal library, a day center or a local social service unit may be integrated with the school.
• Full-service schools	The school participates in a community development initiative, in coordination with public entities and social organizations.
• School as a community hub	Learning activities are integrated with the community development process (and vice versa)

Source: based on Clandfield (2010)

fulfills for the immediate residential context. In Table 4.1 we represent a five-level continuum in the use of schools by the community, proposed by David Clandfield (2010). Collaboration can range from simply providing space for social activities to the full integration of learning with community development. In the middle ground would be the implementation of community services and programs in parallel to regular classroom instruction.

Let us return for a moment to the actions for the prevention of child labor. There are many different ways in which schools can help to reduce children's involvement in work activities. In its most basic form, the school can lend the hall to organize a lecture by a psychologist or health professional to explain the negative consequences of child labor. However, beyond a one-time collaboration, the school can host a training program in social-emotional skills outside of school hours throughout the year. Or it can even integrate preventive activities in a transversal way in the regulated subjects. Ultimately, the fight against child labor could be one of the educational axes approved in the school plan, within the framework of a strategic alliance with other social organizations that share the same community development goals. In each case, we are talking about an increasing level of integration with the community.

As the school strengthens its community character, it becomes an arena for interaction between families and, by extension, also for children outside school hours. A study carried out in the slums on the outskirts of Lima showed that the school was the second most relevant context for interaction in the community, only behind family homes (Maya-Jariego et al., 2018). This is especially relevant if we consider that it is a type of context that can sustain relationships with a preventive value. Firstly, through the systematic analysis of the personal networks of the residents, it was found that in the schools the families of the district usually contact each other and initiate exchange relationships. Secondly, it was shown that such networks of mutual knowledge between households appear to exercise a function of social control and have a protective effect against child labor.

For children, the implementation of psychosocial programs and homework assistance sessions, along with participation in leisure-time activities, can extend their relationship with the school outside of school hours (Dryfoos, 1999). Traditionally, schools are considered "safe havens" that function as an alternative setting to risky contexts. The development of extra-curricular programs can have a positive impact on the organizational climate of schools, sometimes contributing to methodological innovation in regulated subjects, and in general having a positive effect on reducing problem behaviors. In neighborhoods with higher levels of insecurity and violence, there are also experiences in which schools are open outside school hours, simply so that play time can take place in a context of greater protection and, thus, reduce exposure to criminal gangs.

4.2.1   Community Participation and Family Involvement

However, we must bear in mind that not all residential contexts are equally equipped to relate to educational institutions. In some districts the levels of citizen participation and community organization are lower than in others. Both the emergence of effective informal leadership and involvement in decision-making are particularly difficult in low-income families (Sheng, 1990). This is why they sometimes require preparatory actions, focused on motivation and community organization. In addition, to become focal points of community life, schools need to have adequate space and facilities (Haig, 2014). Parental participation can be channeled through communication with program facilitators, involvement in decision-making, collaboration in the development of activities, and attendance at training sessions (Vincent & Beckett, 1993). This is one of the dimensions that distinguishes stressed from flourishing communities (Shultz et al., 2016).

4.2.2   Community Empowerment and Adjustment

Children benefit from participating in learning environments where they feel safe, engage in empowering activities on their own, have the opportunity to interact with their peers, and experience that they are part of a larger community (Graves, 2011). When they establish relationships with community members, children develop a sense of belonging and are integrated into support systems that protect them from adverse circumstances. This requires that families gain control of the situation and have the skills that allow them to be effectively involved in raising their children. By being places for gathering and channeling civic participation, schools can promote the cohesion of local communities and contribute to the empowerment of families (Mansor, 2014; Singh & Woodrow, 2010).

Below, we review two successive ways in which schools are associated with child labor protection factors. On the one hand, the link between families and school forms a bridge between the two contexts of socialization that are possibly most relevant to children at the earliest ages. Secondly, the articulation of relations between families who share a residential environment is associated with mechanisms of social control, and consequently with the monitoring of compliance with children's educational obligations. Both contribute to strengthening the basic microsystems in which individuals are integrated.

> **Box 4.1: The Historical Construction of Childhood**
> In the Middle Ages the idea of childhood did not even exist. The lack of attention, or sometimes interest, of parents towards each individual child corresponded to the existence of large families and to the high rates of infant mortality. Children were seen as small adults, or in any case as imperfect adults. It was not until the seventeenth century that they began to be considered as individuals deserving of protection.
>
> From that point of view, childhood can be conceived as a historical achievement, arising partly as a result of improved public health standards, and later connected to the extension of universal compulsory education. Whereas previously children were expected to participate in adult activities as early as possible, now the majority of social expectation of children is that they will engage in learning and study. Child protection aims to ensure balanced personal development.
>
> Based on "In the Middle Ages there was no such thing as childhood. How perceptions of children have changed through history." *The Economist, January 3rd, 2019.*

4.3   The Relationship of the Families with the School

Schools maintain contact with families through different channels. When the academic year begins, an assembly is called in which the educational project of the center is presented. On a daily basis, teachers maintain regular contact with parents after school or in individual tutorials. For their part, the families are represented in the associations of parents and in the school council. On open days they visit the facilities and observe how work is done in the classroom. Throughout the school year, they also participate in school parties or cultural activities organized by the school.

As we can see, there are several potential connection modalities. In Table 4.2 we describe six common forms of families' relationship with the school (Epstein et al., 2002). Each of these may require different levels of parental involvement, ranging from the mere transmission of information about the school to direct participation on the school board. This is a link that is activated to monitor individual cases, coordinate expectations and teaching-learning practices, train parents, and generally involve families in everything that has to do with the education of their children.

In actions to prevent child labor, ongoing communication between teachers and parents is important to monitor that children are attending school. As teachers are

Table 4.2 Six different ways of family-school relationship

Levels	Description
• Training in raising patterns	Schools provide information to parents on health and child development. They can also organize training courses or "parent schools"
• Communication	The school and in particular the teachers maintain continuous interaction with the parents to resolve doubts about the academic program and to follow up on the progress of their children
• Volunteering	Families can volunteer their time to organize sports and cultural activities at the school
• Home learning activities	Parents help with homework, supervise homework assignments, consult the virtual teaching platform, encourage reading, comment on teaching plans and review exercises done by their children
• Participation in decision making	Parent associations and representation on the school board convey the families' point of view and influence school policies
• Collaboration with the community	Community service activities, outside internships and service-learning also connect families to the school

Source: adapted from Epstein et al. (2002)

usually from a different social background, contact with families helps them to be aware of educational needs in the most disadvantaged social contexts. This allows them to adjust their expectations and modulate their teaching practices. For their part, parents' schools help to promote the value of education in low-income families, contribute to improving intra-family communication, and serve to train strategies for early detection of school drop-out. It is also useful for families to be aware of the logical framework of preventive interventions so that they are in tune with the goals and mode of operation of the program.

Communication with families improves school results in general (Garreta, 2015) and performance in reading and mathematics in particular (González & Jackson, 2013; Herman & Yeh, 1983). More broadly, it contributes to the social and psycho-educational development of children (Comer & Haynes, 1991; El Nokali et al., 2010). However, the direct involvement of parents in their children's learning at home may be more effective than mere participation in scheduled activities at school (Harris & Goodall, 2008).

In the case of families at risk, the connection with the school means facing specific difficulties. Parents with low educational levels or low incomes may feel uncomfortable at school, sometimes not having enough time or lacking the financial resources to participate (Karther & Lowden, 1997). This is why it is necessary to adjust the style of communication, modulate times, eliminate barriers, and introduce incentives to participation. With families of working children or those at risk of child labor, it is necessary to explain clearly how their involvement will benefit the children. Establishing the initial link with families takes time, and then one must be persistent throughout the participation process. In some cases, the provision of educational materials or the organization of a snack has served to motivate initial involvement.

Therefore, while it is important to increase family responsibility, in low-income groups it can become an added burden if not accompanied by adequate support. Families at greater risk often require help in raising their children, training to promote prosocial behavior, alternative spaces in which their children can study when the conditions of the home are not conducive to it, or even adult literacy and school graduation programs (Davies, 2002).

4.3.1   Parent Schools

Interventions to promote effective parenting have been shown to have great preventive value, both in the short and long term. Through training workshops with parents, they produce improvements in a wide range of outcomes for their children, between 1 and 20 years after the intervention (Sandler et al., 2011). Specifically, positive parenting programs reduce academic failure, behavioral problems, delinquency, and substance abuse by their children. They also contribute to the development of skills that correspond to their developmental period.

As a rule, they are implemented through intensive workshops, which allow several factors to be influenced simultaneously. In the workshops with parents at risk of child labor, one can train, among other skills, communication styles with the children, skills for early detection of school dropouts, and strategies for resolving intra-family conflicts. They also try to promote the value of education and raise awareness of the negative consequences of child labor. The possibility of influencing each of these topics in-depth, in small or medium-sized groups, adapting the training to the peculiarities of the participants, are among the factors that help explain why they are effective.

However, parents' participation in this type of workshop is less likely the lower the educational level and the lower the perception of risk faced by their children (Haggerty et al., 2002). This again poses a problem in the case of child labor, since its prevalence is higher among parents with a low level of education or with favorable attitudes towards the involvement of minors in work activities. To the extent that families perceive no need for such services, the coverage of the intervention is negatively affected (Fleming et al., 2015).

4.3.2   Family-School Convergence and Reinforcement Between Microsystems

Another way in which parental involvement can have preventive effects is through the progressive convergence of the educational expectations of families and schools. On the one hand, depending on their learning experiences, children can review the concept they have about their own abilities (Márquez et al., 2019a), influencing, in turn, the degree of convergence with their teachers regarding their level of social and academic competence (Márquez et al., 2020). On the other hand, convergence in educational beliefs, aspirations and expectations could reinforce the results of psychosocial interventions.

According to this idea, we can start from the assumption that child labor prevention programs interact with the participants' microsystems. A program that acts simultaneously in the school and in the family is usually more effective, insofar as the influence that each has on the children's behavior is mutually reinforcing (Pettigrew et al., 2018). Thus, in preventive interventions developed in Peru and Colombia, families needed to know why their children devoted part of the extracurricular sessions to play, or what the reason was for carrying out participatory activities instead of the traditional formats for teaching language or mathematics (Maya Jariego & Holgado Ramos, 2014). Families also needed to count the difficulties they faced in ensuring their children's education. Discussions with psychologists and school heads led to the negotiation of expectations that facilitated the emergence of a shared vision, resulting in better implementation of the program (Márquez et al., 2019b).

Box 4.2: When Child Labor Is Institutionalized

Between Samarkand and Bukhara, the cotton fields follow one another. The omnipresence of this type of plantation is the result of an idea taken to its ultimate consequences. Stalin divided Turkestan into several countries and in the case of Uzbekistan, they allocated cotton production to it. They built canals and put hundreds of thousands of people to work. They transformed the conditions of production in the region. The result was almost two million hectares in need of irrigation. In the second half of the twentieth century, large-scale agricultural production was one of the causes of the drying up of the Aral Sea.

Now the cotton fields are comparatively smaller because they have begun to diversify agricultural production with other types of crops. But it is still Uzbekistan's main industry. Until 3 years ago, universities were also involved in the harvesting season. Professors and students left their academic work to harvest cotton. As in Soviet times, they were given a goal to achieve with each harvest. A teacher in Samarkand privately acknowledges that they paid some farmers to pick their quota.

The involvement of school children in forced cotton harvesting has also been documented, although international pressure seems to have reduced this practice to a minimum in recent years. During the harvest season, children spent up to 2 months in the fields, with the consent of educational institutions, which allowed this form of institutionalized absenteeism.

Source: Maya Jariego, I. (2019). Project field notebook "Alianza universidad—escuela—comunidad para la implementación de estrategias de prevención psicoeducativa en Uzbekistán", 28 de agosto de 2019.

[Uzbekistan]

4.4   Family Relationships and Community Integration

Some of the fundamental behavioral scenarios for the development of relations between neighbors are concentrated in schools. As we have pointed out, the mothers and fathers of the neighborhood initiate relationships at the door of the school, at parties organized by the school, at tutoring sessions, and at parents' schools. Once the relationship is established, it is common to share information and exchange social support. On a day-to-day basis, they talk about school, discuss district problems, or simply lend a hand when a mother is late to pick up her children after school.

A study conducted in several peripheral neighborhoods in Lima, Peru, found that networks between families are less developed in more recent human settlements, with a shorter history of community development (Maya-Jariego et al., 2018). These are less structured communities, where processes of social cohesion are at best under development. However, in these flood plains, where there is a higher risk of child labor, schools often act as a bridge to labor resources and other services available outside the district. So even in the most disadvantaged contexts, schools offer opportunities to develop social capital.

Family relationships sustain community cohesion processes, increase the sense of collective effectiveness, and have a preventive value (Kerrigan et al., 2006; Suglia et al., 2016). Consequently, the establishment of links between households and, in general, community-building strategies can form part of actions to reduce the incidence of child labor. In each context, it is necessary to choose the combination of actions and programs that are best suited to local conditions and interests (Graves, 2011). However, promoting community cohesion and a psychological sense of community, or building consensus and alliances, are initiatives that prepare for a change in a widespread way. It can also serve to reinforce the value that the community places on education.[1]

4.5   The Continuum of Parental Involvement in the Educational Process

As we have seen throughout the book, parents are a key player in the prevention of child labor. On the one hand, the involvement of children in work activities is conceived as a household survival strategy (Basu & Van, 1998) in which parents have a prevalent role in decision-making. On the other hand, parental supervision also influences children's health, learning, and development (Dishion & McMahon, 1998).

---

[1]The articulation of relationships between families in the community context may be another illustration of the African proverb "it takes a village to raise a child".

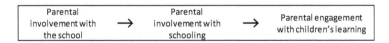

Fig. 4.1 The involvement of parents in the educational process. *Source*: Goodall and Montgomery (2014)

The relationship that parents have with studies translates into their children's educational outcomes. Hence, it is especially relevant to assess how they participate in the teaching and learning processes. It is not only a matter of parents supporting the schools but of making them co-responsible for the educational process. This involves assuming a more active role. To develop this idea, in Fig. 4.1 we have represented the continuum of parental involvement in the educational process (Goodall & Montgomery, 2014). From lowest to highest, this is a progression that begins with the involvement of parents in the school and ends with the commitment to their children's learning. In the first instance, it is the schools that involve parents in the educational process, fundamentally through the transmission of information and the organization of social activities in the schools that are open to family participation. On a second level, there is a more balanced exchange between parents and school personnel regarding the schooling process. Thirdly, the higher level of involvement balances the responsibility of the school and the parents, insofar as the latter are directly involved in the learning process of their children.

As this continuum progresses, children's motivation and academic performance improve, while their educational aspirations increase.

4.6   Strategies to Improve Program Implementation

Schools are a preferential setting for the implementation of child labor prevention programs. It is a context that allows for reaching (potentially) the whole population in a critical developmental period when behaviors are learned, and habits are established that can influence in the medium and long term. It is also an area that, comparatively speaking, provides better accessibility to the target population. In this context, and by way of recapitulation, throughout the chapter we have insisted on three ideas that link schools with prevention strategies:

1. Schools are at the center of community life, facilitate exchange among residents, and in that sense are a key resource for community readiness.
2. The relationships between families that originate in educational institutions underpin the mechanisms of social control, supervision, and monitoring of child labor.
3. In turn, the link between families and schools modulates the learning process of children, influencing their beliefs and educational aspirations.

Program implementation depends on a complex interaction between organizational factors (in this case, schools) and community characteristics (Durlak & Dupre, 2008; Lendrum & Humphrey, 2012; Márquez et al., 2019b). When implementing extracurricular activities, such as reading tutoring sessions, homework support, or mentoring programs, the collaboration of various actors is often necessary (Graves, 2011). Consequently, it involves mobilizing organizational resources and involving the staff of educational institutions and other social organizations.

In dropout prevention programs, the factors that contribute to better outcomes are developing all of the planned intervention components (Wilson et al., 2011), implementing all of the planned sessions (Márquez et al., 2019b), carefully monitoring personal learning environments (Christenson & Thurlow, 2004), and addressing multiple risk factors when implementing early intervention activities (Freeman & Simonsen, 2015). Complementarily, the "principles of effective programs" that have been documented in other intervention settings can also be applied (Nation et al., 2003).

From an organizational point of view, it is beneficial to avoid overloading staff by involving mentors, counselors, and community services (Rumberger et al., 2017). Staff training sessions, technical assistance when needed, and professional development plans are also effective. Both staff who conduct extracurricular activities and those who implement psychoeducational programs must have the necessary experience, along with realistic expectations and a genuine interest in the education of children (Graves, 2011). Finally, leadership and a collaborative environment in educational institutions provide the context for good program performance.

Box 4.3: The Longest Days

"When I was 6 years and 2 months old, I was sent off to work. Fancy that, only just over 6 years of age! This was at the end of February, or early March, and I do not think I shall ever forget those long and hungry days in the fields... My work was about a mile from home, and I had for wages eighteen pence a week and my dinner on Sundays [which] made the Sunday the greatest and happiest day of the week... When the barley was up and the scaring of crows was unnecessary, I had to mind a flock of a hundred sheep... The sense of loneliness and responsibility frequently overcame me, and in my desperation, I would shout 'Mother! Mother! Mother!' But mother could not hear: She was away that time working in the hayfield two miles away... Then I had the job of minding about forty pigs. Pigs are very different animals to mind from sheep. Sheep will keep together: every pig will go its own way careless of the others. The worry, the trouble, the running to and fro..."

Excerpt quoted in Humphries, J. (2013). Childhood and child labor in the British industrial revolution. *The Economic History Review, 66*(2), 395–418.

[Britain]

4.7   Conclusion

Education and child labor are communicating vessels. That is why we have focused on educational institutions in general, and primary schools in particular, to analyze the implementation of preventive programs. As part of their educational activity, teachers relate to families and the wider community. As part of their daily lives, parents develop relationships around the school. Throughout this chapter, we have seen how these two levels of relationships help schools to become catalysts for the kind of psychosocial changes that help to prevent demotivation, academic failure, school drop-out, and, ultimately, child labor.

Based on the existing evidence, three elements stand out that help to enhance the impact of preventive programs: the active commitment of parents, the strengthening of the link between families and schools, and adequate levels of community cohesion. First, the prevention of child labor is most effective when parents place a value on education and are directly involved in their children's learning and personal development. In this area, positive parenting programs improve parents' skills in communicating with their children; establishing appropriate rules of behavior; and monitoring their personal or educational growth. For their part, parents' schools promote awareness of the problem of school drop-out and encourage collaboration with teachers and other socialization agents.

Secondly, the fluid communication of families with the educational system generates a greater level of harmony with preventive purposes; and, thirdly, the strengthening of community cohesion increases control over absenteeism and drop-out. Therefore, as these last two observations show, the family and the community are not only a setting for intervention but also a decisive dispositional context in the effectiveness of programs. In fact, when the family and community context is not available, the effect of the intervention can be significantly reduced.

In the preceding sections, we have seen examples of how inclusive public institutions contribute to the well-being of local communities and promote equal opportunities. As schools unleash their potential as public goods, their beneficial impact is not limited to residents with school-age children but extends to the community as a whole (Neal & Watling Neal, 2012). The shadow of investment in the education system is long-lasting, so it will reappear in our reflection on child labor prevention policies in Chap. 5.

References

Basu, K., & Van, P. H. (1998). The economics of child labor. *American Economic Review, 88*(3), 412–427.

Christenson, S. L., & Thurlow, M. L. (2004). School dropouts: Prevention considerations, interventions, and challenges. *Current Directions in Psychological Science, 13*(1), 36–39.

Clandfield, D. (2010). The school as community hub: A public alternative to the neo-liberal threat to Ontario schools. Our Schools. *Our Selves, 19*(4), 7–74.

Comer, J. P., & Haynes, N. M. (1991). Parent involvement in schools: An ecological approach. *The Elementary School Journal, 91*(3), 271–277.

Davies, D. (2002). The 10th School Revisited: Are School/Family/Community Partnerships on the Reform Agenda Now? *Phi Delta Kappan, 83*(5), 388–392.

Dishion, T. J., & McMahon, R. J. (1998). Parental monitoring and the prevention of child and adolescent problem behavior: A conceptual and empirical formulation. *Clinical Child and Family Psychology Review, 1*(1), 61–75.

Dryfoos, J. G. (1999). The role of the school in children's out-of-school time. *The Future of Children, 9*(2), 117–134.

Durlak, J. A., & DuPre, E. P. (2008). Implementation matters: A review of research on the influence of implementation on program outcomes and the factors affecting implementation. *American Journal of Community Psychology, 41*(3-4), 327–350.

El Nokali, N. E., Bachman, H. J., & Votruba-Drzal, E. (2010). Parent involvement and children's academic and social development in elementary school. *Child Development, 81*(3), 988–1005.

Epstein, J. L., Sanders, M. G., Simon, B. S., Salinas, K. C., Jansorn, N., & Van Voorhis, F. L. (2002). *School, family, and community partnerships: Your handbook for action* (2nd ed.). Thousand Oaks, CA: Corwin Press.

Fleming, C. B., Mason, W. A., Haggerty, K. P., Thompson, R. W., Fernandez, K., Casey-Goldstein, M., & Oats, R. G. (2015). Predictors of participation in parenting workshops for improving adolescent behavioral and mental health: Results from the Common Sense Parenting trial. *The Journal of Primary Prevention, 36*(2), 105–118.

Freeman, J., & Simonsen, B. (2015). Examining the impact of policy and practice interventions on high school dropout and school completion rates: A systematic review of the literature. *Review of Educational Research, 85*(2), 205–248.

Garreta, J. (2015). La comunicación familia-escuela en educación infantil y primaria. *Revista de Sociología de la Educación-RASE, 8*(1), 71–85.

González, R. L., & Jackson, C. L. (2013). Engaging with parents: The relationship between school engagement efforts, social class, and learning. *School Effectiveness and School Improvement, 24*(3), 316–335.

Goodall, J., & Montgomery, C. (2014). Parental involvement to parental engagement: A continuum. *Educational Review, 66*(4), 399–410.

Graves, D. (2011). Exploring schools as community hubs: Investigating the application of the community hub model in the context of the closure of Athabasca School, Regina, Saskatchewan, Canada and other small schools. *Community Research & Action Fund: Community Research Unit.*

Haggerty, K. P., Fleming, C. B., Lonczak, H. S., Oxford, M. L., Harachi, T. W., & Catalano, R. F. (2002). Predictors of participation in parenting workshops. *Journal of Primary Prevention, 22*(4), 375–387.

Haig, T. (2014). Equipping schools to fight poverty: A community hub approach. *Educational Philosophy and Theory, 46*(9), 1018–1035.

Harris, A., & Goodall, J. (2008). Do parents know they matter? Engaging all parents in learning. *Educational Research, 50*(3), 277–289.

Herman, J. L., & Yeh, J. P. (1983). Some effects of parent involvement in schools. *The Urban Review, 15*(1), 11–17.

Humphries, J. (2013). Childhood and child labor in the British industrial revolution. *The Economic History Review, 66*(2), 395–418.

Karther, D. E., & Lowden, F. Y. (1997). Fostering effective parent involvement. *Contemporary Education, 69*(1), 41.

Kerrigan, D., Witt, S., Glass, B., Chung, S. E., & Ellen, J. (2006). Perceived neighborhood social cohesion and condom use among adolescents vulnerable to HIV/STI. *AIDS and Behavior, 10*(6), 723–729.

Lendrum, A., & Humphrey, N. (2012). The importance of studying the implementation of interventions in school settings. *Oxford Review of Education, 38*(5), 635–652.

Mansor, H. N. (2014). *The role of school as community hub and its implications on promoting community cohesion towards sustainable communities* (Doctoral dissertation, University of Salford).

Márquez, E., Holgado, D., & Maya-Jariego, I. (2019a). Conciencia de las capacidades personales y rendimiento académico en la implementación de un programa psicoeducativo. *Universitas Psychologica, 18*(5), 1–18.

Márquez, E., Holgado, D., & Maya-Jariego, I. (2019b). Innovation, Dosage and Responsiveness in the Implementation of the Program "Edúcame Primero Perú" for Reducing Child Labour. *Applied Research in Quality of Life, 14*(3), 617–636.

Márquez, E., Holgado, D., & Maya-Jariego, I. (2020). La Convergencia en la Evaluación Socioacadémica por parte de Docentes y Estudiantes durante la Implementación de un Programa Psicoeducativo para la Prevención del Trabajo Infantil. *Psicología Educativa.* https://doi.org/10.5093/psed2020a3.

Maya Jariego, I., & Holgado Ramos, D. (2014). From Barranquilla to Lima in reducing child labor: Lessons in community action. *Global Journal of Community Psychology Practice, 5*(2), 1–6.

Maya-Jariego, I., Holgado, D., Márquez, E., & Santolaya, F. J. (2018). The community role of schools in Jicamarca and Villa El Salvador (Peru): Crosscutting behavior settings in personal networks. *Psychosocial Intervention, 27*(1), 1–11.

Maya Jariego, I. (2019). Project field notebook "Alianza universidad – escuela – comunidad para la implementación de estrategias de prevención psicoeducativa en Uzbekistán", 28 de agosto de 2019.

Nation, M., Crusto, C., Wandersman, A., Kumpfer, K. L., Seybolt, D., Morrissey-Kane, E., & Davino, K. (2003). What works in prevention: Principles of effective prevention programs. *American Psychologist, 58*(6-7), 449.

Neal, Z. P., & Watling Neal, J. (2012). The public school as a public good: Direct and indirect pathways to community satisfaction. *Journal of Urban Affairs, 34*(5), 469–486.

Pettigrew, J., Segrott, J., Ray, C. D., & Littlecott, H. (2018). Social Interface Model: Theorizing Ecological Post-Delivery Processes for Intervention Effects. *Prevention Science, 19*(8), 987–996. https://doi.org/10.1007/s11121-017-0857-2.

Rumberger, R., Addis, H., Allensworth, E., Balfanz, R., Bruch, J., Dillon, E., & Tuttle, C. (2017). *Preventing dropout in secondary schools.* Washington, D.C.: National Center for Education Evaluation and Regional Assistance, Institute of Education Sciences, US Department of Education.

Sandler, I. N., Schoenfelder, E. N., Wolchik, S. A., & MacKinnon, D. P. (2011). Long-term impact of prevention programs to promote effective parenting: Lasting effects but uncertain processes. *Annual Review of Psychology, 62*, 299–329.

Sheng, Y. K. (1990). Community participation in low-income housing projects: Problems and prospects. *Community Development Journal, 25*(1), 56–65.

Shultz, C., Rahtz, D., & Sirgy, J. (2016). Distinguishing flourishing from distressed communities: Vulnerability, resilience and a systemic framework to facilitate well-being. In R. Phillips & C. Wong (Eds.), *The handbook of community well-being.* Dordrecht, Netherlands: Springer.

Singh, M., & Woodrow, C. (2010). A Research Evaluation of the School-Centred Community Hub Initiative. *Report for Stronger Families Alliance, Connect Child and Family Services Inc., and the Sidney Myer Foundation.*

Suglia, S. F., Shelton, R. C., Hsiao, A., Wang, Y. C., Rundle, A., & Link, B. G. (2016). Why the neighborhood social environment is critical in obesity prevention. *Journal of Urban Health, 93*(1), 206–212.

Vincent, L. J., & Beckett, J. A. (1993). Family participation: DEC recommended practices. In *DEC recommended practices: Indicators of quality in programs for infants and young children with special needs and their families,* see EC 301933.

Wilson, S. J., Tanner-Smith, E. E., Lipsey, M. W., Steinka-Fry, K., & Morrison, J. (2011). Dropout prevention and intervention programs: Effects on school completion and dropout among school-aged children and youth. *Campbell Systematic Reviews, 7*(1), 1–61.

Chapter 5
Child Labor, Psychological Wellbeing, and Public Policy

Abstract In this chapter we review evidence-based practices in the fight against child labor. First, we examine the diversity of child-rearing patterns and the perception of family obligations by children from different social contexts. Second, we describe the most effective prevention strategies. Third, we conclude with some reflections helpful for the design and implementation of community-based policies against child labor. In the final section of the conclusions, we list some recommendations for intervention.

Keywords Child labor · Public policies · Programs · Psychological wellbeing · Quality of life · Evidence-based practices · Community-based approach

5.1   Introduction

When the school holidays arrive and the water level of the rivers starts to rise, many families descend from the high areas of the Andes to Huepetuhe, in the jungle of Madre de Dios. During the 2 or 3 months that they dedicate to the extraction and washing of gold, temporary communities are formed in the artisanal mining camps. These are times when environmental pressure multiplies. Despite the fact that this Amazon region has several natural protected areas, the arsenic and mercury used for gold processing are dumped into the rivers without control. Hydraulic dredges are also used, damaging the fluvial bottoms.

During the summer it is common to see whole families on the river bank. As they dig into the ground until they reach the gravel, they have to remove and move large amounts of sand. The teenagers participate in both the excavation and the transfer of the sand to the hoppers, where the washing and processing of the gold begins. These are physically demanding tasks. Children are particularly agile when transporting gravel and are therefore appreciated by employers for this type of work.

Artisanal mining is a good economic option for rural Andean communities, which migrate in summer to the Amazon region. In the mining camp, employers usually take care of salary and maintenance. During the mining season, each monthly payment is twice the minimum wage. This is a great help for the rest of the year

© The Author(s), under exclusive license to Springer Nature Switzerland AG 2021
I. Maya Jariego, *Community Prevention of Child Labor*, Human Well-Being
Research and Policy Making, https://doi.org/10.1007/978-3-030-70810-8_5

since most of them work in subsistence agriculture. In addition, in the case of children it has the advantage that it does not interfere with the school year.

For minors, however, gold panning is among the "dangerous jobs". Normally, they work 8 h a day in hot and humid conditions, typical of the tropical climate, to which they are not accustomed. They also come into contact with hazardous chemicals. Employers assume that the children are not usually in conflict with working conditions or linked to trade unions. Almost all children working in mining are boys. Adolescent girls are brought from the Andean region to the jungle to work in canteens where they are forced into prostitution.

Intervention on gold panning in Peru can encompass a wide range of preventive, compensatory, and rehabilitative strategies. In the labor field, it has been suggested that it is necessary to fight against the clandestinely in which many of these small mining operations operate and to regularize the work of young people from the age of sixteen (Guillén-Marroquín, 1988). It is assumed that incorporating them into the formal economy would also mean an improvement in their working conditions. In the area of public health, it has been recommended that vaccination campaigns and outpatient medical assistance be carried out with seasonal workers (Piazza, 2001). It is also considered necessary to fumigate work areas to prevent malaria and other tropical diseases related to insect bites. At the institutional level, professional training programs for young people and codes of conduct to prevent child prostitution can be agreed with artisanal miners' organizations. In any case, child labor is a complex problem that requires comprehensive, continuous, and high-intensity action.

In this chapter, we examine the various types of intervention strategies that exist. In the first part, after reviewing the modes of action, we focus on identifying the most relevant evidence-based practices. In the second part, we pay special attention to organizational and community factors. We end the chapter with a list of recommendations derived from the previous analysis.

5.2 Parenting Guidelines and Family Obligations

Recently, there has been a renewed debate, especially in developed countries, about the extent of permissive parenting styles and some loss of parental authority (Sax, 2015). In reaction to such circumstances, some psychologists have recalled that the balanced development of children requires clear rules, the setting of limits and the promotion of a culture of effort. Consequently, it is assumed that the re-establishment of such teaching guidelines would serve to enrich the learning experiences of a generation of irresponsible and undisciplined children.

This contrasts with the cases we have been reviewing in the preceding pages, where children, usually in low-income countries, are pushed to take on certain responsibilities prematurely. In part this may reflect the diversity of socialization patterns, in different national cultures and in different ethnic groups. For example, in the case of the United States, one study showed that adolescents of Asian and Latin

American descent had stronger family values than those of European descent. The former were socialized in a culture that conveyed a high expectation of respect for parents, along with a perceived obligation to help the family (Fuligni et al., 1999).

In any case, it seems that the patterns of upbringing are related to the expectations of compliance with family obligations, generating differentiated contexts of child development. In many African, Asian, and Latin American countries it is likely that older siblings will take care of younger ones while their parents work. It is also very common for girls to take on household chores (or to help their mothers and grandmothers prepare food that the adult members of the family then go to sell at street stalls). There is no doubt that this type of situation is clearly different from the "discipline problems" spoken of in developed countries. At the same time, and although they sometimes do not strictly fall into the category of "child labor", they form diverse contexts of family socialization that must be taken into account in order to adjust interventions to the peculiarities of each group.

5.3 Evidence-Based Practices

In this section we present a typology of strategies to reduce the prevalence of child labor and review the existing evidence on the impact of each modality of intervention. From this overview, we can begin to systematize which actions work, under which conditions and with which specific effects.

The modalities of intervention are different depending on the target population. Thus, programs to reduce the incidence of child labor may target children at risk, working children, or children involved in the "worst forms of child labor". Complementarily, other actions aim to prepare the ground for facilitating the desired social change. In Table 5.1 we have briefly described these four types of intervention. These are preventive, compensatory, rehabilitative, and preparatory actions for the social and political context. In general, we have maintained the original terminology of Rosati and Lyon (2006), which follows economic models of analysis. Later on, we will reinterpret some of these actions from a community point of view.

Firstly, preventive actions are based on a cost-benefit analysis of the decisions made by families on the involvement of their children in work activities. In order to reduce the likelihood of child labor, barriers to access to the education system can be reduced, schooling outcomes can be improved, or financial capital shortages in low-income families can be offset. Examples of preventive actions include programs to prevent school dropouts, early care services, initiatives to improve job opportunities based on educational level, and conditional cash transfers, among others.

Second, school transition programs aim to facilitate the return of working children to the formal education system. To this end, compensatory actions can be implemented with personalized support during their return to the classroom, or after-school preparatory programs that serve as a bridge to re-entry into school under the usual conditions. Flexible schooling modalities have also been experimented with, which provide some kind of educational experience compatible with the children's

Table 5.1 Four types of intervention strategies against child labor

Strategy	Description	Actions
Prevention	Policies affecting relative prices of children's time	• Reduce education costs • Improve the quality of the education system • Accessibility to educational institutions • Increase opportunities for youth employment • Facilitate the transition from studies to work • Improvement of basic infrastructure • Introduction of technological changes in the labor market
	Policies affecting resource constraint and social risk management	• Compensate for the capital and financial credit constraints of vulnerable households • Compensation mechanisms in situations of economic crisis
"Second Chance"	Compensatory policies with working children who have reduced the length of schooling or the quality of their educational experiences	• School transition programs • Reintegration into school with educational support, tutoring or peer mentoring • Extracurricular activities in literacy, math and social-academic skills development • Flexible schooling programs
"Direct Action"	Policies to rescue children from situations that violate their fundamental rights and put their safety or physical integrity at serious risk	• Labor inspections • Community control • Shelters and shelters • Emergency, rehabilitation and psychological support programs
Setting the socio-political context	Preparing the community, social and political ground for the implementation of actions to reduce child labor	• Community awareness programmes • Institutional strengthening • Commitment to international agreements • Community organization and social mobilization • Coordination and information exchange between services

Source: based on Rosati and Lyon (2006)

work experiences. In this case, school schedules are adapted, or curricular adaptations are introduced, assuming that the children will continue to work (at least temporarily). This type of program usually focuses on high-risk children, such as those who work or live on the streets.

Thirdly, the elimination of the worst forms of child labor is associated with the rehabilitation of children. In this context, labor inspections, legal regulation, community control, and, in general, surveillance actions are especially aimed at dangerous work, forced labor, child slavery, and participation in illegal activities. Measures may range from the involvement of state security forces to recover children from trafficking, exploitation, or prostitution, to the establishment of reception institutions where the psychological rehabilitation of minors is promoted. Non-governmental organizations and human rights groups are involved alongside labor inspectors.

Finally, there are a number of other measures that can prepare the ground for the effective functioning of the three levels of intervention above. These are actions that promote a change in attitudes in the population, coordination between existing services, the approval of new legal regulations or the setting up of coalitions of social organizations. The aim is for both institutions and the community to be in the best position to implement preventive, compensatory and rehabilitative actions.

The first three strategies described by Rosati and Lyon (2006) correspond largely to the three traditional levels of primary, secondary and tertiary prevention. It also follows that intervention programs must be adapted to the different risk conditions of the child population. The fourth strategy refers to community preparedness initiatives.

Program evaluation and experimental studies over the past decade have accumulated evidence on which interventions work and which do not. In a systematic review of 33 impact evaluations, programs aimed at reducing household vulnerability were found to have a significant effect on reducing child labor (Dammert et al., 2018). Support to families is often effective, both in terms of income transfers and in providing coverage through health insurance. Paradoxically, programs that promote employment among adults by encouraging entrepreneurial initiatives can increase adolescent and child labor, even though they are effective in reducing poverty. Moreover, in some cases, interventions may not make child labor disappear, but rather shift it to other sectors of activity.

In the following sections we will review some specific modalities of intervention. First, we will look at the three preventive strategies that have shown the best results, to the extent that they can be considered evidence-based practices. As described in previous chapters, this time we will explore some of the open discussions and some of the issues that are pending research in the near future. Secondly, we will review other types of interventions which, although more controversial and with varying results, have attracted public attention in recent years: we refer to programs with street children, fair trade initiatives, corporate social responsibility, and micro-credit.

5.3.1 Three Consolidated Intervention Strategies

In the previous chapters, we have identified three types of interventions that have undergone rigorous experimental evaluations and have consistently shown their effectiveness: conditional income transfers, positive parenting workshops, and school dropout prevention programs. From a theoretical point of view, they illustrate (respectively) the positive impact of strengthening appropriate parenting practices, training parents in the socialization of their children, and promoting schooling and learning. As we have already described in previous chapters, we will now only add some reflections on the conditions in which this impact is produced and the aspects that are currently being researched.

There is consistent evidence in the evaluation of conditional cash transfers on their impact on school attendance, although there is less consensus on their impact on reducing child labor (Duryea & Morrison, 2004). There has also been discussion about whether aid should be in cash or in kind, as a subsidy or as a credit, or whether it should be conditional or unconditional (Tabatabai, 2006). As a general rule, the greater the amount subsidized, the greater the coverage of the program, and the greater the accessibility of the poorest families, the greater the impact of the transfers. However, the effectiveness could vary depending on the previous income level of the families (Pellerano et al., 2019), and function differently when referring to secondary education levels (Barrera-Osorio et al., 2019).

In terms of education policies, in the long term, they are linked to the reduction of income inequality (Velez et al., 2004). However, reducing gender disparity requires specific actions. The differential expectations of families regarding the role their daughters should play are reinforced by the gender segregation of the labor market. Compared to boys, they are more likely to take on household chores, work in domestic service for others, or be responsible for caring for younger siblings. Among other policies, investment in educational infrastructure appears to help reduce the time girls spend on domestic tasks (Agénor & Alpaslan, 2013).

5.3.2 Reintegration Programs for Street Children

Not all street children are working children. However, one of the most common profiles among the former consists of children who started working on the streets to help support the family income. As we have already indicated, both being on the street and living on the street are sources of additional risks. In order to influence these groups, preventive programs and rehabilitation programs have been designed and implemented. Usually, these are initiatives that combine educational activities, professional training, and assistance services. Some of these interventions are carried out in institutions where the participating children reside, while others target children living on the streets.

Programs that have proved effective in this area are characterized by providing individualized care, involving children and the community, collaborating with local services and having professionals trained to ensure coverage of the children most at risk (Volpi, 2002). It is important that they are not limited to providing care services, but that they implement training actions adapted to the child's developmental period and based on mutual trust between children and educators.

Residential services have traditionally been questioned as being too expensive and having a low success rate (Dybicz, 2005). However, in both Brazil and Peru, the combination of residential programs with the participation of social educators on the streets has demonstrated some rehabilitative capacity. In addition to housing, food, and other welfare services, these are interventions that provide behavioral-based training sessions. In this case, about half of the participants in the residential institutions achieved effective reintegration into the community (Harris et al., 2011). For most, it consisted of returning to the original family.

In any case, attempts to get them to return to school always face a high risk of relapse. After returning to school, they often feel discriminated against, experience strong pressure from their former classmates to return to the streets, or lack sustained adult support (Lieten & Strehl, 2014). In addition, teachers often indicate that, especially in classes with a high number of students, they do not have enough time to provide special attention to high-risk children.

5.3.3 Social Labelling and Fair-Trade Initiatives

Social labelling initiatives consist of indicating on the packaging of a product the working conditions under which it has been produced. They originally emerged after a previous history of pressure from some consumer associations in developed countries on local producers in low-income countries. One of the best-known cases is that of the carpet manufacturing industry in India, with a high volume of exports to countries such as Germany or the United States (Ravi, 2001). Non-governmental organizations make labor inspection visits to workshops to certify that no children are working, and they certify the use of a label on those carpets that have been manufactured "child labor free". This label functions as an incentive for companies, which thus obtain better opportunities for marketing their products in international markets.

In addition to human rights groups, a number of foundations, trade unions and business associations have launched such programs. They are usually integrated into an awareness campaign, promoting both international awareness, and changing attitudes among businessmen and local communities (McDonagh, 2002). In general, the various actors involved report a decline in child labor in the sector following its implementation (Ravi, 2001; Rosell & Hansen, 2012; Venkateswarlu et al., 2006). In some cases, however, there is mention of the displacement of child labor to other sectors of the economy or the negative impact on the income of families in lower strata (Sharma, 2002). Hence, the most significant impact, using consumer preferences as a tool, lies in having promoted widespread awareness of the problem, without having to resort to other more aggressive and potentially more harmful forms of pressure such as boycotts of local products (Ravi, 2001; Sharma, 2002).

Documenting fair trade practices is usually quite difficult due to the complex sub-contracting structures involving companies with an international dimension. However, some evidence suggests that the deterioration of working conditions or the presence of child labor does not appear to result directly from involvement in international trade (Edmonds & Pavcnik, 2006). Furthermore, the effects of the impact of "fair trade" certification on small producers, in terms of hiring or involving children in labor, is controversial (Baradaran & Barclay, 2011; Valkila & Nygren, 2010).

5.3.4 Corporate Social Responsibility

Companies can also be involved in actions to prevent child labor (IPEC, 2013). In large factories, it is easier to inspect and control child labor participation. However, when tasks are subcontracted out to the home, as is the case with many craft activities, it is difficult to monitor. In India, this type of outsourced production has been concentrated in community centers, where it can be directly monitored (Bhaskaran et al., 2010). With the same objective, other companies have tried to reduce the length of the production chain and introduce mechanization of certain processes.

For their part, business associations have played an important role in training and raising awareness among employers in selected industry clusters in India, Brazil, and South Africa (IPEC, 2013). In Brazil, employers in the transport industry have signed a code of conduct to prevent the sexual exploitation of girls and adolescents on highways. To this end, they developed a map of the points of risk of sexual exploitation on Brazilian roads and launched a campaign aimed especially at truck drivers. A representative from each company participated in training workshops and then acted as "multipliers" with their fellow drivers.

5.3.5 Microcredit

Low-income families often have problems accessing bank loans and financial services in general. To the extent that they are excluded from the formal economy, they cannot generate the savings that would allow them to invest in their children's education as a social mobility strategy. Moreover, they have no guarantee and no verifiable loan repayment history. As an alternative, microcredit programs have been launched, consisting of small loans to low-income people, to develop small businesses or start up entrepreneurial initiatives (Banerjee et al., 2015). They often target women or self-organized groups in the community, who commit collectively and in solidarity to repaying aid.

In Bangladesh, it has been found that children in families receiving microcredit enjoy better food, clothing, and shelter. They are also more likely to attend school. However, it does not guarantee that parents will withdraw them from work activities. In fact, they sometimes feel the pressure of new income to pay off debt (Smith, 2011), so they expect their children to work. This is why it has been suggested to take into consideration community factors and to collaborate with non-governmental child protection organizations, introducing forms of conditionality similar to those described above.

Box 5.1: Soccer Balls, Global Consumers, and Local Communities

Ensuring procurement standards in supply chains that extend beyond national borders is a challenge for multinational companies. Several sportswear companies have been exposed to reputational crises, as cases of child labor have been documented in their international factory network.

One of the best-known cases is that of the football industry in Pakistan, which provoked a reaction from human rights organizations around the world. Some companies chose to eliminate children from the supply chain. Many of the children who became unemployed in the ball industry ended up in other less regulated or higher risk sectors such as brick making. In contrast, other companies chose to set up a home-sewing system employing women. In this way, it was hoped that child labor would be replaced by adult labor.

In the first case, there is a more direct response to consumer pressure, so it possibly has a greater impact on the company's image. In contrast, the second strategy seems more sensitive to community needs.

Based on Winstanley, D., Clark, J., & Leeson, H. (2002). Approaches to child labor in the supply chain. *Business Ethics: A European Review, 11*(3), 210–223.

[Pakistan]

5.4 Social, Community, and Institutional Prevention Factors

The mere prohibition, through new legal regulations, can have an impact on the reduction of child labor (Piza & Souza, 2016). Although in the previous pages, according to the literature, the economic analysis of the interventions has predominated, some relevant factors of community, social, and institutional character have also been appearing. Among other evidence, we have found that factors such as the commitment of governments to international conventions, the introduction of legal reforms, and institutional alignment with preventive purposes have a decisive weight in obtaining positive results (Dammert et al., 2018).

The policy initiative is reflected in the transformation of labor laws, the application of international standards against child labor, and the incorporation of preventive goals in policies and programs in different areas of administration. The accumulation of small institutional changes has an added preventive effect. In the sections that follow, we illustrate this with the establishment of alliances between different social actors, the participation of academics and researchers in policy reforms, and international cooperation initiatives.

5.4.1 The Institutional Context and Consensus Building for Child Protection

Until very recently, school children regularly participated in forced cotton harvesting in Uzbekistan (Bhat, 2011, 2013). According to the International Labor Organization, "the systematic recruitment of students, teachers, doctors, and nurses has ended".[1] However, the case illustrates in its extreme form the impact of the institutional context on working conditions and ultimately the role assigned to children. Quotas were set by the state and enforced by local officials. Schools were closed during harvest time and children who did not meet their quota could be punished in terms of academic performance. Once in the field, they were exposed to pesticides, long working hours, and poor working conditions.

After the Soviet period, the processes of economic transition in Central Asia still depend mainly on bureaucratic mechanisms (Kandiyoti, 1998). Political institutions have the power to set the terms of the playing field and, consequently, to influence all relevant social actors at the national level. Contrary to what we have described for the case of Uzbekistan, policies that seek to forge consensus through the concertation of employees and employers have a preventive value that spreads throughout the social structure. Households, businesses, and educational organizations respond to a system of incentives established through macro-level policies.

5.4.2 Psychology and Public Policy

Psychological research has provided very consistent evidence on the positive impact of preventive actions with the child population. We know that psychosocial programs implemented during early childhood have long-term effects, sometimes throughout the life cycle; and it has been shown that psychoeducational interventions improve the life opportunities of children from disadvantaged social groups (Woodhead, 1988). On the one hand, intensive early childhood education can have lasting effects on cognitive and academic development (Campbell et al., 2001). On the other hand, programs that target high-risk groups are particularly effective (Kloos et al., 2012).

However, sometimes the experimental evidence and observations obtained through rigorous evaluation of interventions are transferred in a simplistic way to the design of preventive policies. This is not only a matter of generalizing to a type of population that does not match the characteristics of the participants in the interventions evaluated experimentally, but of overlooking the importance of the social, family, and educational contexts in which the program was developed, or which

---

[1]"Major progress on forced labour and child labour in Uzbekistan cotton fields". International Labour Organization (ILO), 22 November 2018. https://www.ilo.org/global/about-the-ilo/newsroom/news/WCMS_650697/lang%2D%2Den/index.htm.

accompany children throughout their growth and development (Woodhead, 1988). For psychological research to inform public policy in a relevant and effective way, it is necessary to consider the characteristics of the population, the peculiarities of the context of application, and the intensity of implementation. Therefore, it is not only a matter of identifying which programs are effective in preventing child labor, but also under what conditions. That is, what are the family, social and educational processes that (potentially) contribute to positive development. The results of child labor prevention initiatives may depend on the degree of community preparedness for them.

Secondly, influence on the design of public policy also depends in part on the ability of psychology professionals to communicate results, capture the attention of the public and influence the politicians who make decisions on the issue of interest. To illustrate this, we can recall that psychologists have participated in parliamentary hearings to demonstrate the consequences on adolescent development of early incorporation into the labor market (Greenberger, 1983). In this regard, public administrations appear to have been more receptive to the generic aims of guaranteeing universal schooling or reducing poverty than to more specific strategies that impact on the mediating role of the family in child development (Woodhead, 1988). However, as we have shown in the preceding pages, here too it can be stated that psychoeducational support for children and their families is not only a cost but an investment. In any case, the political climate of the moment can be decisive, so researchers need to choose carefully when and where they introduce scientific evidence into the public debate (Maccoby et al., 1983).

5.4.3 The Fight Against Child Labor in Development Cooperation Contexts

Part of the preventive programs are developed in the framework of international cooperation initiatives, in which donor countries provide technical and financial assistance (Wabwile, 2010). External aid can boost economic growth processes, although in some cases it has also been used effectively for coercive or deterrent purposes (Arat, 2002). Both the empowerment of communities and the strengthening of trade unions can have far-reaching effects, and even have a (potential) impact at the international level. However, zero tolerance policies against child labor by developed countries have also been interpreted as a way of protecting their respective national labor markets (Winstanley et al., 2002). In fact, programs promoted by international institutions can be seen as external initiatives that do not respect the peculiarities of the local context (Khan et al., 2010; Maya Jariego, 2017).

International organizations have played a leading role in the fight against child labor. The ILO has focused on employment and industrial relations, UNESCO on education and UNICEF on child development in general, while the World Bank promotes economic and community development (Fallon & Tzannatos, 1998).

International cooperation programs aim to reduce poverty, invest in education, and to promote the participation of women and the involvement of civil society. Furthermore, the setting of international standards puts pressure on local governments. All of this is related to the expectation of reducing child labor.

Box 5.2: Two Proper Names in the Fight for Children's Rights
Both were victims of oppressive situations and have become icons of the struggle for the defense of children's rights. Iqbal Masih was killed after denouncing the exploitative situation of children working in carpet making in Pakistan. Malala Yousafzai was attacked by the Taliban for her defense of girls' right to education. Iqbal was given by his father to a carpet manufacturer in exchange for a loan. He worked there, chained to a loom, for more than 12 h a day. Malala lived in an area of Pakistan where the Taliban issued an edict banning girls from school. The former became an activist against child slavery and the latter an active advocate for the right of girls to study.
   "One child, one teacher, one book, one pen can change the world."
   —Malala Yousafzai
   "Kids should have pens and pencils in their hands not tools."
   —Iqbal Masih
   [Pakistan]

5.5   Community-Based Policy Making Against Child Labor

Policies against child labor are not limited to the adoption of new legislation whose compliance is certified through monitoring systems and the enforcement of sanctions. Strategies of prevention, compensation, rehabilitation, and community preparedness are also put in place. Intervention initiatives have progressively given increasing importance to the provision of services and the implementation of psychosocial programs for the protection of minors, together with complementary actions to raise awareness and defend children's rights (Bequele & Boyden, 1988).

Governments have concentrated their efforts on regulating the minimum age for work and preventing the risks associated with the performance of certain jobs, while non-governmental organizations have focused mainly on carrying out community awareness campaigns, and monitoring and social pressure initiatives on employers who hire children. Strategies to reduce child labor are effective in combining action on employers, especially in the informal sector of the economy, and on households that choose to have their children work (Bequele & Boyden, 1988; Grootaert & Kanbur, 1995). Strengthening the education system is also an indirect way to counteract child labor.

In the cases of India and Brazil, much of the progress has been based on the design of a comprehensive policy, with specific plans for those sectors of the economy in which child labor is concentrated, as well as on the establishment of a network of local initiatives that make it possible to sustain community-based actions (Bequele & Boyden, 1988). This perspective is useful because it combines community awareness with the coordination of existing resources. It also generates a shared vision that exerts pressure for change in institutions. In a context where top-down interventions have predominated, initiatives based on community participation and control can open the way to innovation. Psychosocial prevention and advocacy programs fit particularly well into this perspective.

Community interventions have focused on raising community awareness of the harmful effects of child labor, reporting the conditions of risk in which minors carry out their activity, developing social and emotional skills, complying with compulsory schooling, and promoting the positive development of minors. The incorporation into work activities at a very early age and the performance of dangerous work are among the risk factors that can contribute to establishing priorities for action. Small-scale interventions make it possible to develop intensive and comprehensive actions. To strengthen community control, children can also be involved in needs assessment, program design, and monitoring of interventions (Bessell, 2011; Bourdillon, 2006; Tonon, 2012).

Community-based strategies aim to transform the ecological environment, based on bottom-up initiatives that involve citizen participation and the collaboration of different social actors (Jason et al., 2019). To this end, psychologists participate in the implementation of programs and initiatives with a projection on public policies. However, it should be remembered that communities do not form a homogeneous whole but may be subject to conflicts and divisions. Hence, it is advisable to adopt a realistic approach, adapted to each local context (Babo, 2019). Lack of participation and social cohesion problems are two of the elements that can interfere with the proper functioning of community development projects.

Box 5.3: Oliver Twist and Charles Dickens' Working Children

"After a month, Oliver began to mourn, a despicable trade that consisted in mourning all those who passed by the funeral home and took the road to the cemetery, even though he had never seen them alive. His pale face and melancholy expression made him well-suited for the job, according to Mr. Sowerberry. Such were his gifts that in a matter of weeks he was formally hired as an apprentice in the business" (Charles Dickens, 2017, p. 24).

During the industrial revolution, children worked with knitting machines, splitting coal, or as chimney sweeps. In Charles Dickens' novels there are many examples of children in domestic service, working in factories, doing household chores in exchange for maintenance, or even being sold into forced labor. The novel Oliver Twist faithfully depicts some of the forms of child labor in nineteenth-century England and shows how they continually suffer injury, fatigue, malnutrition, and hunger.

(continued)

Box 5.3 (continued)
  The literal quotation corresponds to Charles Dickens (2017). *Oliver Twist.*
Madrid. [The original was published in 1989. The quotation corresponds to the
Spanish version, adapted for a young audience]
  [England]

5.6   Conclusion

Children's early participation in the world of work has long-term effects on the
quality of life of adults. Not only does it relate to the employability profile or health
status, but it can contribute to the maintenance of poverty throughout an individual's
life cycle, or even to its intergenerational reproduction. In this chapter, we have
examined policies and programs that have been directed at countering this social
problem, which has enabled us to identify evidence-based practices and to make new
recommendations based on previous experience.

A comparison of social labelling initiatives, micro-credits and conditional income
transfers has allowed us to see which core elements of the intervention are effective
in practice. On the one hand, social labelling can result in the displacement of child
labor to even more precarious sectors of the economy, if the alternatives available to
families to generate the income needed for household maintenance are not considered. On the other hand, micro-credits counteract economic precariousness without
introducing elements of behavioral conditionality, thus limiting their preventive
impact. The peculiarity of conditional cash transfers lies precisely in the combination
of economic assistance to poor families with the requirement of adequate supervision in the upbringing and education of children.

This opens up the possibility of extending the conditionality of family allowances
to the effective withdrawal of children from child labor. So far, most programs have
incorporated compulsory schooling and medical monitoring as requirements, with
good results. Insofar as the preventive objectives are related to preventing children
from working, the establishment of a higher level of requirements could help to
achieve the preventive results. Only in a few cases has this strengthening criterion
been used.

Secondly, the experience of recent decades has highlighted the importance of the
implementation process itself. As is the case in other areas of intervention (Durlak &
DuPre, 2008), we have seen that the preventive or rehabilitative value of programs
does not depend exclusively on their design, but is related to the degree of community preparedness of the contexts in which they are implemented. Therefore, it is
advisable to take into consideration the peculiarities of each context and adjust the
programs to each receiving system. In this regard, government involvement and
institutional context reform seem to be a preliminary step to making programs truly
effective in practice.

Throughout the chapter we have provided an overview of public policies against child labor, showing the key role of collaboration between schools, social agents in the labor market, and organizations involved in implementing preventive or rehabilitation programs. These are some of the recommendations derived from the previous review:

- Combine the promotion of schooling among low-income families with the fight against poverty. The confluence of both strategies is the most effective option.
- Incorporate (along with compulsory schooling and medical monitoring) the withdrawal of child labor as a precondition for cash transfers to low-income families. This may be particularly relevant in high-risk contexts and in the form of hazardous work.
- Encourage compulsory education and promote educational activities that provide an alternative scenario to involvement in labor activities. Competition of study time with working time is a key factor in preventive actions.
- Take advantage of unused space in schools for the organization of community activities, as well as for the articulation of alliances between schools and surrounding communities.
- Experimenting with curricular adaptations and other forms of flexible schooling with children in high-risk situations (such as working or living on the street), and in general in those cases in which re-entry into school under normal conditions does not seem feasible or immediate.
- Guarantee prior training and professional specialization in rehabilitation programs. Good will and the intention to help may not be enough to achieve the objectives. It is important to have professionals trained to ensure coverage of the highest risk children (such as those living on the streets), and equally trained to implement behavioral-based training sessions.
- Develop individualized rehabilitation programs, adapted to the evolutionary period, and not limited to the provision of care services in residential units. Residential units are expensive and comparatively less effective than other types of community benefits.
- Complement programs to promote adult entrepreneurship with measures to prevent child labor in their children and reinforce as far as possible preventive actions in crisis situations.
- Incorporate the movements of child workers into the social dialogue tables, so that they participate in building preventive consensus.
- Improve impact assessment systems, analyzing the displacement of child labor between sectors of activity, as well as the medium- and long-term effects of interventions.

Public policies against child labor are an area in which very positive results have been achieved in recent decades. This has led to the accumulation of a series of lessons learned that can be used in the design and implementation of programs in the immediate future. First, social dialogue policies and concerted efforts prepare communities to prevent school dropouts, along with the negative consequences of children's involvement in the workplace. Second, compulsory schooling, possibly together with public health systems, are among the political and institutional instruments that have most contributed to improving the population's quality of life. Finally, behavioral-based psychosocial interventions, when properly implemented and in sufficient doses, are particularly effective in preventing and combating child labor.

References

Agénor, P. R., & Alpaslan, B. (2013). *Child labor, intra-household bargaining and economic growth. Centre for Growth and Business Cycle Research (CGBCR) Discussion Paper Series, 181.* Manchester: University of Manchester.

Arat, Z. F. (2002). Analyzing child labor as a human rights issue: Its causes, aggravating policies, and alternative proposals. *Human Rights Quarterly, 24*(1), 177–204.

Babo, A. (2019). Eliminating child labor in rural areas: Limits of community-based approaches in South-Western Côte d'Ivoire. In J. Ballet & A. Bhukuth (Eds.), *Child exploitation in the Global South* (pp. 65–90). London: Palgrave Macmillan.

Banerjee, A., Duflo, E., Glennerster, & Kinnan, C. (2015). The miracle of microfinance? Evidence from a randomized evaluation. *American Economic Journal: Applied Economics, 7*(1), 22–53. https://doi.org/10.1257/app.20130533.

Baradaran, S., & Barclay, S. (2011). Fair trade and child labor. *Columbia Humans Rights Law Review, 43*, 1–63.

Barrera-Osorio, F., Linden, L. L., & Saavedra, J. E. (2019). Medium-and long-term educational consequences of alternative conditional cash transfer designs: Experimental evidence from Colombia. *American Economic Journal: Applied Economics, 11*(3), 54–91.

Bequele, A., & Boyden, J. (Eds.). (1988). *Combating child labour*. Geneva: International Labour Organization.

Bessell, S. (2011). Influencing international child labour policy: The potential and limits of children-centred research. *Children and Youth Services Review, 33*(4), 564–568.

Bhaskaran, R., Nathan, D., Phillips, N., & Upendranadh, C. (2010). Home-based child labour in Delhi's garments sector: Contemporary forms of unfree labour in global production. *The Indian Journal of Labour Economics, 53*(4), 607–624.

Bhat, B. A. (2011). Socioeconomic Dimensions of Child Labor in Central Asia: A Case Study of the Cotton Industry in Uzbekistan. *Problems of Economic Transition, 54*(1), 84–99.

Bhat, B. A. (2013). Forced Labor of Children in Uzbekistan's Cotton Industry. *International Journal on World Peace, 30*(4), 61–85.

Bourdillon, M. (2006). Children and work: A review of current literature and debates. *Development and Change, 37*(6), 1201–1226.

Campbell, F. A., Pungello, E. P., Miller-Johnson, S., Burchinal, M., & Ramey, C. T. (2001). The development of cognitive and academic abilities: Growth curves from an early childhood educational experiment. *Developmental Psychology, 37*(2), 231–242. https://doi.org/10.1037/0012-1649.37.2.231.

Dickens, C. (2017). *Oliver twist*. Madrid.

Dammert, A. C., De Hoop, J., Mvukiyehe, E., & Rosati, F. C. (2018). Effects of public policy on child labor: Current knowledge, gaps, and implications for program design. *World Development, 110*, 104–123.

Durlak, J. A., & DuPre, E. P. (2008). Implementation matters: A review of research on the influence of implementation on program outcomes and the factors affecting implementation. *American Journal of Community Psychology, 41*(3-4), 327–350.

Duryea, S., & Morrison, A. (2004). The effect of conditional transfers on school performance and child labor: Evidence from an ex-post impact evaluation in Costa Rica. *IDB Working Paper No. 418*. https://doi.org/10.2139/ssrn.1818707.

Dybicz, P. (2005). Interventions for street children: An analysis of current best practices. *International Social Work, 48*(6), 763–771.

Edmonds, E. V., & Pavcnik, N. (2006). International trade and child labor: Cross-country evidence. *Journal of International Economics, 68*(1), 115–140.

Fallon, P., & Tzannatos, Z. (1998). *Child labor*. Washington, D.C.: World Bank.

Fuligni, A. J., Tseng, V., & Lam, M. (1999). Attitudes toward family obligations among American adolescents with Asian, Latin American, and European backgrounds. *Child Development, 70* (4), 1030–1044.

Greenberger, E. (1983). A researcher in the policy arena: The case of child labor. *American Psychologist, 38*(1), 104–111.

Grootaert, C., & Kanbur, R. (1995). *Child labor: A review. World Bank Policy Research Working Paper, 1454*. Washington: World Bank.

Guillén-Marroquín, J. (1988). Child labour in Peru: Gold panning in Madre de Dios. In A. Bequele & J. Boyden (Eds.), *Combating Child Labour* (pp. 61–77). Geneva: ILO.

Harris, M. S., Johnson, K., Young, L., & Edwards, J. (2011). Community reinsertion success of street children programs in Brazil and Peru. *Children and Youth Services Review, 33*(5), 723–731.

International Programme on the Elimination of Child Labor (IPEC). (2013). *Business and the fight against child labor: Experience from India, Brazil and South Africa*. Geneva: International Labour Organization.

Jason, L. A., Glantsman, O., O'Brien, J. F., & Ramian, K. N. (2019). Introduction to the field of community psychology. In L. A. Jason, O. Glantsman, J. F. O'Brien, & K. N. Ramian (Eds.), *Introduction to Community Psychology: Becoming an agent of change*. https://press.rebus.community/introductiontocommunitypsychology/chapter/intro-to-community-psychology/.

Kandiyoti, D. (1998). Rural livelihoods and social networks in Uzbekistan: Perspectives from Andijan. *Central Asian Survey, 17*(4), 561–578.

Khan, F. R., Westwood, R., & Boje, D. M. (2010). 'I feel like a foreign agent': NGOs and corporate social responsibility interventions into Third World child labor. *Human Relations, 63*(9), 1417–1438.

Kloos, B., Hill, J., Thomas, E., Wandersman, A., Elias, M. J., & Dalton, J. H. (2012). *Community psychology: Linking individuals and communities*. Boston: Cengage Learning.

Lieten, G. K., & Strehl, T. (2014). *Child street life: An inside view of hazards and expectations of street children in Peru*. New York: Springer.

Maccoby, E. E., Kahn, A. J., & Everett, B. A. (1983). The role of psychological research in the formation of policies affecting children. *American Psychologist, 38*(1), 80.

Maya Jariego, I. (2017). "But we want to work": The movement of child workers in Peru and the actions for reducing child labor. *American Journal of Community Psychology, 60*(3–4), 430–438.

McDonagh, P. (2002). Communicative campaigns to effect anti-slavery and fair trade. *European Journal of Marketing, 36*(5/6), 642–666.

Pellerano, L., Porreca, E. & Rosati, F. C. (2019). The income elasticity of child labour: Do cash transfers have an impact on the poorest children? (August 1, 2019). *CEIS Working Paper No. 466*. https://doi.org/10.2139/ssrn.3430439.

Piazza, M. (2001). *Niños que Trabajan en Minería Artesanal de Oro en el Perú*. Lima: IPEC-OIT.

Piza, C., & Souza, A. P. (2016). *Short-and long-term effects of a child-labor ban*. Washington: The World Bank.

Ravi, A. (2001). Combating child labour with labels: Case of Rugmark. *Economic and Political Weekly, 36*(13), 1141–1147.

Rosati, F. C., & Lyon, S. (2006). Tackling child labour: Policy options for achieving sustainable reductions in children at work. *Understanding Children's Work Project*, Universidad de Roma.

Rosell, P. D., & Hansen, A. (2012). *Children working in the carpet industry of India: Prevalence and conditions*. ICF International.

Sax, L. (2015). *The collapse of parenting: How we hurt our kids when we treat them like grown-ups*. New York: Basic Books.

Sharma, A. N. (2002). Impact of social labelling on child labour in carpet industry. *Economic and Political Weekly, 37*(52), 5196–5204.

Smith, L. C. (2011). Re-evaluating poverty alleviation strategies: The impact of microfinance on child labor in Bangladesh. *Claremont McKenna College Senior Theses. Paper 224*. http://scholarship.claremont.edu/cmc_theses/224.

Tabatabai, H. (2006). *Eliminating child labour: The promise of conditional cash transfers*. Geneva: ILO.

Tonon, G. (2012). *Young people's quality of life and construction of citizenship*. New York: Springer Science & Business Media.

Valkila, J., & Nygren, A. (2010). Impacts of Fair Trade certification on coffee farmers, cooperatives, and laborers in Nicaragua. *Agriculture and Human Values, 27*(3), 321–333.

Velez, C. E., Medeiros, M., & Soares, S. (2004). Schooling expansion in demographic transition: A transient opportunity for inequality reduction in Brazil. In *Inequality and Economic Development in Brazil* (pp. 203–224). Washington, DC: The World Bank.

Venkateswarlu, D., Ramakrishna, R. V. S. S., & Moid, M. A. (2006). *Child labour in carpet industry in India: Recent developments*. Washington, DC: International Labor Rights Fund (ILRF).

Volpi, E. (2002). *Street children: Promising practices and approaches*. Washington, D.C.: World Bank Institute.

Wabwile, M. (2010). Implementing the social and economic rights of children in developing countries: The place of international assistance and cooperation. *The International Journal of Children's Rights, 18*(3), 355–385.

Winstanley, D., Clark, J., & Leeson, H. (2002). Approaches to child labour in the supply chain. *Business Ethics: A European Review, 11*(3), 210–223.

Woodhead, M. (1988). When psychology informs public policy: The case of early childhood intervention. *American Psychologist, 43*(6), 443–454. https://doi.org/10.1037/0003-066X.43.6.

Chapter 6
Epilogue: A Continuum in the Modalities of Child Labor

In the previous five chapters, we have seen that the term "child labor" refers to a wide variety of forms of children's participation in the world of work. Preventive strategies also vary, both in their content and in their impact, depending on the type of child labor on which they are intended to have an impact. In this section, we illustrate this with four examples of child labor that are organized into a continuum according to the severity of their potential consequences, and that require specific policies and programs in each case to counteract them.

- Nahil collaborates with his parents in the cultivation of corn in Yucatan.
- Antonia works as an intern in domestic service in Brasilia.
- Abdul works in a brick kiln in Pakistan.
- Malai works in a brothel for tourists in Bangkok.

The four cases cover a great diversity of situations, with intervention strategies that also adapt to each profile. In the table we distinguish the modalities, effects, and programs that are effective.

The most common form of child labor in the world is agricultural work to support the subsistence economy of the family unit. In this case, labor participation is integrated into the process of socialization and learning, so that it facilitates the development of labor skills and the acquisition of local ecological knowledge. However, early incorporation into the world of work can negatively affect academic motivation and performance, sometimes leading to early school leaving. Although it is at the less harmful end of the continuum, this form of child labor can condition the educational experience of children and, in the medium term, affect employment opportunities or even the maintenance of poverty. Conditional cash transfers and psycho-educational programs to prevent school dropouts are two of the most effective strategies in this case.

Conducting paid activities (either with a contract or as part of the informal economy) often involves a higher level of involvement (in time and effort) by children. Although there is great variability in the level of risk associated, these are usually activities that test the physical and psychological resilience of children. If

© The Author(s), under exclusive license to Springer Nature Switzerland AG 2021
I. Maya Jariego, *Community Prevention of Child Labor*, Human Well-Being
Research and Policy Making, https://doi.org/10.1007/978-3-030-70810-8_6

the work activity exceeds their physical strength, personal maturity or social-emotional competencies, it is highly likely to be detrimental to balanced development. In this case, in addition to the impact on education and employment opportunities, there are significant effects on the health and psychological well-being of children. In addition to the programs mentioned in the previous level, in this case secondary prevention strategies are usually implemented, in order to avoid (or if necessary attenuate) the impact of child labor on health and psychological well-being. Since 1999, the eradication of hazardous work has been one of the priorities of international policy in this area. With this type of population, school reintegration programs are particularly complex and usually face relapses, which must be addressed.

Finally, at the most serious level are cases of child exploitation, such as forced labor, servitude, prostitution, child soldiers and participation in illegal drug trafficking, among others. These are activities that openly violate the rights of children and compromise their moral development or personal integrity. They also generally have a significant psychological impact. Consequently, preventive strategies often involve psychosocial rehabilitation, community reintegration and educational reintegration. Complementarily, they have a component for ensuring compliance with the law, and therefore involve the police, the courts and those other actors involved in the monitoring, control and sanctioning of criminal activities.

The type of child labor does not depend only on the type of economic activity performed, but also (and preferably) on the conditions under which such activity is performed. For example, agricultural activities can be a form of hazardous work when contact is made with insecticides or sharp tools (which can cause injuries), or when long hours are worked in hazardous environmental conditions. Similarly, domestic service can be forced labor when parents give their child to an employer to pay off a debt. Therefore, it is the conditions in which the work activity is performed that determine its risk potential and also the type of intervention that is most relevant in each case.

From the above analysis, it can be deduced that we have a great diversity of policy instruments, which have to be modulated according to the context and the specific goals of intervention. Specifically, the rights approach, legal regulations and agreement among political actors seem particularly relevant to address the worst forms of child labor, ranging from hazardous work to the most severe forms of child exploitation. On the other hand, economic incentives for families to keep their children in school are particularly effective from a preventive point of view (Table 6.1).

Table 6.1 A continuum in the modalities of child labor

	Subsistence economy	Moderate risk wage work	Hazardous work	Forced and Illicit work
Modality	Nahil helps his parents in the cultivation of corn, beans and pumpkin. In the Mayan communities of the southern Yucatan it is a tradition to cultivate the corn in the family garden. This allows them to produce the basic products for the gastronomy of the area	Antonia started working in a house when she was 10 years old. This provides her with room and board, along with a small monthly stipend that she usually sends to her family. In general, domestic workers have worse conditions than other salaried workers. It is usually an invisible job, which requires no qualifications and in which there is a great difference in status with the employer	Abdul works in a brick kiln for 8 h a day, 6 days a week. He began this activity when he was strong enough to lift a brick. His entire family works in the same activity and does not believe that attending school will change the family's occupation	Malai started working in a brothel when she migrated to Bangkok. Most of her clients are tourists. All of her current partners started working when they were 12–15 years old. Only one of them agreed to enter a "foster home" to participate in a reintegration program
Effects	Nahil attends school regularly. However, the time spent on agricultural activities reduces the hours spent on homework. He also has less time to play than his classmates	Antonia had to interrupt her compulsory education when she left her village for Brasilia. However, the most difficult thing for her was to be separated from her family and to live most of the time as an intern in the home. During the first year she cried every night and her mood was very low	Abdul usually has back pain and always ends up very tired. Injuries, wounds, and work accidents are very common. He has also developed a chronic respiratory condition. He shows signs of stress, anxiety, and low self-esteem	Malai has been a victim of abuse and physical violence. She knows of cases of female colleagues who have contracted sexually transmitted diseases and others who have been physically confined as punishment. There are also some cases of unwanted pregnancies in her environment
Prevention	During the last year of elementary school, he participated in an after-school program of educational support. He attended two afternoons per	In her second year, Antonia began participating in an NGO weekend program. Her emotional well-being improved significantly when	Three months ago, a school was built near the brick factory which has launched a program for reintegration into school, with educational	Malai is currently participating in a vocational training course with which the Thai government, in collaboration with several NGOs, is

(continued)

Table 6.1 (continued)

	Subsistence economy	Moderate risk wage work	Hazardous work	Forced and Illicit work
	week, where he received academic orientation and homework help. This improved the results and encouraged the parents to continue with the secondary education	she was assigned to a support group with other child domestic workers. The association also advocates for the regulation of a collective agreement for the sector	support. Abdul has started attending 2 days a week. The Punjab government has announced labor inspections and has committed to having only adults working in the brick industry within 2 years	trying to promote other employment alternatives. They also offer her psychological support to facilitate her personal rehabilitation and community reintegration process. Recently, a local group has been created that meets regularly to monitor preventive actions

Part II
Implementing Child Labor Policies and Programs: Dilemmas and Key Actors in the Practice of Effective Interventions

Chapter 7
Dilemmas in Public Policy Against Child Labor

Abstract In this chapter we examine the dilemmas that exist in the formulation of child labor policies. While public opinion is often sensitive to the needs of children in general, and those of working children in particular, recent years have seen a debate on the most appropriate strategies to address the problem. Despite the fact that children are perceived as a vulnerable population segment, the introduction of the child agency perspective has meant in practice a questioning of the traditional models of protection in social work with children. This has led to qualify the objectives of "eradication" of child labor and to establish limits in international labor standards, with the counterbalance of local needs. In any case, income redistribution policies within a framework of consensus among social actors have proven to be particularly effective. Therefore, despite the controversies regarding the degree of relevance and adjustment, there is sufficient evidence to defend investment in education and health for preventive purposes.

Keywords Child labor · Public policies · Poverty · Consensus · Education · Health · Child protection · International standards

7.1 Introduction

Every year since 2002, the World Day Against Child Labor is celebrated on June 12. In successive editions, public attention has been directed towards the participation of children in agricultural work, child trafficking, the employment of girls in domestic service, child labor in mines and quarries, or the performance of dangerous work in general, among other topics of interest. On several occasions, it has also focused on defending compulsory public education up to the minimum age for admission to employment. This type of campaign aims to raise public awareness of the existence of the problem and to involve governments in the solution. To this end, information is conveyed to the media, debates are organized, and activities are carried out to change attitudes.

Both human rights campaigns and initiatives to protect children often find a positive echo in the general population (Pupavac, 2002). Since the last quarter of

© The Author(s), under exclusive license to Springer Nature Switzerland AG 2021
I. Maya Jariego, *Community Prevention of Child Labor*, Human Well-Being
Research and Policy Making, https://doi.org/10.1007/978-3-030-70810-8_7

the twentieth century, there has been a slow increase in public awareness and concern about the issue (Sood, 2012). In the specific case of World Day Against Child Labor, some NGOs had already paved the way with campaigns against the exploitation of children in the carpet industry in India and Pakistan. Also, with the boycott of sports equipment companies' products made with child labor. Since then, the media have repeatedly paid attention to cases of child abuse, slavery, exploitation, and prostitution. This has generated a certain sensitivity towards the worst forms of child labor, which in the collective imagination become a reference from which to interpret any type of preventive action in relation to this social problem.

The policies of international agencies for the eradication of child labor have been controversial, though. The most widespread criticisms consist of reproaching the lack of sensitivity to local needs, the living conditions of low-income families, and the needs perceived by the child population itself. In this chapter, we will review three key dilemmas in the design and implementation of preventive policies. As we shall see, far from being unproductive, this debate helps to nuance the objectives and modulate the actions of a preventive nature. Secondly, we will show that empirical evidence on what type of actions are effective in practice provides a valid response to these dilemmas. Despite this, they are confronted with opposing socio-political trends that make their implementation difficult.

7.2 A Brief Overview of Child Labor in the World

As a preliminary step to reviewing public policy on the issue, we provide below the basic data on the prevalence and patterns of child labor around the world. In Table 7.1 we have summarized some of the basic descriptive data provided by the latest available estimate from the International Labor Organization (ILO, 2017).

As discussed in Sect. 1.4, most child labor is found in Africa and Asia. Specifically, Africa has 72 million child workers, or 19.6% of the child population, while the Asia and Pacific region has 62 million child workers, or a prevalence of 7.4%. Together, both regions are home to 9 out of 10 child laborers worldwide. However, there may be greater variability if we descend to more specific geographical areas. For example, according to UNICEF data (2019), in Central and West Africa the prevalence is 31%, in Sub-Saharan Africa 29%, and in Eastern and Southern Africa

Table 7.1 Prevalence of child labor and distribution by activity areas in the world

	Prevalence	Agriculture	Industry	Services	Hazardous work
Africa	19.6	85.1	3.7	11.2	8.6
Asia and the Pacific	7.4	57.5	21.4	21.1	3.4
Americas	5.3	51.5	13.2	35.3	3.2
Europe and Central Asia	4.1	76.7	9.7	13.6	4.0
Arab states	2.9	60.3	12.4	27.4	1.5

Source: ILO (2017)

27%, while in the Middle East and North Africa it is only 5%. In general, the prevalence of the problem is significantly higher in lower-income countries.

There are also important differences between regions when we consider the sector of activity. In the case of Africa, child labor is predominantly found in agriculture (85.1%) which means that in most cases it involves unpaid activity within the family unit. In contrast, the Asia-Pacific region has the largest segment of child laborers in industry (21.4%) accounting for most hazardous work and a high risk for children. In the Americas, more than one-third of children work in the service sector.

According to ILO data (2017), the demographic profile shows that children between the ages of 5 and 11 are the largest segment among child workers (47.9%), while the 15–17 age group is the largest among those in hazardous work (51.2%). By gender, children constitute 58% of child workers and perform 62% of hazardous work. However, girls are often responsible for household chores or caring for younger siblings, in a type of activity that is often not reflected in official statistics (Assaad et al., 2010).

Between 2012 and 2016 there has been a 9.7% reduction in the number of child laborers in the world. While this is a positive development, it represents a slight slowdown in the sustained decline observed since 2000. On the other hand, sub-Saharan Africa is the only region where there has been no reduction but a slight increase in the 4-year interval. Both conflict situations and natural disasters in specific regions highlight the fragility of preventive achievements in reducing child labor (Adepoju, 2000; Admassie, 2002; Bass, 2004).

Bearing in mind the above description, international bodies have proposed the need to adapt public policies to each specific regional context, considering the peculiarities of the labor market in each case. Along with tripartite social dialogue as a basic approach, it is recommended that access to education, the protection of the most vulnerable families and the promotion of quality youth employment be established as priorities. However, as we will see below, despite this basic consensus in general actions, there are several fundamental dilemmas in the design of public policies on the subject. This is what we propose to review below.

7.3   Three Alternatives in the Design of Preventive Policies

Child labor is both a by-product of traditional local cultures and of international trade and is attempted to be regulated through legal instruments (Smolin, 1999). On the one hand, there are traditions, social norms, and attitudes favorable to the early incorporation of children into the world of work. On the other hand, the internationalization of the economy generates a demand for labor that also reaches the most vulnerable groups in low-income countries. The movements to defend the rights of the child seek to counteract both influences by introducing regulations on the minimum age for access to employment, promoting the commitment of states to protect children from hazardous work, and preserving compulsory education.

In practice, this translates into (a) the approval of international standards to (b) eradicate child labor and (c) promote the protection of children. These three elements constitute three pillars of the policies of international organizations which, as we explain below, have been questioned by social movements and local organizations.

7.3.1 International Standards and Local Needs

One of the most widespread reactions to preventive initiatives is to point out that international bodies design their interventions without considering the cultural and ethnic characteristics of local contexts. Among other paradigmatic cases, the work is considered part of the education of children in Andean culture (Campoamor, 2016), and in general in rural contexts, where it functions as a form of informal learning about agricultural tasks. Gender roles are also culturally determined, so strategies to counteract stereotypes may face reactions from local people.

From alternative ideological frameworks, there are certain social movements in developing countries that interpret preventive policies as neocolonial practices that seek to neutralize the relative advantage of lower labor costs (Smolin, 1999), or that restrict their own forms of cultural organization. In reaction, they defend their autonomy to define their own policies and maintain idiosyncratic social practices at the local level. This is the case, for example, with the Movement of Adolescent and Child Workers, Children of Christian Workers in Peru, and other movements of child workers in Latin America (Maya Jariego, 2017), to which we will return later. Also, in the Indian sub-continent, in line with previous approaches, it has been noted that trade sanctions or product boycotts can have a negative impact on the local labor market in developing countries (Edmons, 2003). Hence, European or North American activism that does not cater to local needs is sometimes criticized (Brooks, 2005).

7.3.2 Eradicate or Mitigate

Secondly, it has been questioned whether the goal of preventive policies must necessarily be the complete abolition of child labor. Instead, the introduction of regulations is suggested, either to alleviate the most negative consequences of child labor involvement or to achieve a relative reduction in the prevalence of the problem (Ballet & Bhukuth, 2019). One of the central arguments of this second point of view consists in anticipating the consequences of the elimination of child labor in low-income families. As it is a phenomenon directly linked to poverty, the withdrawal of children from the labor market can have a negative impact on the economic sustainability of family groups. Ultimately, the dilemma between abolishing and regulating refers to the operational definition of child labor. In this respect, there is evidence of possible positive effects of early labor experiences, or even the possibility of reconciling labor activities with studies in a balanced manner (under certain circumstances), which makes it pertinent to question the modalities of child labor that are intended to be eliminated and those that are not.

7.3.3 Protection or Agency of Children

Thirdly, a group of non-governmental and professional intervention organizations has been formed to propose alternative policies to those promoted by international bodies. More specifically, they defend the incorporation of the children's point of view through their participation in decision making. To do so, they assume that children are active individuals with the capacity to build their future. In this case, it is considered that the emphasis on the protection of children involves in part denying children's agency by setting arbitrary limits on children's autonomy to define their own interests. Especially in the field of anthropology, a discourse has emerged that attributes to the very concept of child labor a vision of children based on dependence and passivity (Nieuwenhuys, 1996), so it is proposed to replace an "adult-centered" perspective by the recognition of children's capabilities (Ballet et al., 2011; Hart & Brando, 2018; Reynaert & Roose, 2014). A simple way to do this is to seek the views of children through participatory procedures (Biggeri et al., 2006).

Ultimately, the three above arguments are related insofar as it is assumed that different social constructions of childhood emerge in different cultures. International instruments against child labor encounter diverse local realities, with different visions of what children can (or cannot) do at certain ages, and sometimes face counter-reactions from those segments of the population who question the ultimate goals of the intervention.

Box 7.1: The Global March Against Child Labor
The "Global March Against Child Labor" is a community-based movement created to defend the rights of children, with a special emphasis on the right to education. The original mobilization began in 1998, with the participation of non-governmental organizations, trade unions, and other social entities around the world. Under the strong leadership of Kailash Satyarthi, who would later receive the Nobel Peace Prize in 2014, a broad international alliance was formed to promote effective regulation against the worst forms of child labor. Today it is considered an example of transnational activism with positive results.

However, in some contexts, it has been noted that such campaigns "ignore the key role that children play in the global flexible labor market". In the case of children working in the vineyards in South Africa, Levine (1999) argues

(continued)

Box 7.1 (continued)

that international legislation prohibiting child labor perpetuates the economic conditions that produce it. According to this analysis, it is important to take into consideration both the contribution of children's wages to the domestic economy and the labor exploitation to which adults may also be subjected. Many children defend their right to work because their removal from the vineyards does not imply the disappearance of the conditions of poverty and labor exploitation to which their families are exposed.

Based on Levine, S. (1999). Bittersweet Harvest: Children, work, and the global march against child labor in the post-apartheid state. Critique of Anthropology, 19(2), 139–155.

[South Africa]

7.4   What Is Effective in Preventing Child Labor

Despite all the criticism, the preventive strategies implemented in recent decades have yielded results. In just 15 years there was a reduction of more than a third in the prevalence of child labor in the world. Among other things, we have effective strategies to involve families in their children's education, to monitor that employers do not hire underage children, and to improve the functioning of primary schools. The levels of impact of preventive policies in some countries and regions have been so high that not only are there "lessons learned" that can be replicated in other contexts, but they constitute exemplary practices that could also guide intervention with other social problems and be extended to other populations with different needs.

Public health, education, and social service programs have a direct impact on the quality of life of the population. More specifically, conditional economic incentives, coalition-building for preventive purposes, and the development of psychoeducational programs to prevent school dropouts have proven particularly effective. However, these types of measures are confronted with opposing social and political trends, which can significantly hinder their implementation. Social policies of income redistribution, as well as investment in public health and education systems, face financial difficulties and a political climate that puts their sustainability at risk. For their part, social dialogue instruments face high levels of social and political polarization, which makes their regular functioning more difficult. We develop these ideas below.

7.4.1   Redistributive Policies

Financial support programs for low-income families seem to be working, especially when combined with the requirement for adequate parental supervision of children. They are usually implemented on a large scale, through benefits provided by the state. This emphasizes the importance of national institutions and policies in reducing inequality. Among other factors, both the reduction of public spending on social policies and the transformation of social security systems have shown a significant empirical association with the increase in income inequality in OECD countries (Caminada & Goudswaard, 2001). This takes on its full meaning in the poorest countries, which have a lower capacity for redistribution (Ravallion, 2009). Furthermore, it seems necessary to achieve a minimum level of economic development for redistribution policies to be viable. Hence, low-income countries need to be particularly sensitive to the alternatives available to them to combine economic growth and income redistribution policies according to the different stages of their development (Bardhan, 1996).

However, it is worth drawing attention to the fact that conditional cash transfers have proved effective even in countries with comparatively unprogressive tax systems. In the case of Latin America, despite high levels of inequality, the state's redistributive capacity is relatively small. However, cash transfers to low-income groups have introduced significant improvements in recent decades (Goñi et al., 2008; Lustig et al., 2011). Part of this positive contribution may depend on combining income redistribution with an immediate impact on improving human capital, which may have indirect repercussions in terms of efficiency.

However, transfers to families need to be properly accompanied by investments in public policies for them to work effectively (Hasan, 2010). Otherwise, when families are obliged to guarantee schooling or regular medical check-ups, there is an increase in pressure on the education and health systems, for which they are likely to be completely unprepared. For example, to the extent that pupil/teacher (or doctor/patient) ratios increase, the quality of education or health care could be adversely affected. It is therefore interesting to explore the extent to which these programs are conditioned by economic growth cycles.

7.4.2   Policies Based on Consensus

Cross-cutting agreements between employers and workers, sometimes involving other social groups, create the right climate to ensure that children below the minimum age for employment are not part of the workforce. Instruments such as collective bargaining, cross-cutting political alliances, and community coalitions facilitate the regulation of social issues of concern, through the involvement of diverse actors in the development of shared social standards. The institutionalization of social conflict is one of the central characteristics of modern societies

(Dahrendorf, 1990), in which mutual tolerance between adversaries and political contention are two of the fundamental informal mechanisms that sustain the system of checks and balances of democracies (Levitsky & Ziblatt, 2018).

However, these types of dynamics based on social dialogue are facing more and more difficulties, in the context of increasing fragmentation and social conflict. Since the last quarter of the twentieth century, there has been a parallel increase in income inequality and political polarization, both in the United States and in Europe (McCarty et al., 2003; Neal, 2020; Winkler, 2019). This process seems to correspond in part to an intergenerational divergence (Boxell et al., 2017) and is expressed simultaneously in attitudinal differences and some relational segregation (Baldassarri & Bearman, 2007). Simultaneously, in the last decade, the economic crisis has led to a scenario of confrontation and the breaking of consensus in labor relations, in which the unions have lost representation and negotiating power (Sánchez-Mosquera, 2018).

7.4.3   Investment in Education and Health

Both public health policies and investment in education have a widespread impact on the population's quality of life, contribute to equal opportunities, and reduce inequality. A well-functioning education system is directly related to reducing the risk of child labor. However, adequate financing of education is a particularly complex challenge, especially in developing countries (Psacharopoulos, 1988). On the one hand, adverse economic conditions and the increase in the school-age population can result in scarce public resources available in relation to identified needs (Psacharopoulos, 1986). On the other hand, many other social needs are competing for the same resources.

In the case of developing countries, it has been very common to favor higher education at the expense of primary education, despite evidence that the latter is particularly productive from both an economic and social point of view (Gupta et al., 2002; Jones, 2001). Financing is finally connected to the provision of infrastructure, the availability of scholarships and credits for students, or the salary levels of teachers, among other factors that can be key in the educational process. On the contrary, both the inefficient management of resources and budget cuts in crisis situations have a negative impact on the capacities of the educational system.

In this context, both in the development of public health policies and in sustaining the education system, complementary funding mechanisms have been explored, either through taxes, credits, private contribution and tuition payments (Birdsall, 1996; Nkrumah-Young & Powell, 2011), or through community-based innovations (Abel-Smith & Dua, 1988; Moens, 1990). In all cases, however, the bulk of funding remains state-dependent.

Box 7.2: When Schools are Closed
During the Ebola outbreak in Liberia and Sierra Leone, the temporary closure of schools had a negative impact on academic performance, sexual exploitation, unwanted pregnancies, and child labor. On a larger scale, the 2020 coronavirus pandemic led to population confinement and temporary school closures in many countries. Presumably, these circumstances not only reduce the labor productivity of parents, who have to take care of their children but also negatively affect the learning opportunities of children and will in turn have a reflection on the development of their capacities.

It has been shown that even temporary interruptions due to summer vacations have an impact on the skills acquired during the school year. According to some estimates, each year of schooling increases annual income by 10%, so it can be expected that interrupting the academic year will have a negative impact on human capital. Moreover, this impact is greater among children at risk.

Based on: Closing schools for covid-19 does lifelong harm and widens inequality. *The Economist, April 30th, 2020.*

7.5   Changes in the Goals, Modalities, and Focus of Preventive Policies

The debate we have summarized in the previous sections does not remain at a theoretical level but has had concrete consequences in the formulation of policies against child labor. In the first place, it has been reflected in the gradual shift in intervention priorities towards the worst forms of child labor. Secondly, it has led to the design of intervention strategies that are more sensitive to the peculiarities of the context, that are adjusted to the characteristics of each community, and that adapt to the pace of change that is feasible in each case.

On the one hand, when the potential impact of the policies on low-income families is taken into consideration and, at the same time, the subjective point of view of the children affected by the intervention is taken into account, the natural result is to rethink the very notion of child labor. While there are modalities whose regulation may be more controversial, the prevention of those labor activities that entail a greater physical risk, that involve the performance of illegal activities, or that are based on the ruthless exploitation of the labor force, usually elicits a greater consensus. The corollary has been to admit that different forms of child labor require different solutions. A more pragmatic approach has also been established, giving priority to action over those forms that (because they are more serious) are less contested when trying to guarantee children's rights.

On the other hand, community adjustment strategies have been gaining importance. This means in some cases rethinking program objectives, replacing them with less ambitious but viable ones. It also often involves adapting the pace of change,

Table 7.2 Demands, challenges and innovations in preventive policies

Local demands	The challenges	The innovations
• Consider local needs	• Keep the reduction of inequality and poverty as priorities	• Involve families in the learning process
• Adapt to the pace of change	• Prevent political polarization and social fragmentation	• To generate transversal alliances
• Incorporate participatory practices	• Guarantee the financing and sustainability of public policies	• Strengthen the coverage and quality of the educational system

Source: Own elaboration

with medium- and long-term plans (Márquez et al., 2019). Ultimately, it is a matter of respecting the needs perceived by the population, adapting to local traditions and acting appropriately, according to the values prevailing in each context. There are communities that are not prepared to consider the eradication of child labor but may be receptive to programs to strengthen primary education or to prevent dropouts. Each specific intervention has to be adjusted to the context in which it takes place. Thus, the representation of governments, workers, and employers in the design of interventions, as well as negotiation and community participation during implementation are particularly relevant.

In Table 7.2 we have summarized some of the changes that have been introduced in public policies as they attempt to reflect local demands, or when they seek to overcome the challenges of intervention and introduce evidence-based innovations. The overall picture shows that this is an area in which there are effective models of intervention, but in which an institutional approach has been followed that has not always been sensitive to the reality of local communities (Khan et al., 2007). In addition, the triggers for effective interventions are faced with opposing social trends that put their sustainability at risk.

Low-income countries do not share that the local labor market can be assessed with the same labor standards as developed countries (in terms of working conditions, labor rights, or protection of the most vulnerable groups) (Smolin, 1999). We also know that countries often go through different phases before reaching a level of community preparedness that allows them to consider the reduction of child labor as a goal (Hindman & Smith, 1999). On the other hand, the (targeted) fight against the worst forms of child labor is not only considered more relevant but is generally accepted by the population in poorer countries as well.

The use of the language of universal rights (or, more broadly and non-specifically, resorting to maximalist discourses), "faces a possible reaction from those who are concerned about their cultural, family or personal autonomy" (Smolin, 1999, p. 400). In contrast, the emphasis on the regulation of labor standards refers to a negotiated perspective that, paradoxically, may be more effective in guaranteeing in practice those rights advocated by universalist approaches (Hindman & Smith, 1999). This implies developing a commitment to certain idiosyncratic cultural attitudes and practices. Reformist policies against child labor derive precisely from this double link: on the one hand, they are guided by the rights they seek to promote, and on the other, they strive to respect the pace of change in local communities.

On a purely pragmatic level, low-income countries largely have those public services that they are in a position to finance. We know that investment in primary schools, at the compulsory education level, is directly related to reducing the risk of child labor and produces valuable returns in adult life. But for this to be viable, it is necessary to generate sufficient resources to provide the educational system with adequate amounts and in a sustained manner over time. Such provision also depends in part on efficiently managing the available budget. In addition, resources may be depleted by other social needs competing for the budget, or by cases of corruption and hoarding of resources by local elites.

In this context, it may be useful for social workers and other intervention professionals to be aware of financial difficulties and to be aware of the institutional context in which social policies are developed. Regardless of whether they need to be sensitive to local needs, as we have depicted in Table 7.2, it is also interesting to anticipate the type of barriers that may face the implementation of evidence-based programs. This type of knowledge, focused on action and results, can help keep inequality and poverty reduction as social policy priorities.

Box 7.3: Four Stages in Regulating the Minimum Age for Admission to Employment

The International Labor Organization (ILO) has gone through four different stages in regulating the minimum age for access to employment. The first stage, between 1919 and 1932, consisted in establishing 14 years as the minimum age for working in the industry and the maritime sector, and in ensuring that children under 14 go to school even when participating in agricultural activities. This is a stage in which specific regulations are established in each sector of the economy and some exceptions are allowed in some geographical areas, such as Japan and India. From the outset, the difficulty of establishing a universal standard becomes apparent. In the second stage, between 1936 and 1965, the minimum age was revised upwards in the industrial and maritime sectors, setting it at 15 years.

In 1973, the Convention on the Minimum Age for Admission to Employment (Convention 138) was adopted, initiating the third stage, which established a generic regulatory framework to replace the sectoral agreements. In addition, the "complete abolition of child labor" is proposed as the ultimate goal of the intervention. It is expected that the countries will commit themselves to this objective and progressively raise the minimum age for admission to employment. However, regulation is flexible, allowing low-income countries to set the minimum age at 14, if required, and to regulate light work even at a lower age.

(continued)

Box 7.3 (continued)

In the 1990s, child labor became a central element of the ILO's mission. In this fourth stage, the minimum ages determined by the states range from 14 to 16 years. This is a time when tensions have arisen between developed countries and low-income countries over the implementation of policies to eradicate the problem. It is in this context that the convention against the worst forms of child labor was formulated and approved in 1999.

Based on Smolin, D. M. (1999). Conflict and ideology in the international campaign against child labor. *Hofstra Labor & Employment Law Journal*, 16 (2), 383.

7.6   Conclusion

Child labor creates a division between poor countries (where it has a higher incidence) and rich countries (where it is comparatively less frequent) and positions them differently with respect to preventive policies. The importance of taking into account local needs, the assessment of the impact of restrictive legal regulations on poor families, and the interest in taking into account the point of view of children have emerged precisely in those regions where child labor participation has more weight in the national economy.

Awareness campaigns on child exploitation are the instrument that has received the most public attention. However, it is the programs with a direct impact on the behavioral and economic aspects of the population at risk that are most directly associated with reducing the prevalence of child labor. The former promotes community preparedness, while the latter has been especially effective in practice. The review carried out throughout this chapter has allowed us to distinguish between dispositional policies (which aim to change social attitudes towards the issue), regulatory policies (which modify the regulatory framework of labor relations) and policies focused on results (which normally affect family income and the behavior of children and their families). Each of these may be more or less relevant depending on the stage each specific region is at with respect to the child labor problem.

Since the first estimates of the prevalence of the problem in 1995 (ILO, 1996), the experience of intervention on child labor has been positive. Evidence-based practices have been documented and a significant impact on social needs has been achieved. Criticism of abolitionist policies, on the other hand, has led to a more pragmatic approach, with specific strategies for adaptation to the community contexts in which programs are developed and a priority focus on the worst forms of child labor. This has been reflected above all in the incorporation of participatory strategies and in the modulation of the pace of change. The most effective policies act at multiple levels simultaneously, through medium- and long-term initiatives. As we have seen, they can also benefit from a community-based approach to intervention.

However, despite their proven effectiveness, the continuity of such policies may be at risk if some of the trends we have described are consolidated. Political polarization increases the confrontation around preventive campaigns and makes the implementation of concertation initiatives considerably more difficult. Budgetary restrictions limit the scope of redistribution policies and the capacity to invest in the education system. Similarly, the coverage of social welfare programs is also being reduced.

In the following two chapters we will propose some specific actions to improve the implementation of preventive programs. First, we will review the transfer strategies that can be developed by the different stakeholders in the intervention. Secondly, we present a practical guide to use organizational capacities, adapt programs to community contexts, and adequately implement evidence-based practices.

References

Abel-Smith, B., & Dua, A. (1988). Community-financing in developing countries: The potential for the health sector. *Health Policy and Planning, 3*(2), 95–108.

Adepoju, A. (2000). Issues and recent trends in international migration in Sub-Saharan Africa. *International Social Science Journal, 52*(165), 383–394.

Admassie, A. (2002). Explaining the high incidence of child labour in Sub–Saharan Africa. *African Development Review, 14*(2), 251–275.

Assaad, R., Levison, D., & Zibani, N. (2010). The effect of domestic work on girls' schooling: Evidence from Egypt. *Feminist Economics, 16*(1), 79–128.

Baldassarri, D., & Bearman, P. (2007). Dynamics of political polarization. *American Sociological Review, 72*(5), 784–811.

Ballet, J., & Bhukuth, A. (2019). *Child exploitation in the global South.* Cham: Palgrave Macmillan.

Ballet, J., Biggeri, M., & Comim, F. (2011). Children's agency and the capability approach: A conceptual framework. In M. Biggeri, J. Ballet, & F. Comim (Eds.), *Children and the capability approach* (pp. 22–45). London: Palgrave Macmillan.

Bardhan, P. (1996). Efficiency, equity and poverty alleviation: Policy issues in less developed countries. *The Economic Journal, 106*(438), 1344–1356.

Bass, L. E. (2004). *Child labor in Sub-Saharan Africa.* London: Lynne Rienner Publishers.

Biggeri, M., Libanora, R., Mariani, S., & Menchini, L. (2006). Children conceptualizing their capabilities: Results of a survey conducted during the first children's world congress on child labour. *Journal of Human Development, 7*(1), 59–83.

Birdsall, N. (1996). Public spending on higher education in developing countries: Too much or too little? *Economics of Education Review, 15*(4), 407–419.

Boxell, L., Gentzkow, M., & Shapiro, J. M. (2017). Is the internet causing political polarization? Evidence from demographics. *NBER Working Paper Series, No. w23258.* National Bureau of Economic Research.

Brooks, E. (2005). Transnational campaigns against child labor: The garment industry in Banghladesh. In J. Bandy & J. Smith (Eds.), *Coalitions across borders: Transnational protest and the neoliberal order* (pp. 121–139). Lanham: Rowman & Littlefield.

Caminada, K., & Goudswaard, K. (2001). International trends in income inequality and social policy. *International Tax and Public Finance, 8*(4), 395–415.

Campoamor, L. (2016). "Who are you calling exploitative?" Defensive motherhood, child labor, and urban poverty in Lima, Peru. *The Journal of Latin American and Caribbean Anthropology, 21*(1), 151–172.

Dahrendorf, R. (1990). *The modern social conflict: An essay on the politics of liberty.* Berkeley: University of California Press.

Edmons, E. V. (2003). Should we boycott child labor? *Ethics and Economics, 1.* http://hdl.handle. net/1866/3289.

Goñi, E., López, J. H., & Servén, L. (2008). *Fiscal redistribution and income inequality in Latin America. Policy Research Working Paper 4487.* Washington, D.C.: The World Bank.

Gupta, S., Verhoeven, M., & Tiongson, E. R. (2002). The effectiveness of government spending on education and health care in developing and transition economies. *European Journal of Political Economy, 18*(4), 717–737.

Hart, C. S., & Brando, N. (2018). A capability approach to children's well-being, agency and participatory rights in education. *European Journal of Education, 53*(3), 293–309.

Hasan, A. (2010). *Gender-targeted conditional cash transfers: Enrollment, spillover effects and instructional quality. Policy Research Working Paper, 5257.* Washington, D.C.: The World Bank.

Hindman, H. D., & Smith, C. G. (1999). Cross-cultural ethics and the child labor problem. *Journal of Business Ethics, 19*(1), 21–33.

ILO. (1996). *Child labor: Targeting the intolerable.* Geneva: ILO.

International Labour Organization. (2017). *Global estimates of child labor: Results and trends, 2012–2016.* Geneva: ILO.

Jones, P. (2001). Are educated workers really more productive? *Journal of Development Economics, 64*(1), 57–79.

Khan, F. R., Munir, K. A., & Willmott, H. (2007). A dark side of institutional entrepreneurship: Soccer balls, child labour and postcolonial impoverishment. *Organization Studies, 28*(7), 1055–1077.

Levine, S. (1999). Bittersweet Harvest: Children, work and the global march against child labour in the post-apartheid state. *Critique of Anthropology, 19*(2), 139–155.

Levitsky, S., & Ziblatt, D. (2018). *How democracies die.* Portland: Broadway Books.

Lustig, N., Higgins, S., Jaramillo, M., Jimenez, W., Molina, G., Arauco, V. P., ... & Yañez, E. (2011). Fiscal policy and income redistribution in Latin America: Challenging the conventional wisdom. *Commitment to Equity Initiative, Inter-American Dialogue y Tulane University.*

Márquez, E., Holgado, D., & Maya-Jariego, I. (2019). Innovation, Dosage and Responsiveness in the Implementation of the Program "Edúcame Primero Perú" for Reducing Child Labour. *Applied Research in Quality of Life, 14*(3), 617–636.

Maya Jariego, I. (2017). "But we want to work": The movement of child workers in Peru and the actions for reducing child labor. *American Journal of Community Psychology, 60*(3–4), 430–438.

McCarty, N., Poole, K. T., & Rosenthal, H. (2003). Political polarization and income inequality. *SSRN.* https://doi.org/10.2139/ssrn.1154098.

Moens, F. (1990). Design, implementation, and evaluation of a community financing scheme for hospital care in developing countries: A pre-paid health plan in the Bwamanda health zone, Zaire. *Social Science & Medicine, 30*(12), 1319–1327.

Neal, Z. P. (2020). A sign of the times? Weak and strong polarization in the US Congress, 1973–2016. *Social Networks, 60,* 103–112.

Nieuwenhuys, O. (1996). The paradox of child labor and anthropology. *Annual Review of Anthropology, 25*(1), 237–251.

Nkrumah-Young, K. K., & Powell, P. (2011). Exploring higher education financing options. *European Journal of Higher Education, 1*(1), 3–21.

Psacharopoulos, G. (1986). *Financing education in developing countries: An exploration of policy options.* Washington, D.C.: The World Bank.

Psacharopoulos, G. (1988). The financing of education in developing countries. *Higher Education Policy, 1*(1), 12–16.

Pupavac, V. (2002). The international children's rights regime. In D. Chandler (Ed.), *Rethinking Human Rights* (pp. 57–75). London: Palgrave Macmillan.

Ravallion, M. (2009). *Do poorer countries have less capacity for redistribution?. Policy Research Working Paper 5046*. Washington, D.C.: World Bank.

Reynaert, D., & Roose, R. (2014). Children's rights and the capability approach: Discussing children's agency against the horizon of the institutionalised youth land. In D. Daniel Stoecklin & J. M. Bonvin (Eds.), *Children's rights and the capability approach* (pp. 175–193). Dordrecht: Springer.

Sánchez-Mosquera, M. (2018). Trade unionism and social pacts in Spain in comparative perspective. *European Journal of Industrial Relations, 24*(1), 23–38.

Smolin, D. M. (1999). Conflict and ideology in the international campaign against child labour. *Hofstra Labor & Employment Law Journal, 16*(2), 383.

Sood, R. S. (2012). *Efficacy and effectiveness of the role of media as an important tool for human rights campaigners: A case study of 'global march against child labour' campaign*. Department of Mass Communication. Shri Jagdish Prasad Jhabarmal Tibrew Ala University. Vidyanagari, Jhunjhunu, Rajastan. Doctoral Dissertation.

UNICEF. (2019). *Global databases based on Demographic and Health Surveys (DHS), Multiple Indicator Cluster Surveys (MICS) and other national surveys, 2010–2019*.

Winkler, H. (2019). The effect of income inequality on political polarization: Evidence from European regions, 2002–2014. *Economics and Politics, 31*(2), 137–162.

Chapter 8
From Science to Practice in the Prevention of Child Labor

Abstract In this chapter, we describe how empirical evidence on the causes of child labor is translated into preventive policymaking. The transfer of scientific research results is a two-step process, involving (a) the dissemination of knowledge and (b) community ownership. Accordingly, we first examine the role of science-practice chains in the dissemination of innovations; and second, we analyze the role of the different parties involved in the process. A better systematization of the types of child labor could contribute to the formulation of more precise and consistent intervention projects, with results indicators adjusted to theoretical expectations. Similarly, the detailed description of the progressive process of incorporation into the world of work would allow the implementation of long-term prevention strategies, with proximal and distal result indicators. Throughout the chapter, recommendations are made to develop a systemic approach to intervention, as well as to carry out preparatory actions to create an environment conducive to the reduction of child labor.

Keywords Child labor · Research results-transfer · Community preparedness · Science-practice chains · Stakeholders · Implementation

8.1 Introduction

The two largest cocoa producers in the world are located in West Africa. According to the latest U.S. Department of Labor estimates, up to 60% of production is concentrated in Ghana and Côte d'Ivoire, where more than two million children are estimated to be engaged in hazardous work.[1] Among other tasks, they clear brush and plant, as well as harvest, transport, and open pods with a machete. Consequently, children's involvement in cultivation and processing involves the use of sharp tools, the transport of heavy loads, and sometimes the application of pesticides (Nkamleu

---

[1]The descriptive data in this section is based on the Bureau of International Labor Affairs: https://www.dol.gov/agencies/ilab/our-work/child-forced-labor-trafficking/child-labor-cocoa

© The Author(s), under exclusive license to Springer Nature Switzerland AG 2021
I. Maya Jariego, *Community Prevention of Child Labor*, Human Well-Being Research and Policy Making, https://doi.org/10.1007/978-3-030-70810-8_8

& Kielland, 2006). This results in more than half of the children reporting injuries or accidents during the course of their work.

In this area, prevention programs face significant challenges. In the case of Ghana, despite having ratified most of the international conventions to protect children's rights and eradicate child labor, labor inspections, and other mechanisms to ensure compliance with the law are inefficient. In addition, the population, especially in rural areas, is hardly aware of the legal regulations for the sector (Mull & Kirkhorn, 2005). On the other hand, initiatives to eliminate child labor in the cocoa industry often involve, among other stakeholders, governments, chocolate manufacturers, civil society representatives, and international organizations. Simply bringing to the table and, where appropriate, mobilizing the capacities of such diverse actors is a challenge in itself.

However, despite these difficulties, some actions have proved effective. For this, the previous disposition and the evolution of the local communities seem to be decisive. For example, monitoring and labor inspections are more successful when local opinion leaders contribute to the creation of preventive standards, when parents are more aware of the risks of their children working on the cocoa plantation, and when local institutions are involved throughout the intervention process (Bayer, 2014). Similarly, both task mapping with the collaboration of children and occupational risk analysis based on community participation have been used effectively to design educational materials and implement awareness campaigns (Mull & Kirkhorn, 2005). In practice, they can serve as an observation guide for labor inspectors. This has highlighted the importance of "local ownership" of preventive interventions (Bayer, 2014).

In this chapter, we will review the role of different actors in the implementation of public policies against child labor. As we have illustrated with the case of cocoa production, the impact of preventive actions depends in part on the involvement and performance of different stakeholders. On the one hand, the dissemination of evidence-based practices requires some kind of connection between academic researchers and intervention practitioners. Community service providers need to receive up-to-date information on which activities and programs produce positive results. On the other hand, in each local context, social cohesion and relationships among different segments of the population determine the degree of community preparedness for the change that the intervention is intended to promote. Throughout the chapter, we will propose concrete recommendations to improve the participation of each specific subgroup.

Box 8.1: Using Implementation to Improve Early Education Outcomes
Early education produces immediate results on both the social and cognitive development of minors. Moreover, when early education is of good quality, it is reflected in academic performance (in the medium term) and in labor insertion during adult life.

(continued)

Box 8.1 (continued)

The first research on early education focused on the results obtained by minors. Instead, the most recent research focuses on the program implementation process. For example, an attempt is made to determine how the context in which the programs are applied affects the results of the interventions. It also looks at how to ensure that evidence-based practices continue to have a positive impact when applied on a large scale. In addition, it seeks to avoid differences in implementation that could lead to inequalities between different groups of children when programs are implemented.

One of the results of this new approach has been the discovery of the importance of community contexts and local conditions of implementation of early education. On the other hand, researchers need to establish collaborative relationships with policymakers and practitioners.

The quality of the interaction of caregivers with minors continues to be the center of the educational process, although it is assumed that it is clearly influenced by the contexts in which it occurs.

Based on: Foundation for Child Development (2020). *Getting it Right: Using Implementation Research to Improve Outcomes in Early Care and Education*. New York, NY.

8.2 Strategies for Transferring Scientific Knowledge

The knowledge available on the factors that precede the involvement of minors in work activities allows the formulation of policies with which to counteract the phenomenon. For example, if we find that the incidence of child labor is higher among large low-income families, we can deduce that those initiatives that seek to control the number of children per household, or that provide financial assistance to the poorest families, could have a preventive effect. Following this logic, we have summarized in Table 8.1 some of the types of interventions that can be derived from previous empirical research on the subject (Grootaert & Kanbur, 1995).

Two of the priorities that have emerged precisely from the preceding academic studies are (a) to reduce the cost of and barriers to schooling and (b) to diversify the alternatives available to families to obtain economic income. When it was realized that, under certain conditions, academic and work activities are in competition with each other, measures were put in place to affect the distribution of children's time between studies and work. When it is assumed that the parents make decisions with which they intend to guarantee the economic sustainability of the household, measures are designed that intend to offer alternative income to the families. Compulsory schooling for children and work opportunities for adults counteract, on paper, child labor.

However, low-income countries often lack the administrative capacities to implement such actions effectively. Moreover, to become "evidence-based practices,"

Table 8.1 Translation of empirical evidence into policy interventions

Intervention type	Empirical foundation
Family planning	Research has shown a positive correlation between the number of children and the likelihood of child labor in the household. Fertility regulation policies would therefore have a preventive value.
Anti-poverty policies	The incidence of child labor is higher in low-income families. Credits, tax policies, and financial insurance can contribute to improving the situation of families and reducing the risk of child labor in the medium term.
Introduction of technological changes	The mechanization of those agricultural or industrial activities in which children work as unskilled laborers would reduce the probability of their incorporation into the world of work.
Guaranteeing compulsory schooling	Work time can compete with the completion of academic activities (either attending school or doing homework). That is why reducing the cost of education for families and providing the population with local educational infrastructures makes it more likely that parents will try to ensure the schooling of their children.
Education of girls	When mothers are educated, their children are less likely to work and it impacts the educational aspirations of the family as a whole. Community development policies could be more sustainable and efficient when they aim to improve the relative situation of women.
Improved employment opportunities	Employment and opportunities in the labor market for adults indirectly affect the situation of minors. To the extent that parents have alternative sources of income, they are less likely to turn to their children to ensure the survival of the household.
Legal regulations	International conventions, national regulation of labor relations and legal recommendations are some of the most widespread instruments. However, inspectors usually encounter difficulties in visiting workplaces and in enforcing sanctions in case of non-compliance with the legislation. Instituting compulsory education introduces another way of regulating protection during childhood.

Source: based on Grootaert and Kanbur (1995)

they have to go through a rigorous process of impact evaluation and demonstrate that they are effective in different intervention settings. It should also be remembered that definitive implementation is conditioned by the decisions of the political bodies competent to invest in such measures (and not in others), together with the decisions of the intervention professionals to prioritize such actions (and not others). Therefore, the translation of empirical evidence into policy interventions is not a unilateral and automatic process, but rather one that involves the mobilization of community capacities, communication among different social agents and the activation of the appropriate institutional levers. This is why it is also necessary to analyze it systematically, in order to gain greater control over the transfer of results.

As we will see below, the dissemination of knowledge and community ownership are two sides of the same coin. The transfer of research results is in part a process of innovation dissemination that leads from science to practice. However, as we have just seen, there are multiple actors involved in order for this process to run in a functional way. Therefore, it is necessary to pay attention also to the organizational capacities and community dynamics that are part of the context of the intervention. This is what we intend to develop in the sections that follow.

8.2.1 The Science-Practice Chains

Elementary school teachers sometimes develop educational performances that are not based on evidence, or whose effectiveness is at least questionable (Dagenais et al., 2012). In the case of child labor, programs with preventive purposes are often proposed and promoted by external entities, such as universities and non-governmental organizations (Márquez et al., 2019). However, there are also cases in which they are prescribed by the school itself or even depend on the initiative of the teachers, who seek information to select educational materials of interest. In this regard, it has been found that educators' interpersonal contacts with academic researchers (and with experts in general) play a prominent role in the adoption of certain psychoeducational programs (Neal et al., 2015). In other cases, information circulates within the same group of professionals, reducing the likelihood of accessing up-to-date information on evidence-based preventive practices (Neal et al., 2019). This has led to renewed interest in studying the type of informal chains that facilitate the dissemination of theoretical innovations in professional practice.

Based on this same social network analysis approach, one of the ways to promote the transfer (and facilitate the adoption of certain intervention models) is the selection and training of opinion leaders in informal professional information exchange networks. Thus, in three public health units in Canada, it was found that both the individuals who participated in specialized training courses and their more direct connections were more likely to adopt evidence-based practices (Nooraie et al., 2017). This same relational approach has also been used to monitor and improve the coordination of health services (Nooraie et al., 2019). This approach often improves the cultural relevance and community fit of interventions, so it may be especially appropriate in child labor prevention initiatives.

We have verified in the implementation of psycho-educational programs against child labor that the relationships between teachers are essential for the proper functioning of the intervention, as well as for obtaining positive results (Márquez et al., 2019). Teachers' relationship networks can condition their motivation to participate in extracurricular activities, the use of certain scientific models in their daily activities, their degree of professional commitment and even the results of their students. In these networks, there are usually some teachers who are key actors, since they connect colleagues with each other, encourage them to participate or disseminate some good intervention practices of which they have been aware. Identifying such teachers can facilitate educational innovation as well as the implementation of evidence-based practices. Participatory management of these resources can be a method of improving the quality of the education system in developing countries (Masino & Niño-Zarazúa, 2016).

8.3   Strategies for Community Preparation

The concept of community preparedness refers to the degree to which a community is prepared to take action on a given problem (Edwards et al., 2000), for example, child labor. This requires certain levels of awareness of the problem, along with a minimum of community participation and effective local leadership. For example, a study in the primary care system in Andalusia found that in those health districts where there was no adequate level of community organization, where citizen participation was low, and where primary care teams did not operate in an integrated manner, social workers were forced to forego the prevention and community promotion programs prescribed by the public health system in order to focus exclusively on individual care benefits (Maya Jariego et al., 2010).

Accordingly, each community context may vary in the degree to which it is prepared for preventive intervention, ranging from a total lack of awareness of the problem in question to local settings with connected community-based organizations, active local leaders, and a favorable social climate for serving at-risk groups. This sometimes makes it necessary to carry out preparatory actions before implementing a preventive program. The most common is to carry out sensitization activities to increase awareness of the problem, together with community organization activities to stimulate citizen participation and local leadership. Adaptations to the program can also be made according to the local community's disposition.

In the case of child labor, some of the most common preparatory actions are awareness-raising campaigns with the general population, the organization of local coalitions, information visits to employers' federations, and training sessions with parents and teachers, among others. When there is a favorable culture in the population towards the early labor involvement of children, preventive actions can face strong resistance from the community against the goals of the intervention (Maya-Jariego, 2017).

Box 8.2: Comprehensive Community-Based Action in Brazil
In the area of policies against child labor, Brazil is recognized as one of the pioneering countries in the implementation of national conditional income transfer programs, as well as for having achieved one of the greatest reductions in the prevalence of child labor in developing countries since records began.

As in other cases, Brazil has combined legal reforms with the application of economic incentives. However, in the phases with the greatest preventive

(continued)

Box 8.2 (continued)

impact, the active role of the government in promoting comprehensive policies (Rosati et al., 2011) stands out, along with a certain community approach.

For example, the family health program established a decentralized system to provide health services at the community level, with teams of health professionals who traveled to local settings, including the most disadvantaged areas. The program had positive results in reducing mortality, reducing adult unemployment, reducing fertility, and increasing school attendance (Rocha & Soares, 2010).

Government action has been complemented by a community-based strategy, in which local coalitions were formed to mobilize volunteer resources and community-based organizations in large urban areas. This approach has been particularly beneficial in protective actions with street children (Myers, 1988). Thus, systemic action with public resources was reinforced by bottom-up initiatives with community participation.

[Brazil]

8.4   The Role of Different Stakeholders in the Implementation of Policies and Programs

Models designed to reduce the gap between preventive research and practice have highlighted the importance of communication between different stakeholders, such as intervention professionals, academic researchers, trainers, funders, and public administration managers, among others (Wandersman et al., 2008). Information exchange, dissemination of innovations, and multi-sector collaboration can contribute to the continuity of services and to prioritizing evidence-based actions. In Table 8.2 we have summarized some of the actions that the different stakeholders can carry out to promote preventive actions based on available scientific evidence.

8.4.1   Researchers

Researchers can help determine which programs are most effective in each area of intervention. The empirical demonstration is an unavoidable step in the development of evidence-based practices, even though it is not always taken into account in the justification of the policies that are intended to be promoted. For example, it is widely believed that improving the quality of the education system leads to a reduction in child labor, even though not enough evidence has been accumulated in this regard (Dammert et al., 2018; Paruzzolo, 2009).

From an eminently theoretical point of view, psychosocial research could advance with the elaboration of an inductive typology of the diverse modalities of

Table 8.2 Strategies to bridge the gap between science and practice in child labor prevention

Roles	Actions
Researcher	• It is a priority to document the sequence of psychological changes that link the results of academic motivation, educational performance, school dropout and child labor • It is also necessary to demonstrate that improving the quality of education has an effective impact on reducing child labor
Program evaluators	• Rigorous and systematic evaluations of the impact of interventions are needed • To this end, it is recommended that outcome indicators be collected to document everything from immediate educational changes to the impact on child labor in the medium term • It is also important to examine the differential effect of each component of the intervention
Intervention professionals	• Explicitly define the intervention's logic model • During program selection or design, ensure the evaluability of programs
National or regional intervention agencies	• Results-based management is a mechanism with a great capacity to influence the content and format of interventions • Alliances between social organizations generate their own environment for the effective implementation of evidence-based programs
Program managers, facilitators, and monitors	• Establishing networks of facilitators who exchange experiences accelerates the dissemination of innovations • The management staff has a relevant role in the deployment of organizational capacities and in the creation of a positive work climate
Unions and employers	• The agreement generates a suitable climate for the proper functioning of preventive actions

child labor, together with the exploration of the sequence of cognitive, motivational and behavioral processes that lead, first, to school abandonment and then to early incorporation into the labor market. From a practical point of view, researchers can facilitate the transfer when they incorporate intervention professionals into their work teams or when they carry out activities to translate theoretical knowledge into recommendations for intervention (Maya Jariego, 2010).

8.4.2 Program Evaluators

The impact assessment is intended to check whether the intervention has had the intended effects on individuals, families, and the community. To do this, methodological designs are used that allow the changes observed among the participants to be directly attributed to the program. This is why they are particularly useful both to account for the results and to introduce improvements in the interventions.

Systematic impact evaluations have been relatively rare in child labor projects (Paruzzolo, 2009).[2] Among the most common reasons are evaluability limitations arising from the design of the intervention itself. When objectives are vaguely defined, actions are diffuse in nature, or the program covers a wide range of potential outcomes and multiple fields of action, it is especially difficult to use a design against which to contrast the effects of the intervention. In preventive programs, it is advisable to trace the sequence that links school dropout with early incorporation into the labor market. Thus, the combination of direct and indirect result indicators provides a better understanding of the program's operation.

On the other hand, evaluations have focused preferably on short-term results (Boateng, 2017). However, longitudinal designs would allow an assessment of the extent to which the psychological damage or negative health impact experienced by working children is sustained over time and persists into adulthood (Dammert et al., 2018). Only in a few unique cases have the long-term effects on the entry of young adults into the labor market been documented. This type of evidence is especially useful from a theoretical point of view, since it helps to clarify the very concept of child labor. It is also important for evaluators to ensure that they have parental consent and adequately protect the identity of the minor (Paruzzolo, 2009).

Evaluators have an important role in connecting theory and practice, as they often mediate between intervention professionals and the scientific literature (Maya Jariego, 2010). Evaluators can recommend evidence-based theoretical and practical models to program facilitators. They can also train them to select and design appropriate logic models. In addition, they can collaborate with intervention practitioners to systematize program implementation experience, document lessons learned, and publish results in scientific journals.

8.4.3 Intervention Professionals

Among intervention professionals it is not as usual as in the academic field to publish the results of the intervention. However, documenting the successes and failures of program implementation is useful for documenting "lessons learned" and informing researchers about what works and what does not in practice (Maya Jariego, 2010). This establishes a mechanism for learning and continuous improvement, which contributes inductively to the formulation of appropriate interventions. In the case of child labor, it has been pointed out that it is advisable for the interveners to be explicit in the definition of the program's logical framework and to be concerned with formulating it in a way that is evaluable, with precise operationalization

---

[2]Perhaps one of the exceptions is assessments of conditional cash transfers. Among other possible results, the short- and long-term impact has been examined in schooling, medical care, labor insertion during adulthood, the reduction of child labor and the reduction of health problems in adolescence (Baez & Camacho, 2011). However, econometric analyzes have also predominated over the evaluation of the psychosocial impact on the ground.

(Boateng, 2017). The internal consistency of the project facilitates its connection with the theoretical contents of preventive value.

In practice, intervention professionals act as intermediaries between the different stakeholders, thus playing a central role in improving program implementation and articulating theory and practice. This requires not only the skills needed to communicate with the different stakeholders, but also the time needed to establish trusting relationships (Dobbins et al., 2009). Among other groups of interest, it is important that they are connected to professionals in social and health services, as well as child protection programs.

8.4.4   National or Regional Intervention Agencies

The agencies that finance and manage the intervention have enormous power to modulate the nature of the programs implemented in their geographical environment of reference. Not only do they decide which actions they finance and which they do not, but they can establish organizational, methodological, or substantive requirements about the type of interventions they intend to promote. Results-based management establishes a system of incentives for the continuity of programs that can affect everything from the duration of the project to the type of intervention strategies considered eligible. In some cases, public administration agencies play a role in standardizing program application criteria, defining priorities, establishing practical recommendations, and systematizing experiences by areas of action and population segments (Maya Jariego, 2010).

In the case of child labor, the clearest reference is the International Labor Organization (ILO), which promotes the involvement of local governments, contributes to building partnerships, and plays a key role in defining intervention models and strategies (Boateng, 2017). This has marked a style of intervention with some emphasis on legal regulations and tripartite cooperation.

Otherwise—be it in the educational, social, or public health field—individual projects have predominated, focusing on one type of child labor activity in a given geographical area. This is reflected in the profusion of sectoral actions, focused on a type of specific result indicators (such as school attendance or medical follow-up, considered separately[3]). A unique case is the systemic approach developed by UNICEF. The United Nations Children's Fund has sought to replace small-scale, issue-focused projects with comprehensive prevention strategies that address the needs of children, families, and the community as a whole (Boateng, 2017; UNICEF, 2014). Thus, the emphasis is placed on the coordination of social, labor and educational policies aimed at children.

---

[3]Part of the success of conditional cash transfer programs has been attributed precisely to the combination of income redistribution policies with more or less comprehensive monitoring of the child's situation

Box 8.3: Public Policy Recommendations in Latin America

The International Labor Organization (ILO) and the Latin America and Caribbean Regional Child Labor Free Initiative (LACTI network) have published a document aimed at decision makers and technical professionals to prevent child labor and "redouble progress towards the achievement of target 8.7 of Agenda 2030 of the Sustainable Development Goals, which calls for ending child labor in all its forms by 2025". (ILO & LACTI Network, 2020, p. 3).

Assuming that immigrant children are a high-risk group, the document suggests ten specific prevention strategies:

1. Designing evidence-based interventions on the link between migration and child labor and systematizing available knowledge.
2. Establishing a single registration system on child labor cases to facilitate collaboration between different countries and institutions in the region.
3. Develop awareness-raising actions aimed at the population in general and at officials of care and inspection services in particular.
4. Take advantage of information technologies to facilitate the identification and reporting of cases, as well as to ensure the continuity of services.
5. Establish defined systems of work in the judicial system, both at the national level and in international collaboration.
6. Put intervention with migrant children in the context of family vulnerability, livelihood needs, and reunification processes.
7. Manage programs with reference to the local communities receiving the immigrant population.
8. Engage all actors involved in the production process of the primary sector, insofar as some of the immigrant children are seasonal agricultural workers.
9. Promote education and training for employment as resources that, at different ages, can contribute to the adaptation process of migrant minors.
10. Promote services that are sensitive to the cultural diversity of indigenous communities.

As we can see, one of the conditions that increases the risk among immigrant minors is geographical mobility itself, to the extent that it makes it difficult to follow up cases and provide continuity of services. Community strategies can improve the sustainability of actions and can therefore be a method of preserving services despite the geographical displacement of recipients.

The recommendations also highlight the multitude of actors that may be involved in child labor cases. Consequently, when geographical displacement occurs, coordinated action becomes an added challenge. Ultimately, public policy depends on the involvement of a wide range of actors.

(continued)

Box 8.3 (continued)
Based on: OIT & Red LACTI (2020). *El vínculo entre migración y trabajo infantil.* [The link between migration and child labor]. https://www. iniciativa2025alc.org/es.

8.4.5   Program Managers, Facilitators, and Monitors

As a general rule, the implementation of a program is not reduced to the interaction between the intervention professionals and the participants, but potentially involves a great diversity of actors. If we think, for example, of the interventions in an educational context, families, heads of studies, volunteers, school management, teachers, educational inspectors, etc. may emerge as interest groups. Each one of them can play a relevant role in how the intervention is carried out. Some facilitate the adaptation of the program to the local reality.

In the implementation of preventive programs, it has been proven that coordination among program facilitators accelerates the dissemination of "good practices" of intervention and improves the adaptation of psychoeducational activities to each local context (Holgado et al., 2014). Also in primary schools, principals and heads of studies exercise a leadership role in selecting the type of educational programs and materials to be implemented in each school, while at the same time influencing the establishment of a constructive social climate among teachers (Maya-Jariego et al., 2015).

Many of these resources are usually channeled through strategic alliances for the defense of children's rights, which also have a self-training component in the technical aspects of child labor prevention (Boateng, 2017). These alliances facilitate the coordination of services for children and usually have an awareness and activism component to defend the most vulnerable groups. In addition to improving regional coordination, the link between non-governmental organizations increases their bargaining power. This has been particularly reflected in campaigns to put pressure on producers and manufacturers who use child labor.

8.4.6   Unions and Employers

A characteristic element of child labor policies is the prominent role of unions and employers. The ILO usually channels its policies through local governments and the tripartite social dialogue tables that they promote in each country. Unions assess the working conditions of children and, in addition to direct action, can incorporate children's interests into collective bargaining processes. Employers can play an active role by introducing codes of conduct and other self-regulatory mechanisms. Chambers of Commerce and business federations provide technical training and can develop awareness-raising activities in the sector (Haspels & Jankanish, 2000). In general, the climate of consensus-building creates an environment conducive to preventive action.

8.5 Prevention, Protection, and Comprehensive Interventions

Prevention and protection strategies usually base the program logic model on available knowledge about the causes and consequences of child labor. Previous research has identified some of the most relevant risk factors (to influence) and some of the most significant protective factors (to counteract). Based on the available evidence, actions have been designed with which to increase the income of families in a situation of poverty or to reduce the barriers to access to education among the most vulnerable families.

However, the previous sections have also revealed aspects susceptible to development in research that could contribute to introducing improvements in preventive actions. In the first place, the systematic analysis of the modalities of child labor would make it possible to be more precise in the formulation of the preventive projects and in the selection of the indicators of results. In other words, the diffuse nature of the program activities or the imprecise nature of the evaluation criteria reveal the need to qualify the concept of child labor and the diversity of forms it takes. Secondly, early incorporation into the world of work is a progressive process in which each phase (or each level of work involvement) may require specific actions. The differentiation between prevention, protection, and direct-action strategies (Rosati & Lyon, 2006) refers precisely to measures with which to counteract, respectively, the risk, damage or aggravation of child labor situations. With a longitudinal perspective, it is also possible to explore the traceability between the living conditions of children in the short and long term. In that sense, it has been proven that investment in education during early childhood not only significantly reduces the risk of child labor, but also increases the probability of attending school at later ages (Paruzzolo, 2009).

In terms of intervention, we have also identified two elements that can contribute to improving effectiveness. These are the adoption of a systemic or comprehensive approach to prevention, along with the development of preparatory actions to improve the community's readiness for the proposed behavioral changes. First, in line with the United Nations Children's Fund child protection strategy (UNICEF, 2014) and in order to mobilize preventive resources in a comprehensive and coordinated manner, it would be beneficial to adopt an overall view of the living conditions and needs of the child population in a given geographical area. Secondly, the experience of intervention in the last decades has shown that, in order to be effective, prevention and protection measures require (preferably) an adequate legal regulatory framework, institutions with sufficient organizational capacities, a climate of agreement in labor relations, efficient coordination agencies at the local level and an active community, aware of the problem and receptive to the introduction of changes in its ways of proceeding (Paruzzolo, 2009). Thus, the adoption of a community and participatory approach could bring innovations with an added value, in an area of prevention that has been obtaining positive results in recent decades.

Prevention strategies have been largely inspired by models of family economic decision-making to ensure the sustainability of households (Rosati & Lyon, 2006). To do so, a balance is made between (a) how parents value the immediate economic return of children's work and (b) the long-term results expected from the investment (in time and resources) in their children's education. Among the most common preventive actions, the intention is to promote the obtaining of alternative income or to reduce the cost associated with education. Hence, increasing the availability of credit for families, reducing the financial risk or improving accessibility to educational infrastructure are all of preventive value.

From the review of the transfer processes we have verified the existence of a set of factors of community character on which it is also possible to operate with preventive purposes. In addition to the preparation for change, we have verified the influence of local networks for the dissemination of information, levels of citizen participation, coordination of services, leadership in organizational contexts, the formation of community alliances, or the creation of cohesive environments, among many other valuable elements. On this type of evidence, a community-based approach to intervention can be based that complements the prevention strategies already consolidated.

While programs based on economic incentives have already proven effective on their own, their impact can be enhanced by community actions that promote parent involvement or community participation. Both the collaboration of local associations and the advocacy of international nongovernmental organizations can have an empowering effect and improve families' socioeconomic choices (Myers, 1991). In the case of schools, it is effective to communicate with parents, invite them to participate, transfer decision-making power to them, and reorganize the structure of schools to facilitate mutual understanding (Menheere & Hooge, 2010). When such conditions exist, teachers are more likely to provide a positive model of how to interact with children and to guide parents on how to help them with homework or facilitate learning.

Box 8.4: Employer Collaboration in Prevention in India

In India, there is a legal framework that prohibits the performance of hazardous work by children under 14 years of age, since the second half of the 1980s. Employment and non-formal education programs have also been developed with adults to provide alternatives in areas with a higher incidence of child labor.

(continued)

Box 8.4 (continued)

However, the case of India in the public imagination is often associated with international pressure on certain industrial sectors where there have been cases of child exploitation, such as carpet manufacturing and sportswear distributed in the global market.

In some industrial clusters, such as handicraft manufacturing, the replacement of household subcontracting by in-house production has been effective. With the collaboration of employers, it has been possible to reduce the hiring of minors. Complementarily, these types of changes are facilitated when adults enjoy better wages or when schools offer midday meals to children attending school. Pressure from the government to ensure compliance with the law is also important. In any case, prevention is always more difficult when it comes to countering the dynamics of the informal economy.

Based on: International Program on the Elimination of Child Labor (IPEC) (2013). *Business and the fight against child labor: experience from India, Brazil, and South Africa.* Geneva: International Labor Organization.

[India]

8.6 Conclusion

Although there is empirical evidence that child labor policies have been accompanied by positive results, both the evaluation of impact and the systematic study of interventions have been relatively rare (Paruzzolo, 2009). Consequently, even with effective actions, child labor prevention and child labor protection measures are still susceptible to improvement. Among other aspects, we have found that progress could be made towards the formulation of comprehensive policies, sensitive to the different phases and intensities of the incorporation of children into the labor market, complemented by a community intervention approach:

- In those cases where impact evaluation has been conducted, the impact on educational outcomes has been more widely documented than the reduction of child labor. There is a need for experimental and quasi-experimental evaluations of those interventions that have child labor as a direct objective. The indirect impact of educational actions on child labor can also be evaluated.
- Early education, channeled through day-care centers, seems to have a potential of special interest because of its long-term effects on educational and labor indicators of young adults. Longitudinal action-research designs can improve our knowledge in this regard.
- In turn, evidence-based practices seem to be reinforced when accompanied by community-based initiatives, which improve the implementation process. The creation of local multi-stakeholder committees is an especially appropriate tool for this purpose.

The educational level of mothers, the diversification of incentives to promote school attendance and the transition from studies to work are some of the aspects that could contribute to the emergence of innovations in the educational field. With respect to financing and credit to families, the community dimension, and the prominent role of women in local development initiatives could also be deepened.

Policies against child labor have been articulated around tripartite social dialogue, with the participation of national governments, employers and trade unions. In this chapter we have shown how participation in preventive actions can also be extended to other community actors that contribute to improving preparedness for change, the relevance of actions and, ultimately, the effectiveness of interventions.

References

Baez, J. E., & Camacho, A. (2011). *Assessing the long-term effects of conditional cash transfers on human capital: Evidence from Colombia*. Washington, D.C.: The World Bank.

Bayer, C. N. (2014). *The effects of child labor monitoring on knowledge, attitude, and practices in cocoa growing communities of Ghana* (Doctoral dissertation, Tulane University, Payson Center for International Development).

Boateng, P. (2017). *Interventions on child labour in South Asia. K4D Helpdesk Report*. Brighton, UK: Institute of Development Studies.

Dagenais, C., Lysenko, L., Abrami, P. C., Bernard, R. M., Ramde, J., & Janosz, M. (2012). Use of research-based information by school practitioners and determinants of use: A review of empirical research. *Evidence & Policy: A Journal of Research, Debate and Practice, 8*(3), 285–309.

Dammert, A. C., De Hoop, J., Mvukiyehe, E., & Rosati, F. C. (2018). Effects of public policy on child labor: Current knowledge, gaps, and implications for program design. *World Development, 110*, 104–123.

Dobbins, M., Robeson, P., Ciliska, D., Hanna, S., Cameron, R., O'Mara, L., ... Mercer, S. (2009). A description of a knowledge broker role implemented as part of a randomized controlled trial evaluating three knowledge translation strategies. *Implementation Science, 4*(1), 1–9.

Edwards, R. W., Jumper-Thurman, P., Plested, B. A., Oetting, E. R., & Swanson, L. (2000). Community readiness: Research to practice. *Journal of Community Psychology, 28*(3), 291–307.

Foundation for Child Development. (2020). *Getting it Right: Using Implementation Research to Improve Outcomes in Early Care and Education*. New York, NY.

Grootaert, C., & Kanbur, R. (1995). *Child labor: A review. World Bank Policy Research Working Paper, 1454*. Washington: DC.

Haspels, N., & Jankanish, M. (2000). *Action against child labour*. Geneva: International Labour Organization.

Holgado, D., Maya-Jariego, I., Ramos, I., & Palacio, J. (2014). El papel de los facilitadores en la implementación de los "Espacios para Crecer": Evaluación formativa del programa con menores trabajadores "Edúcame Primero, Colombia". *Universitas Psychologica, 13*(4), 1441–1460.

International Programme on the Elimination of Child Labor (IPEC). (2013). *Business and the fight against child labor: Experience from India, Brazil and South Africa*. Geneva: International Labour Organization.

Márquez, E., Holgado, D., & Maya-Jariego, I. (2019). Innovation, dosage and responsiveness in the implementation of the program "Edúcame Primero Perú" for reducing child labor. *Applied Research in Quality of Life, 14*(3), 617–636. https://doi.org/10.1007/s11482-018-9608-1.

Masino, S., & Niño-Zarazúa, M. (2016). What works to improve the quality of student learning in developing countries? *International Journal of Educational Development, 48*, 53–65.

Maya Jariego, I. (2010). De la ciencia a la práctica en la intervención comunitaria: La transferencia del conocimiento científico a la actuación profesional. *Apuntes de Psicología, 28*, 121–141.

Maya Jariego, I., Holgado, D., Santolaya, F., Gavilán, J., & Ramos, I. (2010). *Comunidades preparadas para la salud. Preparación comunitaria y práctica profesional de los trabajadores sociales de Atención Primaria en Andalucía.* Madrid: Bubok.

Maya-Jariego, I. (2017). "But we want to work": The movement of child workers in Peru and the actions for reducing child labor. *American Journal of Community Psychology, 60*(3–4), 430–438.

Maya-Jariego, I., Aceituno, I., Santolaya, F. J., & Holgado, D. (2015). Diagnóstico de la preparación comunitaria para la reducción del trabajo infantil en dos comunidades de Lima (Perú). In J. En Fialho, C. Silva, & J. Saragoça (Eds.), *Diagnóstico Social. Teoria, metodologia e casos práticos* (pp. 199–214). Lisboa: Edições Silabo.

Menheere, A., & Hooge, E. H. (2010). Parental involvement in children's education: A review study about the effect of parental involvement on children's school education with a focus on the position of illiterate parents. *Journal of European Teacher Education Network, 6*, 144–157.

Mull, L. D., & Kirkhorn, S. R. (2005). Child labor in Ghana cocoa production: Focus upon agricultural tasks, ergonomic exposures, and associated injuries and illnesses. *Public Health Reports, 120*(6), 649–655.

Myers, W. (1988). Alternative services for street children: The Brazilian approach. In A. Bequele & J. Boyden (Eds.), *Combating child labour* (pp. 125–143). Geneva: International Labour Organization.

Myers, W. E. (Ed.). (1991). *Protecting working children.* London: Zed Books.

Neal, J. W., Neal, Z. P., Kornbluh, M., Mills, K. J., & Lawlor, J. A. (2015). Brokering the research–practice gap: A typology. *American Journal of Community Psychology, 56*(3–4), 422–435.

Neal, J. W., Neal, Z. P., Mills, K. J., Lawlor, J. A., & McAlindon, K. (2019). What types of brokerage bridge the research-practice gap? The case of public school educators. *Social Networks, 59*, 41–49.

Nkamleu, G. B., & Kielland, A. (2006). Modeling farmers' decisions on child labor and schooling in the cocoa sector: A multinomial logit analysis in Côte d'Ivoire. *Agricultural Economics, 35* (3), 319–333.

Nooraie, R. Y., Marin, A., Hanneman, R., Lohfeld, L., & Dobbins, M. (2017). Implementation of evidence-informed practice through central network actors; a case study of three public health units in Canada. *BMC Health Services Research, 17*(1), 208.

Nooraie, R. Y., Khan, S., Gutberg, J., & Baker, G. R. (2019). A network analysis perspective to implementation: The example of health links to promote coordinated care. *Evaluation & the Health Professions, 42*(4), 395–421.

Organización Internacional del Trabajo & Red Lacti. (2020). *El vínculo entre migración y trabajo infantil.* [The link between migration and child labor]. Retrieved from https://www.iniciativa2025alc.org/es.

Paruzzolo, S. (2009). The Impact of Programs Relating to Child Labor Prevention and Children's Protection: A Review of Impact Evaluations Up to 2007. *Understanding Children's Work Working Paper Series.* ILO, World Bank & UNICEF.

Rocha, R., & Soares, R. R. (2010). Evaluating the impact of community-based health interventions: Evidence from Brazil's Family Health Program. *Health Economics, 19*(S1), 126–158.

Rosati, F. C., & Lyon, S. (2006). Tackling child labour: Policy options for achieving sustainable reductions in children at work. *Understanding Children's Work Project*, Universidad de Roma.

Rosati, F. C., Manacorda, M., Kovrova, I., Koseleci, N., & Lyon, S. (2011). Understanding the Brazilian success in reducing child labour: Empirical evidence and policy lessons. *Understanding Children's Work report*, ILO. Universidad de Roma.

UNICEF. (2014). *Child labour and UNICEF in action: Children at the centre.* New York: UNICEF.

Wandersman, A., Duffy, J., Flaspohler, P., Noonan, R., Lubell, K., Stillman, L., . . . Saul, J. (2008).
Bridging the gap between prevention research and practice: The interactive systems framework
for dissemination and implementation. *American Journal of Community Psychology, 41*(3-4),
171–181.

Chapter 9
A Practical Guide to Improving the Results of Preventive Actions Against Child Labor

Abstract Scientific knowledge about the causes, consequences, and effective actions against child labor is necessary but not sufficient for the prevention of the problem. The implementation of programs depends on the capacities of the facilitators, on the quality and intensity of the activities developed and on the reaction of the community contexts on which they act. In this chapter, we examine how to improve implementation through science-practice transfer, organizational support and service delivery. After presenting an integrated model for bridging the gap between science and practice, we compile a series of concrete recommendations with which to improve both the implementation of behavioral-based preventive interventions and legal regulations to prevent the worst forms of child labor.

Keywords Child Labor · Policy · Programs · Effectiveness · Transference · Organizational capacities · Community adjustment · Evidence-based practices

9.1 Introduction

In previous chapters, we have shown the existence of evidence-based practices that can be effective in preventing child labor. However, as with other social problems, such practices need to be implemented with sufficient quality and intensity to generate the desired results (Chinman et al., 2008).

Although we have programs that we know work, because they have been proven experimentally, in practice we may encounter difficulties when we implement them in specific communities. To achieve effective functioning, it is necessary to (a) translate scientific knowledge so that it is applicable in a specific context, (b) develop service delivery with the fidelity and dose required to obtain results, and (c) deploy the organizational capacities that make the two previous elements possible.

In this chapter, we provide some practical guidelines for the proper functioning of child labor prevention programs. To this end, we will differentiate between two basic types of actions, as summarized in Table 9.1. On the one hand, behavioral-based strategies that seek to modify the community contexts in which child labor arises. In

© The Author(s), under exclusive license to Springer Nature Switzerland AG 2021
I. Maya Jariego, *Community Prevention of Child Labor*, Human Well-Being
Research and Policy Making, https://doi.org/10.1007/978-3-030-70810-8_9

Table 9.1 Two types of intervention strategies against child labor

Behavioral approach and context modification	Rights and law enforcement approach
• Provide economic incentives to low-income families	• Prohibition of hazardous work, forced labor, and child exploitation
• Psychoeducational actions to improve academic performance and prevent school dropouts	• Establishment of the minimum age for employment
• Measures to protect working children	• Legal regulations and defense of the rights of minors
• Primary prevention strategies	• Rehabilitation and reinsertion strategies

Source: Own elaboration

this area, evidence-based practices have a preferential impact on poverty conditions and educational experience. Primary prevention strategies have contributed to reducing the prevalence of the problem. On the other hand, international organizations (in particular the ILO) have focused a large part of their efforts on the approval of legal regulations to prevent the participation of children in the labor market. These actions are carried out with the commitment of employers, unions, and local governments, which since 1999 have focused preferably on the worst forms of child labor.

These two types of actions can be related. For example, the formation of political consensus and the approval of legal instruments translate into social norms that exercise coercive power over behavior. Behaviorally based preventive strategies may have better results when the socio-political context is more sensitized and involved in the protection of children's rights. In other words, the emphasis on the adoption and enforcement of regulations on minimum age for access to employment impacts on preparedness for change, so it could improve the outcomes of primary prevention psychosocial strategies.

9.2   A Framework for Program Design and Implementation

To facilitate an adequate match between program design and implementation, it is necessary to take into account and mobilize the capacities of a wide range of actors, from academic researchers to program facilitators, including managers, funders, and intervention evaluators, among many others.

In Fig. 9.1 we have highlighted the three fundamental components that contribute to bridging the gap between science and practice of preventive actions (Wandersman et al., 2008). These are successively the actions to disseminate innovations with preventive value, to provide the organizational support necessary for program

Translation and transfer system	→	Prevention support system	→	Service delivery

Fig. 9.1 Three systems to communicate science and practice. Source: Wandersman et al. (2008)

implementation, and to apply preventive innovations in the field. We will now review these three systems, starting with service delivery: We focus first on the implementation of programs themselves, and then we review the two instrumental systems that seek to improve their operation.

9.2.1   Service Delivery

Implementation depends on the program operator, as well as the organizational and community context in which it takes place. At the individual level, the levels of training, experience and motivation of the facilitators are directly related to the quality of implementation. At the organizational level, the type of leadership and size of the organization can be very important. Finally, at the community level, readiness for change, levels of community participation, and a sense of collective self-efficacy are important (Wandersman et al., 2008).

We can illustrate this with the specific case of child labor. In the implementation of a psychoeducational program in three schools in Lima, Peru, we found that the intervention evolved differently in each school (Holgado et al., 2015). Both the leadership of the directors and the heads of studies, as well as the size of each school, made it necessary to adapt the intervention strategies to the peculiarities of each context. On the other hand, the organizational characteristics of the schools interacted with the degree of community organization of the neighborhoods in which each one of them was located (Maya-Jariego et al., 2015). Specifically, both the workload of the teachers collaborating with the program and the degree of involvement of the parents' associations were two decisive factors in the operation of the intervention.

9.2.2   Prevention Support System

Preventive actions do not only depend on having information about which activities are appropriate and which are not. Putting them into practice also depends largely on the organizational capacities that are made available to the program. Among other factors, the organizational climate, infrastructure, and material resources are relevant. Human resources, competencies, and motivation of the staff are also decisive. All this can be improved through organizational development strategies, specialized training, and management of incentives (Wandersman et al., 2008).

In the case of child labor, training, technical assistance, and advice on how to implement a program have been shown to improve the quality and sustainability of the intervention (Maya-Jariego & Palacio, 2014). This may be especially relevant when the program's implementers are elementary school teachers, who need sustained technical support from those who have designed or are driving the program (Márquez et al., 2019). Similar effects are also achieved when the interaction between facilitators is promoted through continuous program monitoring procedures (Holgado et al., 2014). These types of strategies help maintain motivation and raise standards about what is considered appropriate implementation.

9.2.3   Translation and Transfer System

Preventive interventions are usually based on prior knowledge of the causes, consequences, and effective actions against child labor. However, it is sometimes necessary to have a good "translation" of such knowledge so that it can be easily used. This means summarizing research on the topic, selecting the best intervention practices, and identifying the central components of those programs that have had positive results (Wandersman et al., 2008).

With respect to child labor prevention, there are systematic reviews and compendia of good practices that provide a synthesis that can guide intervention. Specifically, tools include a typology of interventions (Rosati & Lyon, 2006), a systematic review of impact evaluations (Dammert et al., 2018), several collections of experiences of effective intervention in different regional contexts (e.g., Bequele & Boyden, 1988; Grootaert & Kanbur, 1995), and an inductive analysis of the central elements in prevention programs (Maya Jariego, 2014).

On the other hand, implementation is facilitated when quality educational materials exist or when outreach activities (or training actions in general) are carried out that simply transmit available knowledge and facilitate the appropriation of "know-how" by program facilitators and other stakeholders. In this area, the International Labor Organization (ILO) and more specifically the International Program on the Elimination of Child Labor (IPEC) provide practical materials on the implementation and evaluation of preventive actions. Both the statistical reports and the information sheets contribute to a better understanding of the phenomenon, promote awareness of some of the key factors in its prevention, and provide practical recommendations for intervention.[1] Another recognized resource center is the Regional Initiative "Latin America and the Caribbean Free of Child Labor" (Red LACTI), which has a toolbox and a map of good practices in the region.[2] Both the ILO and the LACTI network function as clearinghouses for information and play the role of generic child labor clearinghouses that systematize available knowledge. This translation work has facilitated the transfer of preventive actions.

---

[1]Most of these materials are available on the ILO website https://www.ilo.org/global/topics/child-labour/lang%2D%2Den/index.htm and in the IPEC section https://www.ilo.org/global/about-the-ilo/how-the-ilo-works/flagships/ipec-plus/lang%2D%2Den/index.htm (access: 12 June 2020).

[2]The contents of the LACTI network are available at https://www.iniciativa2025alc.org/es.

> **Box 9.1:   Child Soldiers in Uganda**
> "Where the fighting has been going on for decades (as in Angola or Sudan), most of the adults have died long ago, from hunger or epidemics; the children remain, and it is they who continue the wars. In the bloody chaos that is devastating to different countries in Africa, tens of thousands of orphans, starving and homeless people have appeared. They are looking for someone to feed and shelter them. Where there is an army, it is easier to find food, because the soldiers have the best chance of getting it: in these countries, weapons are not only used in combat, but also as a means of survival, sometimes the only one that exists.
>
> Lone and abandoned children go where troops are stationed, where there are barracks, camps or detachments. By dint of helping and working, they end up becoming part of the army: they are 'children of the regiment'.
>
> Fragment of Ryszard Kapuściński (2000). *Ébano*. Barcelona: Editorial Anagrama. The original was published in 1998. The quotation corresponds to the Spanish version. Own translation.
>
> [Uganda]

9.3   Ten Steps in the Implementation of Programs

In this section, we draw on the Getting to Outcomes® (GTO) model, which provides a logical framework to facilitate program implementation and accountability (Wandersman et al., 2000). With a list of ten questions, this model allows you to review the main components of any intervention, provides a user-friendly follow-up guide, and, as its name suggests, is results-oriented. Among many other social issues, it has been successfully applied in the design of child welfare services (Barbee et al., 2011; Pipkin et al., 2013).

The use of this logical framework facilitates the selection of evidence-based practices and improves the implementation of programs so that results are closer to the expected (Chinman et al., 2016; Mattox et al., 2013). Throughout the process, model users need to focus on needs assessment, program design, organizational framework, implementation of activities, and adaptation to the community context. Also, in the strategies for evaluation, improvement, and sustainability of the intervention.

Next, we are going to review the ten components of the model applying them in each case, successively, to the preventive strategies of behavioral basis and to the legal regulations against the worst forms of child labor. In Table 9.2 we make a schematic comparison of both types of interventions. Then, in Box 9.2, we illustrate them with two specific programs.

Table 9.2 Strategic components of prevention and legal actions

	Behavior-based prevention	Legal regulations against the worst forms of child labour
Needs	• Prevalence of child labor • Type of work activities • Working conditions • Characteristics of the families • Attitudes towards child labor	• Cases of rights violations • Conditions of exploitation/abuse • Characteristics of the sector • Assessment of unions and employers
Goals	• Reduce the prevalence of the problem • Preventing school dropouts • Promote playtime and alternative behaviors • Improve motivation and academic performance	• Abolish unauthorized activities • Promote the involvement of employers and unions • Prevent work under a certain age • Forming agreements between social agents
Evidence-based practices	• Positive parental styles • Development of social-emotional competencies • Risk reduction in low income families • Discontinuing school dropouts	• Consensus policies and social dialogue • Community coalitions • Strengthening of social norms • Knowledge of evolutionary development
Community Adjustment	• Adaptation to the local culture • Attitudes of parents • Community preparedness	• Distribution of power • Balance in decision making • Involvement of local institutions
Organizational capabilities	• Characteristics of the educational centers	• Participation in international organizations
Actions	• Psychoeducational actions • Income distribution.	• Awareness and attitudinal change • Negotiation, agreement and legislation
Development and evaluation	• Impact evaluation • Systematization	• Inspection, monitoring • Complaints and defense of rights
Results	• Reduction of prevalence • Improvement of working conditions • Reduction of the intensity or qualitative changes	• The signing of international agreements • Changes in regulations • Local level agreements
Improvement	• Conditioned to child labor • Community focus	• Incorporate local variations • Reformist approach
Continuity	• Community reactions • Economic crisis	• Political polarization • Local needs

Source: own elaboration

9.3.1 Identification of Needs

The first step consists of assessing needs and identifying available resources in the community. In order to describe the problems faced by the population and establish priorities for action, it is recommended that different sources of information be tapped and that different types of data be used (Wandersman et al., 2000). In child protection services, it is especially informative to collect data on court cases involving registered children (Pipkin et al., 2013). At the policy level, it has been recommended to generate social indicators that take into account the perception of children and adolescents themselves about their living conditions (Casas, 2011).

Reliable data on the prevalence of child labor in the geographic area of reference, along with a description of the type of work activities children perform and the conditions under which they work, is critical to the development of preventive programs. All of this allows us to estimate the dimension of the problem, assess its seriousness, and describe the context in which it occurs. Complementarily, knowing the attitudes of the families towards child labor helps to assess the disposition for change on the part of the population in case it is necessary to implement previous actions of community preparation.

For its part, the fight against the worst forms of child labor can be based on data provided by labor inspections and complaints made by non-governmental organizations that defend the rights of children. It is also important to obtain a diagnosis from the social agents, in order to take into consideration, the "normative needs" according to the judgment of the experts in the labor market. Furthermore, while preventive actions are preferably based on the identification of risk factors, in this second case it is more practical to identify the potential barriers that the processes of rehabilitation and reintegration of working children may face. In this way it is possible to assess the dimension of the problem.

9.3.2 Establishment of Goals

The second step is to delimit the target population and define what the intended results are. It is desirable that objectives be formulated in a realistic, precise, and measurable manner (Wandersman et al., 2000). Goal setting is not an automatic process; it depends on decision making. For example, when defining the target population, the intervention strategy is also being decided upon. In other words, it is part of the program design.

The central focus of preventive actions is usually the reduction of the prevalence of child labor (or to achieve relative improvements, at the lower end, in the quantity or quality of work activities performed by children). However, instrumental objectives can also be formulated aimed at alleviating the conditions of poverty of families, preventing school dropouts, improving academic skills, or increasing the time devoted to leisure activities, among others.

For their part, legal instruments aim to abolish forms of child labor considered undesirable. This is the case of the rules and regulations that establish a system of sanctions against forced labor, child exploitation, and dangerous work performed by minors. In this case, the instrumental objectives are focused on the formation of alliances among social actors, as well as on the creation of consensus and norms of preventive value. They may also be aimed at encouraging the involvement of employers and trade unions in the monitoring and control of the worst forms of child labor, or at changing public attitudes in this regard.

9.3.3 Evidence-Based Design

Third, it is recommended that the intervention use "evidence-based practices," that is, programs (or program components) that have been shown to be effective in previous implementation experiences (Wandersman et al., 2000). This requires relying on the scientific literature or on repositories that systematize good intervention practices with which to address different social problems and needs. With regard to child protection programs, a useful resource is the "California Evidence-Based Clearinghouse for Child Welfare" (CEBC)[3] which selects and systematizes the most effective practices in social work with families (Barbee et al., 2011). Regular contact with university researchers or technical advice from government agencies can also play a similar role (Pipkin et al., 2013).

In the case of preventive programs, two protective factors have been identified whose strengthening and development improve the results of the intervention: the social-emotional competencies of children and positive parental styles. Social skills, together with adequate intergenerational communication, can anticipate the emergence of problems. Among the risk factors, it is effective to counteract the incidence of poverty and early dropout from compulsory schooling.

To act against the worst forms of child labor, the creation of a shared vision among different social organizations has proven particularly effective, as well as the strengthening of informal norms that contribute to community control of the problem. Social dialogue policies (at the macro level) and community coalitions (at the meso level) are major recurrent components in initiatives with positive results. Studies on child and adolescent development are also useful in regulating the type of activities allowed at different ages (Greenberger, 1983).

9.3.4 Adjustment to the Community Context

Community adjustment of interventions refers to the adaptation of the program to the characteristics of the community context and the peculiarities of the population. This ranges from cultural adaptations to design tailored to local specificities. It also involves ensuring that it does not interfere with other pre-existing programs or cause duplication of services (Wandersman et al., 2000). It is important to

---

[3]Both the programs and the tools to improve their implementation are available on the web: https://www.cebc4cw.org/.

incorporate the perspective of families in some way (Barbee et al., 2011), with special adaptations for ethnic minorities (Pipkin et al., 2013).

The adjustments required vary depending on the type of program. On the one hand, preventive programs need to adapt to community readiness levels, slowing the pace of change when the population's cultural values and parental attitudes are more favorable to children's involvement in work activities. On the other hand, the commitment to international conventions is facilitated to the extent that they are derived from a participatory process in which local governments have the possibility of contributing and influencing.

9.3.5 Organizational Context of the Intervention

Human resources, technical resources, leadership, organizational climate, and funding, among other organizational factors, can condition program implementation (Wandersman et al., 2000). Also important is the definition of roles and the workload of the different actors involved in the intervention. Staff training is one of the factors related to a good implementation of planned activities (Barbee et al., 2011).

In the case of child labor prevention programs, primary schools have played a prominent role. It has been shown that the size of the school and the social climate among the teaching staff influence both the implementation process and the results obtained. On the other hand, in low-income countries schools often lack specialized psychological support. This makes the psychosocial content function as a hook for the participation of the educational community in the programs. However, due to the existence of pressing needs, there is also a risk that the original objectives of the intervention will be overshadowed.

As for the conventions that regulate child labor, their ratification depends in part on the internal dynamics of international bodies. As a general rule, for local entities, participating in international initiatives offers an opportunity for learning and organizational training. However, despite the interest in attracting resources, local organizations are often sensitive to power imbalances or openly perceive their capacity to influence decision-making as comparatively weak.

9.3.6 Program Actions

The action plan involves the temporary organization of activities, the anticipation of the resources needed in each case, and the distribution of responsibilities among the different participants in the implementation (Wandersman et al., 2000). Both a logical sequencing and the anticipation of which activities are instrumental to others, guarantee the proper functioning of the program. Piloting interventions can introduce an iterative process of improvement in the implementation of activities (Barbee et al., 2011).

Psychoeducational actions and income redistribution are the two central components of preventive interventions; while the regulation of the worst forms of child labor is usually due to awareness raising actions, formulation of agreements and elaboration of legal texts. Being clear about the central components of the intervention, such as those just highlighted, contributes to better implementation of activities. In this way, recruitment, training, or resource management activities, which are of a secondary nature, are put at the service of the main intervention strategies.

9.3.7   Evaluation and Implementation

With regard to the implementation of the intervention, in this section we refer to the monitoring of activities and the follow-up of the program's progress. This provides us with information about the fidelity, quality, and intensity of implementation (Wandersman et al., 2000). This section also includes aspects related to program evaluation, such as the evaluation design, the results indicators used, or the degree of reliability and validity of the information collected to assess the intervention.

In the case of preventive programs, it is essential to have an impact evaluation and to summarize "lessons learned" through periodic systematic reviews. In this way, knowledge is generated about which actions obtain which results in which child labor conditions. With regard to legal regulations, both labor inspections and monitoring to ensure compliance with the law can have evaluative value.

Programs against child labor are complex interventions, with multiple components, so in the evaluation of programs it is necessary to make the model on behavior change explicit, and to propose designs that allow a reasonable attribution of the impact to the actions carried out (Perrin & Wichmand, 2011). Furthermore, most impact evaluations only collect short-term results and it is necessary to obtain evidence of the long-term effects of the interventions (Dammert et al., 2018).

9.3.8   Results

Obtaining results, as its name suggests, is the central element around which the GTO model revolves. Ultimately, we are interested in knowing the impact of the intervention to see if the set of strategies deployed succeed in modifying the problem that gave rise to the program (Wandersman et al., 2000). Among other aspects, we can evaluate the reaction of the participants, the acquisition of knowledge or skills throughout the intervention, the changes in behavior or the final impact on the social problem.

The impact of preventive programs is measured preferably through the decrease in the labor participation of minors, whether evaluated in quantitative or qualitative terms. Although the reduction in the prevalence of child labor is the most convincing data, the improvement in living and working conditions is also a very interesting indicator. If we take a pragmatic approach, sometimes just reducing the number of working hours or preventing working hours from overlapping with school hours can be significant achievements of the intervention. With a broader perspective, we can consider the impact of work activity on children's health, psychological well-being, and educational experience.

With regard to regulations against the worst forms of child labor, the impact could be assessed, for example, in terms of the number of signatories to international conventions or by documenting changes in labor relations introduced by governments at the local level. It may also be informative to count the number of children reintegrated into compulsory schooling.

9.3.9   Quality Improvement

After implementing the program, "lessons learned" can be drawn for the next implementation by collecting suggestions for improvement based on experience (Wandersman et al., 2000). This makes the intervention part of a continuous learning cycle and subject to continuous improvement.

Child labor policies have been very effective over the past few decades. However, they have also been subject to a continuous process of transformation and improvement. For example, conditional cash transfers, despite their generally good results, are being subjected to a process of systematic evaluation in order to understand the conditions under which better performance is achieved. For its part, the regulation of the minimum age for access to employment began by establishing the same standard for all countries that were committed to ILO Convention 138. Over time, it was applied in a more flexible manner, allowing the introduction of local variations. In general, preventive strategies have incorporated community-based innovations, while legal regulations have progressively adopted a more pragmatic and reformist approach.

9.3.10   Sustainability of the Intervention

Continuity of the program into the future depends on having the necessary funding, support from the referral administration, sufficient staff with the required technical skills, and overcoming negative community reactions (Wandersman et al., 2000).

Both lack negative community reactions and lack of financial resources can interfere with the continuity of preventive actions. In the case of legal regulations, they may be more affected by processes of political polarization or the reactions of local institutions that do not see their needs or views on local people's problems adequately represented.

9.4 Organizational Capacities, Community Adjustment, and Evidence-Based Practices

The 'Edúcame Primero" (Educate Me First) program is a psycho-educational intervention that aims to prevent school dropout, acting on protective factors of behavioral basis, with a special emphasis on social-emotional skills. In a case of application of the program in Tegucigalpa, the implementation was part of a project of cooperation for development with the collaboration of a Spanish university and a Honduran university (Holgado, 2019). The intervention was made operational through an international team of program facilitators, made up of interns from the local university and Spanish students who were doing a short stay as international volunteers.

The facilitators functioned as a semi-autonomous working group: once they had received the program guidelines and were trained in the educational materials, the group had the autonomy to make decisions about the development of the intervention, for which they were jointly responsible. This was reflected in a positive social climate, which kept morale high throughout program implementation and facilitated collaboration within the team. The small group was coordinated by a facilitator with previous experience in the implementation of the program in Colombia and Peru. This allowed for a background in the operation of the program in various schools and with different types of families. However, again, it was necessary to adapt it to the peculiarities of the educational communities in Honduras.

In its different applications, the impact of this program goes beyond reducing the risk of child labor. Along with the program's impact on the receiving communities, it is a service-learning experience in which participating students develop intercultural competencies and specific skills for the implementation of psycho-educational activities. It also has an impact on the sensitivity towards groups at risk in general and the problems of developing countries in particular. Furthermore, the intervention has had continuity through the appropriation of the preventive action by the local universities, which in some cases have continued to implement the program as part of the external practices of their students.

"Edúcame Primero" is an evidence-based program. However, as we have just illustrated, the results depend not only on the content of the intervention (or the activities foreseen in the educational materials) but also on the organizational capacities that are put in place, together with the effort to adapt to the specific application contexts. In previous editions (in Colombia and Peru), the program had a more complex organizational structure. In Honduras, on the other hand, the organization of an international team that functioned autonomously not only made the management of the intervention more efficient, but also introduced the necessary flexibility to accommodate each educational center in the most convenient way. Ultimately, it is this complex process of interaction between organizational factors, context characteristics, previous experience, and program preventive content that is expressed in a unique implementation history and associated results.

This case of implementation in Tegucigalpa is consistent with previous literature that has stressed the importance of local partners, participatory strategies, and small changes in the program to adapt them to the target population (Nápoles et al., 2013). In particular, organizational structure and processes play a critical role in practice, so manipulating these factors can increase the preventive potential of interventions (Yano, 2008). Therefore, it can be concluded that the interaction between organizational capacities and the characteristics of the community context inform the level of preparedness for change (Maya Jariego et al., 2010). Consequently, operating on such an organizational-community interface is an indirect and efficient way to enhance the impact of programs.

Box 9.2: A History of Two Programs

Below, we describe two intervention programs, following the ten-step outline in Sect. 9.3. This example allows us to illustrate the differences between behavior-based prevention and political-legal actions against the worst forms of child labor. In parentheses, each number corresponds to the 10 intervention components of the GTO model

The family health program in Brazil is a system for providing primary care. (1) In different regions there are great health disparities. (2) The program aims to improve health care for the most disadvantaged groups. (3) To this end, it focuses on risk and protective factors in the accessibility of health services. (4) Each team is responsible for a group of families. (5) The program introduces an organizational innovation, through the decentralization of the public health system. (6) The program is implemented through teams of health professionals distributed in the communities. They focus on prevention strategies, early detection, and the promotion of healthy habits. (7) The intervention was subjected to an econometric study and an impact evaluation. (8) The program has reduced infant mortality and improved levels of compulsory schooling. It has also improved health coverage. (9) In order to improve the impact on the reduction of child labor, it is recommended that conditionality criteria be established. (10) The continuity of the program depends on the financing of the national government. Based on Rocha, R., & Soares, R. R. (2010). Evaluating the impact of community-based health interventions: evidence from Brazil's	Among the pacification initiatives in Colombia, programs have been carried out to promote the demobilization of minors from armed groups. (1) Colombia is the fifth country in the world in terms of the recruitment of child soldiers, who often suffer from post-traumatic stress. (2) The intervention was carried out to promote the reintegration of child soldiers into civilian life. (3) The Convention on the Rights of the Child prohibits the recruitment of children under 18 years of age. Public officials were involved in raising awareness of the need to demobilize minors. (4) An alliance was created with community leaders and non-governmental organizations. (5) UNICEF, SIDA and local entities participated in the program. (6) Actions were implemented for: personal protection and security; family tracing and reunification; and legal advice for community reintegration. (7) An international cooperation agency carried out the external evaluation. (8) Participants received emergency assistance. The community was sensitized to the risk of anti-personnel mines. (9) The location of minors and the identification of differentiated profiles is one of the challenges to improve the intervention. (10) There are sufficient funding and

Family Health Program. *Health Economics,* 19(S1), 126–158.	involvement of local entities to maintain this line of action. Based on Jesús, J. (2005). Demobilization and reintegration of child soldiers in Colombia. *SIDA Evaluations 05/25.*

9.5   Drop Out of School and Get Off the Street

Dropping out of school and leaving the street are two opposing processes that underpin many of the policies and programs against child labor revolve. On the one hand, the interruption of compulsory studies is relatively frequent among minors who carry out work activities before the permitted age. That is why early detection and early prevention are two preferred action strategies to avoid a process of progressive deterioration leading to the substitution of compulsory education by child labor and living on the street at the worst. On the other hand, once the process has started, rehabilitation, family reintegration and community reintegration strategies are required to reverse the situation.

Figure 9.2 illustrates the direction in which psychosocial prevention and rehabilitation strategies work. Some child labor prevention programs seek to counteract the risky conditions that lead children to drop out of school to engage in income-generating activities. Other interventions try to get children to go back to school, to reintegrate them into their families, and to regain a normalized lifestyle. Paradoxically, the more serious the psychological consequences and, therefore, the more necessary the intervention, the more difficult it is to obtain positive results. Consequently, although action on the worst forms of child labor generates a greater consensus on the need to act, preventive interventions are those that have a better prognosis in terms of their effectiveness on paper.

Although in reverse, both strategies are based on creating trusting relationships with adults and providing children with a safe and stimulating environment, which encourages learning and personal development. Both tutors and mentors consist of developing an effective personal relationship that sustains the exchange of social and academic support on an ongoing basis. For their part, family reintegration strategies

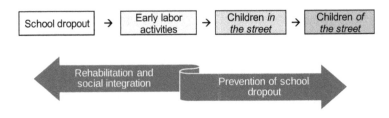

Fig. 9.2 Prevention and rehabilitation strategies. Source: own elaboration

Table 9.3 Roles of tutors in prevention and rehabilitation programs

Prevention of school dropouts	Rehabilitation and reintegration programs
• Motivate tutored students	• Encourage contact with rehabilitation services
• Provide academic support	
• Facilitate positive personal experiences at school	• Connect with families and the school
	• Preparing the family and the community
• Provide support and positive role models	• Ensure coverage of high-risk groups

Source: own elaboration

work insofar as they involve the re-education and preparation of children and parents before reconnecting both parties. In this second case, the residential units transcend their merely care function to the extent that they are used as an incentive to implement rehabilitation actions and allow intensive educational interventions.

When children drop out of compulsory education, they are no longer exposed to the equalizing effect of school and to the diversity of interventions that help promote healthy lifestyles. Programs to prevent school dropout reveal the relevance of early action, with multiple components of primary prevention. When children live on the streets, reversing the situation becomes an even more complex challenge with a more uncertain outcome. Rehabilitation and family reintegration programs continually face problems of coverage and the risk of relapse, which must be countered with specific actions.

As summarized in Table 9.3, guardians have different roles in EDP and community reintegration programs. To prevent drop-out, tutors encourage students' academic motivation, provide academic support, and promote participation in activities that provide a positive school experience. To promote reintegration into the community, tutors encourage students to commit to behavioral change and initiate the process of rehabilitation, act as intermediaries with the family and the school, and prepare the community context for the successful reintegration of children on the streets.

To compare these two types of strategies, in Annexes A and B we include two practical cases that summarize each area of intervention. Annex A is a review of the risk factors, exemplary programs, and principles of effective prevention to reduce dropouts. In Annex B, we do the same with the community rehabilitation of street children. Both are illustrated with a practical case, with a concrete program in which the basic components of the intervention are analyzed.

Box 9.3: Military Camps and Child Sexual Exploitation
Sexual exploitation tends to occur more frequently among boys and girls living on the street, either because they have been expelled from home or as a result of immigration and forced displacement. Risk factors are having been sexually abused or, in the case of girls, joining street gangs. Although they are sometimes sexually exploited by their own relatives, it is increasingly common

(continued)

Box 9.3 (continued)

for them to be recruited by organized crime gangs to engage in prostitution, sometimes as part of the international trafficking of minors (Estes & Weiner, 2001).

The prevalence of child sexual exploitation has also been associated with those local contexts in which there is a large community of men who are passing through, such as the military, truck drivers or those attending conventions. In the case of Korea, Japan or the Philippines, settlements, neighborhoods and in some cases small towns have been documented in which local women offer sexual services to soldiers of the United States Army (Moon, 1997). One such town in South Korea is called "American Town".

This situation occurs both outside and within the United States: "The problem is especially pronounced where: (1) substantial concentrations of military personnel are found; (2) a large percentage of this personnel are sexually "unattached"; (3) the communities that surround military bases are poor; and (4) law enforcement (both in the community and on the military bases) is comparatively lax." (Estes & Weiner, 2001, p. 101).

Based on:

Estes, R. J., & Weiner, N. A. (2001). *The commercial sexual exploitation of children in the US, Canada and Mexico*. Philadelphia: University of Pennsylvania, School of Social Work, Center for the Study of Youth Policy.

Moon, K. H. (1997). *Sex among allies: Military prostitution in US-Korea relations*. Columbia University Press.

[Korea]

9.6   Conclusion

In this chapter we have described the implementation of interventions as a complex process in which program content, organizational factors, and characteristics of community contexts interact. The same program can achieve different results depending on the organizational and community context in which it is implemented, as well as on the interaction between the two. Using the GTO model as a reference, we have identified some key factors that can result in greater program impact:

- With regard to the content of the activities, we have distinguished (a) preventive interventions in risk contexts, normally aimed at poor families, and (b) actions to involve local institutions in the transformation of the regulatory framework of labor relations.
- Primary schools often appear as a preferential context for preventive programs, both because of their centrality in community life and because of their role as a catalyst for relations between families. The size, structure and social climate of educational institutions condition the results of the intervention.

- Also among the organizational factors, the dynamics of power and influence in international organizations stand out. On the one hand, policies led by the ILO and development cooperation projects offer opportunities for the training of organizations in low-income countries. On the other hand, the latter aspire to have greater representation and influence on international policies.
- In terms of adaptation to local contexts, it is necessary to adjust the program to the attitudes of families and the cultural values of the population. Community reactions against the objectives of the intervention are among the most common barriers and can diminish the impact of preventive actions.
- Also, among the contextual factors, it is necessary to take into consideration the degree of regulation of child labor and the degree of compliance with the law. The political system and the legal framework are dispositional factors for promoting changes in the behavioral base.
- Finally, it is advisable to follow a participatory approach involving children, families, unions, employers, and public officials.

Through the comparative analysis, we were able to identify two types of differentiated actions. On the one hand, behavioral-based psychosocial interventions promote protection resources in groups at risk of child labor. On the other hand, consensus-building and legal-institutional reforms aim to have an impact on the worst forms of child labor. These two types of intervention are not incompatible with each other and can in fact be mutually reinforcing.

Box 9.4:   Child Labor in 7 Questions
What is child labor? Child labor is all work done by children under the minimum legal working age, which in most countries is set at about 15 years of age, according to ILO Convention 138.

   What are the worst forms of child labor? The worst forms of child labor include forced labor, slavery, prostitution, involvement in illicit activities (such as drug trafficking), and the performance of "hazardous work" as defined in ILO Convention 182. This is the first international ILO Convention to achieve universal ratification.

   What is "hazardous work"? Dangerous work is work that puts children's health, safety and personal integrity at risk. Among others, they include mining, informal street work, or "scavenging" and recycling of rubbish, as well as those activities that require the use of dangerous machinery or the handling of toxic substances. In addition, particularly harsh working conditions in relation to age can make an activity considered "hazardous", such as working at night, working long hours or being exposed to noise, lack of air and other precarious environmental conditions.

   What are children working on worldwide? More than two-thirds of the world's child workers are in agriculture, doing unpaid work within the family unit. Child labor is therefore strongly associated with the subsistence economy

(continued)

Box 9.4 (continued)

in the primary sector. However, in certain regions there are significant segments of the child population working in industry or the service sector. Finally, about 5 per cent of the world's children are engaged in hazardous work.

What are the causes of child labor? Child labor is significantly concentrated in low-income families and is associated with poverty. There is evidence of an intergenerational cycle of poverty, so if adults worked when they were young, their children are also more likely to work. Migration, forced displacement and armed conflict create situations of vulnerability that often result in child labor. Another important factor is favorable public attitudes towards the involvement of children in labor activities.

What are the consequences of child labor? Child labor can have a direct impact on the physical health and psychological well-being of children. Hazardous work is associated with a higher incidence of accidents, injuries, and health problems. In the short term, it can have a negative impact on academic performance and increases the likelihood of dropping out of school. In the long term, it reduces job opportunities in adulthood and is often reflected in lower wages.

What is effective in preventing child labor? Conditional cash transfer programs reduce the prevalence of child labor. Combining social protection measures for the most vulnerable families with educational support for children is the type of action that has had the best results. Behavioral-based psycho-educational interventions can prevent school absenteeism and facilitate the process of community reintegration of child workers. Coordinated action by employers, trade unions and other social actors is an element of community preparedness that contributes to the development of social norms with preventive value.

References

Barbee, A. P., Christensen, D., Antle, B., Wandersman, A., & Cahn, K. (2011). Successful adoption and implementation of a comprehensive casework practice model in a public child welfare agency: Application of the Getting to Outcomes (GTO) model. *Children and Youth Services Review, 33*(5), 622–633.

Bequele, A., & Boyden, J. (Eds.). (1988). *Combating child labour.* Geneva: International Labour Organization.

Casas, F. (2011). Subjective social indicators and child and adolescent well-being. *Child Indicators Research, 4*(4), 555–575.

Chinman, M., Hunter, S. B., Ebener, P., Paddock, S. M., Stillman, L., Imm, P., & Wandersman, A. (2008). The getting to outcomes demonstration and evaluation: An illustration of the prevention support system. *American Journal of Community Psychology, 41*(3–4), 206–224.

Chinman, M., Acosta, J. D., Ebener, P. A., Sigel, C., & Keith, J. (2016). *Getting to Outcomes guide for teen pregnancy prevention.* Santa Monica: RAND Corporation.

Dammert, A. C., De Hoop, J., Mvukiyehe, E., & Rosati, F. C. (2018). Effects of public policy on child labor: Current knowledge, gaps, and implications for program design. *World Development, 110*, 104–123.

Estes, R. J., & Weiner, N. A. (2001). *The commercial sexual exploitation of children in the US, Canada and Mexico*. Philadelphia: University of Pennsylvania, School of Social Work, Center for the Study of Youth Policy.

Greenberger, E. (1983). A researcher in the policy arena: The case of child labor. *American Psychologist, 38*(1), 104–111.

Grootaert, C., & Kanbur, R. (1995). *Child labor: A review. World Bank Policy Research Working Paper, 1454*. Washington: World Bank.

Holgado, D. (2019). Edúcame Primero en Honduras. Impacto psicológico y transmisión del conocimiento ecológico local en menores trabajadores en el sector pesquero. *Convocatoria de Ayudas para Actividades y Proyectos de Cooperación al Desarrollo 2017/2018*. Universidad de Sevilla.

Holgado, D., Maya-Jariego, I., Ramos, I., & Palacio, J. (2014). El papel de los facilitadores en la implementación de los "Espacios para Crecer": Evaluación formativa del programa con menores trabajadores "Edúcame Primero, Colombia". *Universitas Psychologica, 13*(4), 1441–1460.

Holgado, D., Santolaya, F. J., Maya-Jariego, I., Cueto, R. M., & Anaya, R. H. (2015). Preparación comunitaria y organizativa contra el trabajo infantil en tres colegios de barrios periféricos de Lima (Perú). *Apuntes de Psicología, 33*(3), 103–116.

Jesús, J. (2005). Desmovilización y reintegración de niños soldados en Colombia (2003–2004). In *SIDA Evaluations 05/25*. Stockholm: Swedish International Development Cooperation Agency and UNICEF.

Kapuściński, R. (2000). *Ébano*. Barcelona: Editorial Anagrama.

Márquez, E., Holgado, D., & Maya-Jariego, I. (2019). Innovation, dosage and responsiveness in the implementation of the program "Edúcame Primero Perú" for reducing child labor. *Applied Research in Quality of Life, 14*(3), 617–636. https://doi.org/10.1007/s11482-018-9608-1.

Mattox, T., Hunter, S. B., Kilburn, M. R., & Wiseman, S. H. (2013). *Getting To Outcomes® for home visiting: How to plan, implement, and evaluate a program in your community to support parents and their young children*. Santa Monica: RAND Corporation.

Maya Jariego, I. (2014). Elementos centrales en la reducción del trabajo infantil: Acceso a una educación universal de calidad, transferencia condicionada de efectivos y coaliciones de agentes sociales. *Jornada por la erradicación del trabajo infantil. Por una justicia social para una globalización equitativa*. Organización Internacional del Trabajo (OIT), Agencia Española de Cooperación Internacional (AECI) y Universidad de Sevilla. 17 de marzo de 2014.

Maya Jariego, I., Holgado, D., Santolaya, F., Gavilán, J., & Ramos, I. (2010). *Comunidades preparadas para la salud. Preparación comunitaria y práctica profesional de los trabajadores sociales de Atención Primaria en Andalucía*. Madrid: Bubok.

Maya-Jariego, I., & Palacio, J. E. (2014). La red de facilitadores de los "Espacios para Crecer" en Barranquilla (Colombia). Estrategias de continuidad, ajuste comunitario y mejora de la implementación en los programas de prevención del trabajo infantil. *Journal de Ciencias Sociales de la Universidad de Palermo, 2*, 61–70.

Maya-Jariego, I., Aceituno, I., Santolaya, F. J., & Holgado, D. (2015). Diagnóstico de la preparación comunitaria para la reducción del trabajo infantil en dos comunidades de Lima (Perú). In J. En Fialho, C. Silva, & J. Saragoça (Eds.), *Diagnóstico Social. Teoria, metodologia e casos práticos* (pp. 199–214). Lisboa: Edições Silabo.

Moon, K. H. (1997). *Sex among allies: Military prostitution in US-Korea relations*. New York: Columbia University Press.

Nápoles, A. M., Santoyo-Olsson, J., & Stewart, A. L. (2013). Methods for translating evidence-based behavioral interventions for health-disparity communities. *Preventing Chronic Disease, 10*, 130133. https://doi.org/10.5888/pcd10.130133.

Perrin, B., & Wichmand, P. (2011). Evaluating complex strategic development interventions: The challenge of child labor. In K. Forss, M. Marra, & R. Schwartz (Eds.), *Evaluating the complex:*

Attribution, contribution and beyond (pp. 243–891). New Brunswick, NJ: Transaction Publishers.

Pipkin, S., Sterrett, E. M., Antle, B., & Christensen, D. N. (2013). Washington State's adoption of a child welfare practice model: An illustration of the Getting To Outcomes implementation framework. *Children and Youth Services Review, 35*(12), 1923–1932.

Rocha, R., & Soares, R. R. (2010). Evaluating the impact of community-based health interventions: Evidence from Brazil's Family Health Program. *Health Economics, 19*(S1), 126–158.

Rosati, F. C., & Lyon, S. (2006). Tackling Child Labour: Policy options for achieving sustainable reductions in children at work. *Understanding Children's Work Project,* Universidad de Roma.

Wandersman, A., Imm, P., Chinman, M., & Kaftarian, S. (2000). Getting to outcomes: A results-based approach to accountability. *Evaluation and Program Planning, 23*(3), 389–395.

Wandersman, A., Duffy, J., Flaspohler, P., Noonan, R., Lubell, K., Stillman, L., . . . Saul, J. (2008). Bridging the gap between prevention research and practice: The interactive systems framework for dissemination and implementation. *American Journal of Community Psychology, 41*(3–4), 171–181.

Yano, E. M. (2008). The role of organizational research in implementing evidence-based practice: QUERI Series. *Implementation Science, 3*(1), 29.

Chapter 10
Epilogue: The Sustainability of the Impact of Preventive Interventions

Ratification of ILO Convention 182 on the worst forms of child labor by all its member states was completed in August 2020 (Annex III). This is the first time in the history of the organization that universal ratification has been achieved. This is good news insofar as a large part of the achievements in the fight against child labor have been based precisely on international collaboration, within the framework of multi-lateral organizations. However, in the current political situation, the network of multilateral institutions seems to be under strong pressure, so the need to renegotiate the agreements and commitments established after World War II has been suggested. Rights that are now assumed to have been acquired could be questioned, and if necessary, finally revised, depending on the political or economic circumstances. The preceding pages can be read in part as a reaffirmation of the rights, values, and social conquests of more recent history in addressing the needs of children and the protection of minors.

Despite age being an objective fact, the notion of childhood is a concept that has been built up throughout history and, consequently, has been reflected in a variety of ways both in social policies and in the prevailing patterns of upbringing in each social context (Gittins, 2009). In a way, the drive of international agencies has contributed to a greater convergence among countries in the legal treatment of children. These regulations are in turn based on assumptions that convey a certain vision of children, such as the degree of responsibility attributable to their actions, the (greater or lesser) need for protection and care, and the set of prerogatives they enjoy. The ways in which childhood is understood are indirectly crystallized in the legal instruments on children's rights. In this sense, the consideration of the active role of minors is an element of innovation that can contribute to the development of participative policies, although it seems necessary to implement it by foreseeing possible paradoxical effects contrary to the protection of children.

Prevention policies and programs have been shown to be effective in reducing the prevalence of child labor worldwide. Specifically, specific interventions have been developed with children at risk of early entry into the labor market, with children already experiencing the negative consequences of working, and with children

© The Author(s), under exclusive license to Springer Nature Switzerland AG 2021   143
I. Maya Jariego, *Community Prevention of Child Labor*, Human Well-Being
Research and Policy Making, https://doi.org/10.1007/978-3-030-70810-8_10

suffering from some of the "worst forms" of child labor (Paruzzolo, 2009). Each target group involves different intervention strategies. In recent years, greater attention has been given to those cases that require immediate action, because they are labor activities (or situations of child exploitation) that have a serious personal impact and where protection measures are urgent. On the other hand, primary and secondary prevention strategies have proved to be particularly effective, which has made it possible to generate a body of evidence-based practices that can be replicated in different intervention contexts.

Most of the most effective actions are behavioral-based interventions, consisting of the prevention of school dropouts, the administration of incentives to vulnerable families and the development of skills in children. Although it has been indicated that psychology has paid little attention to the phenomenon of child labor (Hobbs & Cornwell, 1986), the truth is that risk and protection models, together with reinforcement and social learning strategies, among others, have been used as a reference in the design of interventions and have proven to have preventive value in practice. However, it also seems necessary to strengthen systematic studies on the psychological impact of child labor, the specific interferences of early labor initiation on development, and the individual differences related to the various forms of child labor. After two decades oriented preferably towards obtaining immediate results, the research could contribute both to a better understanding of the phenomenon and to the systematic evaluation of the impact of interventions. At the same time, it seems an appropriate way to guarantee the long-term sustainability of the good results obtained in this area of intervention.

As we write these pages, in the context of the coronavirus disease pandemic that began in 2019, the United Nations has warned of the generational impact that prolonged school closures could have, as well as the problems of educational continuity to which children, adolescents, and youth are exposed. Prolonged school closures, coupled with economic difficulties, increase the risk of dropping out of school and may reverse some of the progress made in recent decades in reducing child labor around the world. This risk is greater among the most vulnerable groups. This is why it is pertinent to reinforce policies that have proven to have a preventive impact, basing interventions on the lessons learned in recent decades. Among other initiatives, it seems appropriate to develop compensatory actions with low-income households, support families and caregivers, protect children at risk, ensure the continuity of services and adapt interventions to the peculiarities of each context. It is also an opportunity to promote innovative strategies for preparedness, adjustment, and community building that we have described in previous chapters.

Prolonged school closures have negative health and social consequences for children in poverty, and it can increase inequalities (Van Lancker & Parolin, 2020). For instance, it tends to broaden the achievement gap between children of different socio-economic status, as well as have a detrimental effect on their mental health and well-being. In addition to interrupting the daily routine, for many children, it means losing access to the resources they normally get through school (Lee, 2020). Both children with special educational needs and those with mental disorders are especially sensitive to social distancing measures. As a consequence of

Table 10.1 Challenges in the sustainability of preventive achievements against child labor

	Describing the challenges
Protect vested rights	Child protection is a historical achievement and, as such, may be subject to review depending on the social and political context
Balancing participation and protection	The emphasis on the participation of minors has to be compatible with the objectives of child protection
Promote behavioral and community-based interventions	Both behavioral-based practices and the community approach to intervention offer opportunities for innovation and reinforcing the impact of policies to combat child labor
Sustaining achievements in reducing child labor in the context of the pandemic	The COVID-19 pandemic puts at risk the achievements made in reducing child labor in recent decades: compulsory schooling, the equalizing effect of school and the maintenance of a time reserved for growth and learning during childhood are subjected to new pressures in the context of crisis

the prolonged closure, they miss compensatory programs for risk groups that are normally channeled through the educational context. Therefore, it is recommended to be proactive and mitigate as much as possible the impact on the populations at the highest risk (Ahad et al., 2020; Armitage & Nellums, 2020). Strategies to ensure the preservation of services have come to occupy the center of concern in many intervention contexts.

In this book, we assume that a better understanding of the causes and consequences of child labor provides policymakers and implementers with the tools necessary to improve child protection outcomes. Throughout the process we have learned that by the very term "child labor" we are referring to a great diversity of situations of vulnerability that require specific interventions in each case. On the other hand, despite being an area in which a 40% reduction in the prevalence of the problem has been achieved in the period 2000–2016 (ILO, 2017), we have seen the need to improve the degree of systematization and theoretical formalization of the interventions. Among other measures, systematic research and a community approach could contribute to maintaining the previous trajectory of high effectiveness in addressing the problem (Table 10.1).

As we have seen, children have the same rights as adults, but at the same time they are the recipients of special protection. The policies we have described aim to preserve childhood as a territory reserved for personal development and learning (based on the assumption that education offers children a passport to the future). As the literature on preventive interventions shows, early action can provide lifelong benefits. When they also target groups at risk, they are particularly efficient. For this reason, efforts should not be spared to prevent those life events, such as early employment, that may hinder the development of children, harm their health, or deteriorate their well-being. We trust that this book will provide models, strategies, and recommendations for the implementation of effective interventions to prevent children's adversity and build a better future for the new generations.

References

Ahad, M. A., Parry, Y. K., & Willis, E. (2020). Spillover trends of child labor during the coronavirus crisis-an unnoticed wake-up call. *Frontiers in Public Health, 8,* 288. https://doi.org/10.3389/fpubh.2020.00488.

Armitage, R., & Nellums, L. B. (2020). Considering inequalities in the school closure response to COVID-19. *The Lancet Global Health, 8*(5), e644.

Gittins, D. (2009). The historical construction of childhood. In M. J. Kehily (Ed.), *An introduction to childhood studies* (pp. 25–38). UK: McGraw-Hill Education.

Hobbs, S., & Cornwell, D. (1986). Child labour: An underdeveloped topic in psychology. *International Journal of Psychology, 21*(2), 225–234. https://doi.org/10.1080/00207598608247587.

International Labour Organization. (2017). *Global estimates of child labour: Results and trends, 2012–2016.* Geneva: ILO.

Lee, J. (2020). Mental health effects of school closures during COVID-19. *The Lancet Child & Adolescent Health, 4*(6), 421.

Paruzzolo, S. (2009). The impact of programs relating to child labor prevention and children's protection: A review of impact evaluations up to 2007. In *Understanding Children's Work Working Paper Series.* ILO: World Bank & UNICEF.

Van Lancker, W., & Parolin, Z. (2020). COVID-19, school closures, and child poverty: a social crisis in the making. *The Lancet Public Health, 5*(5), e243–e244.

Chapter 11
Coda: A Lesson Well-Learned?

"The commitment between social justice policies, liberal institutions, and the market led to a virtuous circle in which public education and universal health care were established. Progressive taxation, social services and public goods helped to reduce inequalities within the nation state. However, with globalization the balance between production and distribution was broken"—Tony Judt (2011)

At the start of our exploration into child labor, we learned about the case of Orlando, a child who fishes in the mangroves of western Honduras. This is a typical example of the involvement of children in the subsistence activities of the family unit in the primary sector of the economy. Later on, we learned about other cases that brought us closer to the great diversity of situations faced by working children, from informal sales on the streets of Colombian cities, to harvesting on cocoa plantations in Ghana, to child sexual exploitation in Thailand, to physically demanding activities in artisanal mining in the Peruvian Amazon region.

This diversity of the contexts in which children's labor takes place allowed us to verify that working conditions are determinants of both the type of child labor and its psychosocial impact. Aspects such as the number of working hours, the overlap of working hours with academic hours, the performance of physically demanding tasks, and the occupation of night shifts, to name but a few, have a decisive influence on the probability of dropping out of compulsory education, as well as on the psychological and health risks to which children are exposed. Therefore, the potential to interfere with normal developmental progress is highly variable depending on working conditions.

Secondly, the diversity of work contexts also allows for the establishment of a gradation in the modalities of child labor, and even to glimpse a possible route of progressive deterioration of the circumstances in which the work involvement of minors takes place. To illustrate this with a specific case, there is evidence that the collaboration of minors with the family business generally entails less exposure to psychosocial risk factors than salaried work in the industrial sector. In turn, children who work as factory workers do so without necessarily reaching the levels of coercion, violence or threat that characterize forced labor. Thus, there are activities

© The Author(s), under exclusive license to Springer Nature Switzerland AG 2021   147
I. Maya Jariego, *Community Prevention of Child Labor*, Human Well-Being
Research and Policy Making, https://doi.org/10.1007/978-3-030-70810-8_11

which, by their very nature, put the moral integrity of the child at risk, such as prostitution, illegal drug trafficking or life on the streets.

The typology we have just mentioned is not made up of watertight compartments, but rather the individual can move between the different forms of child labor depending on his or her personal circumstances. Moreover, to the extent that participation in early work reduces the opportunities available to individuals during their development, such transitions may in practice reflect a gradual worsening. We know, for example, that dropping out of school to help out at home can be the precursor to some girls ending up in domestic service. There is also evidence that children who sell on the streets may be at some risk of ending up living in the open. It is the passage from children *in the street* to children *of the street*.

Consequently, the psychosocial impact of child labor depends largely on the ways in which the child labor is carried out. For example, agricultural work within the family unit often carries a risk of educational abandonment, while industrial waged work sometimes involves the performance of dangerous tasks, with a risk of accidents and injuries. Both the sexual exploitation of children and the recruitment of child soldiers are the kind of activities that usually have a severe psychological impact and interfere with balanced personal development. Therefore, preventive action on each of these modalities also has the indirect effect of avoiding the possible worsening of working conditions (through the implementation of potentially more dangerous activities).

In this book we have focused on public policies for the prevention of child labor and the protection of children. This is an area in which programs have proved very effective in reducing the prevalence of the problem. This has been achieved by combining behavioral-based preventive actions with the introduction of legal regulations and institutional reforms for rehabilitation and community reintegration purposes. The former have been aimed at reducing school absenteeism, preventing early entry into the world of work and interrupting the processes of progressive personal deterioration among children at risk. The latter have set as a priority the elimination of the "worst forms" of child labor.

As we have seen, these are two intervention strategies which, in practice, reinforce each other. Firstly, conditional cash benefits for low-income families are an evidence-based practice, which emphasizes certain behavioral mechanisms to counteract poverty, while ensuring the educational inclusion of children. It is a type of action that can interrupt the intergenerational reproduction of poverty and that prevents children from having their personal opportunities reduced during a critical developmental period. In this context, both the establishment of standards in labor relations (such as the minimum legal age for employment, Annex D) and the building of consensus between trade unions and employers can enhance the results of behavioral-based programs. Although legal reforms and dialogue between social partners aim to transform the socio-cultural context, in practice they pave the way for preventive programs to work. By taking into account the institutional side and incorporating participatory strategies, they allow programs to be adapted to each local context. They also facilitate the process of community ownership, thus reducing the risk of negative reactions to the intervention among the target population.

Public policies against child labor act on dispositional factors (such as public attitudes), behavioral factors (such as parenting styles), and the legal framework for industrial relations. In their operation, we have detected two mechanisms that are directly associated with the effectiveness of interventions: the conditionality of economic support to vulnerable families and the community preparedness strategies that precede the implementation of programs. On the one hand, monetary incentives are used to reinforce the desired patterns of parenting and parental supervision. On the other hand, awareness and prior organization of the community environment improve the implementation of programs. Thus, among other factors, the functions of the education system depend in part on the involvement of parents in their children's learning, the relationship of families with the school and the levels of community cohesion.

Despite the positive results in reducing the prevalence of child labor since registration, serious threats to the sustainability of effective programs have also been identified. This is the case with political polarization, budgetary constraints and, more recently, the COVID-19 pandemic. Anti-child labor policies provide a good example of the benefits (and limits) of establishing universal public education and health. They also illustrate the need not to take for granted the rights and institutions that have underpinned achievements in this area. This is why it is still an area open to the development of comprehensive policies, sensitive to the diversity of forms taken by the phenomenon and with a community approach to program implementation. Even though we are experiencing far-reaching social transformations, the lessons learned over the last few decades should still have value to illuminate the future.

Reference

Judt, T. (2011). *Ill fares the land: A treatise on our present discontents*. London: Penguin.

Annex A: School Dropout Prevention

Tutoring or mentoring programs that provide personalized academic support, promote positive school experiences, and manage absences.

The educational context is a privileged resource for prevention. Both the equalizing role of the school and its contribution to the development of healthy lifestyles mean that the interruption of compulsory education has more far-reaching social and psychological consequences than the mere achievement of a given academic grade. Dropout prevention programs combine compensatory academic support activities with behavior-based strategies to improve the educational experience of high-risk children. Although experimental trials to assess impact are scarce, there are promising programs to reverse demotivation and absenteeism. These are individualized and small group interventions that improve the educational experience, promote academic performance, and help integrate children into their immediate school environment. Among other factors, we know that the development of positive relationships with peers and teachers is an element that prevents dropouts. Tutoring or mentoring programs are an efficient way to articulate the academic, psychological, and relational components through individualized interventions.

The abandonment of compulsory education has medium and long-term effects that carry a significant social cost. For example, among those who do not complete their secondary education, unemployment, mental health problems, low income work activities, or participation in criminal activities, among other social problems, are comparatively more likely during their adult life. In the short term, it is sometimes inextricably linked to child labor.

As we will see below, the factors that lead to such absenteeism are very varied and range from the rejection of school due to anxiety, stress or depression, to academic

© The Author(s), under exclusive license to Springer Nature Switzerland AG 2021
I. Maya Jariego, *Community Prevention of Child Labor*, Human Well-Being
Research and Policy Making, https://doi.org/10.1007/978-3-030-70810-8

problems, lack of parental supervision or participation in criminal gangs. As a general rule, preventive interventions aim to interrupt a progressive deterioration process in which occasional absenteeism leads to habitual absenteeism and this in turn is a precursor to permanent school desertion.

Interventions that have shown promising results in this area usually provide individualized attention to children at high risk. This not only makes it possible to respond to their specific needs but also facilitates the development of attachment relationships with the school and teachers. On the other hand, the most effective programs usually link participation in compensatory academic activities with obtaining greater status and recognition for the student in the school. It is also important that students perceive the completion of their studies as an achievable goal that will contribute positively to the development of the subsequent work path. For children from low-income families, scholarship programs and paid internships provide an incentive to avoid the premature replacement of compulsory education by work activities that will help their parents financially.

Risk and Protective Factors

The first problems of motivation and academic performance are a direct antecedent of absenteeism and school dropout. Students who repeat grades or who have consistently poor grades are more likely to drop out of school. Normally, there is a process of progressive disconnection, before leaving school more or less definitively. This is why recurrent absences are an early sign of school dropout and can be used for early detection of dropout. Dropout also has a higher incidence in children who suffer from previous cognitive or emotional problems.

Attendance problems occur more often when there are negative attitudes towards academics, and when there are incidents of aggression or misbehavior at school. Especially among adolescents, it can be linked to relationships with problematic friends or those who engage in risky behaviors. Among other events at the individual level, teenage pregnancy and child labor can be the trigger for the definitive interruption of studies.

The prevalence of school dropouts is higher in low-income families, with parents who have low educational levels and low aspirations for their children's academic performance. These parents also tend to have less contact with teachers and generally a poor relationship with the school. Both dysfunctional families and those with a high level of geographic mobility are more likely to have their children fail to complete compulsory education. Accordingly, seasonal agricultural workers are a high-risk group, since they frequently change their school of reference and sometimes resort to having their children collaborate in the family's economic activity.

As can be deduced from the risk factors summarized in Table A.1, supervision by parents and teachers can help prevent early school leaving. Systems for monitoring and controlling school attendance reduce the incidence of the problem, while serving to establish the appropriate preventive measures. Educational institutions can also

Table A.1 Risk factors for dropping out of School

Individual	• Low educational performance • Repeat course • Low academic performance expectations • Lack of effort, commitment, and continued attendance • Aggressiveness and behavioral problems in school • Having friends with high-risk behaviors • Maternity • Child labor • Learning disabilities and special educational needs
Family	• Low socioeconomic level • Low educational level of the parents • High geographic mobility of the family • Family disorganization • Low educational expectations on the part of the parents • Little contact and involvement of parents with the school
School environments	• Poor learning environment at the school • Security and infrastructure problems in the school • Classroom overcrowding and poor quality of teachers • Lack of contact with the families

play a protective role by developing a positive climate within the school and by maintaining continuous contact with families. This has a greater impact when there is also an adequate communication pattern between parents and children.

Exemplary Programs

A basic strategy for preventing dropouts has been to improve academic performance and promote a positive educational experience. To this end, the central components of the intervention are individualized academic support, the assignment of tutors or mentors, and the monitoring and control of attendance problems. At-risk students participate in extracurricular activities or summer courses in which they receive academic support in those subjects in which they normally have the most difficulty, such as language and math. Compensatory courses are usually given individually or in small groups so that students receive personalized treatment. At the same time, cases of absenteeism are closely monitored since absences are a direct antecedent to dropping out of school.

Two types of intervention with very good results consist of the assignment of tutors or mentors, which allow for a personalized follow-up of the school experience. Mentors not only provide academic support and guidance, but also train students in functional school management skills, set short-term goals that can be achieved by students, and promote the creation of positive student/teacher relationships. Establishing effective supportive relationships with some adults in the school prevents dissatisfaction and subsequent dropout. Alternatively, the involvement of peer mentors facilitates an appropriate communication style while connecting them to positive role models. This strategy has worked particularly well with members of minority and disadvantaged groups. On the other hand, at-risk students themselves can mentor or participate in volunteer actions. When they are involved in prosocial activities and exercise high-status roles, with which they gain greater recognition in school, they are also less likely to drop out.

At the secondary school level, multi-component interventions are more effective in both reducing the dropout rate and increasing the completion rate. Programs with better preventive outcomes often combine academic support activities, training in study skills, specific actions on absenteeism, and behavior-based strategies. Organizational changes in the school are also effective. In general, at-risk students benefit when they participate in individualized tutoring in language and math, when they receive specific instruction on how to organize their homework or how to prepare for a test, when teachers contact their parents in case they miss class, and when incentives are applied to reinforce continued attendance and improve academic expectations. Organizing the school into semi-autonomous teaching-learning groups can also improve sensitivity to special educational needs.

Creating a positive social climate in the school reduces the risk of absenteeism and dropout. Students benefit from a safe and stimulating environment, where they have opportunities to participate, with a cohesive atmosphere and where adults are concerned about the welfare of their children. In secondary schools, the importance of combining clear rules, which establish behavioral discipline, with a strong emotional bond with the school has been proven. Dropout rates are lower when students perceive that teachers have high expectations about their academic performance, convey a high level of demand, and are available to provide the necessary support. Both the dynamics of the teaching staff and the degree of openness to the involvement of families and the community have a direct impact on the atmosphere of the school. For their part, school principals can contribute to a positive climate by promoting connectivity and a sense of belonging. Organizational consulting strategies can also be used to improve the school environment (Table A.2).

Learning Communities Learning communities are a project of educational transformation based on dialogical learning, educational community participation, and the application of inclusive, evidence-based practices. This initiative has been developed in preschools, primary and secondary schools.

The classroom is organized into small interactive groups and follows a dialogical model to promote coexistence and learning. Parents are also trained to actively participate in the educational process, both in family life and in the school. The intervention has proven to have a positive impact on both the children and their communities of reference. The program improves academic results, reduces school dropouts, and improves the social climate in the school.

(continued)

This is an action that not only reduces absenteeism among students, but also increases the involvement of parents in their children's school activities and in the learning process more widely. Due to its potential for community dynamization, it is usually implemented in underprivileged neighborhoods as a tool for social transformation

Table A.2 Some successful programs in the prevention of dropouts from compulsory education

Achievement for Latinos through Academic Success (ALAS)	It is an intervention for high school students that acts on the factors that influence school dropout. Each student is assigned a counselor or mentor who monitors attendance, behavior, and academic performance. The counselor makes suggestions, represents the students' interests, and coordinates with families and teachers. Students receive training in problem-solving skills, self-control, and assertiveness. Parents receive specialized training in solving problems with their children. They are also provided training on how to participate in school activities, how to communicate with teachers and school principals to address their children's needs. Therefore, it is an intervention that combines individualized counseling with behavioral training for the children and their parents. The program has been shown to be effective in reducing school dropouts
"The Effective Learning Program"	It is a program that follows the "schools within the school" model to adapt the educational context to children with special educational needs. Participants are referred to the program when they have low academic performance and have missed more than 15 days of class during the course. Students participate in 3 h of academic support, in classes with a significantly lower ratio than the school average. In this way they receive individualized attention and are trained in communication skills according to their personal profile. Teachers are in permanent contact with parents and academic advisors. In addition, they care about maintaining a positive climate in combination with high academic standards. Therefore, it is an intervention in which the monitoring of class attendance is reinforced with academic, organizational, and behavioral components

Principles of Effective Prevention

The programs we have reviewed are intended to improve academic performance and reverse the demotivation process that leads to school dropouts. They do this by providing personalized support to students and promoting positive school experiences. In this way they contribute to establishing a link between the student and the educational center that is more difficult to break. The development of positive relationships with peers and teachers can be complemented with the following specific suggestions:

- It is advisable to segment the population at risk of dropping out according to the profile of the students, carrying out specific interventions in each subgroup. In the most extreme cases, we find the set of individuals who do not like school, who have the poorest academic performance, and who are frequently absent. However, there is another group of students who struggle to overcome their academic problems and who maintain a comparatively higher frequency of school attendance. Logically, preventive measures have to be adapted differently for each group. In the first case, it may be necessary to adapt the goals and contents of educational activities, while in the second group, the introduction of incentives and the implementation of motivational strategies may be sufficient.
- Secondly, it is advisable to integrate the set of initiatives that are implemented to improve the school and its educational impact. It is frequent that in each school there are programs to reduce absenteeism, boost academic performance, guarantee the completion of studies, prepare for the development of a productive professional career, etc. Many of these results are interrelated, so it is necessary to adopt an overall vision and, consequently, an integrated management of the psychosocial programs implemented in each school.
- In this sense, processes at the meso-social level, which affect the whole school, have an impact on all students who share the same learning environment. Hence the importance of organizational factors and leadership in each educational center. For example, when there is a generalized environment of indiscipline, or a high percentage of students who misbehave, preventive actions at the individual level may find it very difficult to be effective.
- It is also useful to use available data to identify students who are at risk of dropping out of school as early as possible. Once identified, individualized programs are particularly effective. Academic support needs to be tailored to the personal learning environment. It is also useful for each student to have at least one adult reference who provides support and responds to his or her specific educational needs.
- Finally, structured training on social skills and behavior-based programs to improve classroom behavior are a timely complement to preventative measures. These programs should be student-centered and involve families as much as possible Fig. A.1.

Fig. A.1 A mother accompanies her children to school in a suburb of Lima, Peru. School is one of the few community resources in a peri-urban settlement without infrastructure. In these neighborhoods, schools are not only a learning context for children but also a fundamental place for the formation of relationships between neighbors, and contribute to community building. Photo: José Orihuela, Laboratory of Personal Networks and Communities®

Case Study: A Dropout Prevention Program Among High-Risk Youth in the Urban Context

Adolescents living in disadvantaged urban districts are prone to academic failure, absenteeism, and dropout[1]. As a rule, these are neighborhoods with a high prevalence of crime, drug abuse, unwanted pregnancies, and behavioral problems. These problems often function as risk factors in the interruption of compulsory education.

In the United States, the percentage of students who do not complete compulsory secondary education is more than 10%. As a result, this group has fewer job opportunities and a significantly lower earning capacity than their peers who complete compulsory education.

In Baltimore, a program was implemented in six high schools in the poorest neighborhoods, targeting students with a defined academic risk profile: repeaters, with below-average grades, and who missed more than 20 days of class in the last academic year. This list of characteristics was used to select the participants in the program. All those students who met at least two of these characteristics were admitted.

The FUTURES program is an intervention to prevent school dropouts among high-risk adolescents, which is implemented in secondary schools. The intervention

---

[1]The program description is based, with minor adaptations, on the article by Lever et al. (2004).

lasts for 4 or 5 years, so it accompanies students throughout their secondary education. Among other contents, it provides academic support, psychological care, and personal skills training. The tutors also work on academic motivation and provide career guidance sessions. The program provides specific actions to facilitate entry into secondary education and the transition to the job market.

Before entering high school, students who meet the risk profile participate in a summer course to facilitate the transition to secondary education. As an incentive, they receive a scholarship that compensates them for participating. In addition to receiving academic reinforcement classes, they participate in "life skills" training sessions and job preparation workshops. A psychologist is available throughout the summer to provide personalized attention if needed. He is also responsible for identifying which students will need intensive support when they start the school year.

During the course, at-risk students are assigned to classes with a lower ratio. They have a tutor who advises them in a personalized way. In the afternoons they receive supplementary sessions from teachers who are motivated to work with the "most difficult" students. Periodically, they meet with the psychologist to review their progress and make individual plans for personal development.

In recent years they have been participating in the highest ratio classes, although they continue to receive academic reinforcement sessions. The tutors accompany them throughout their academic life in the institute. In addition to monitoring class attendance, tutors have a role in providing academic guidance and social support if necessary. The tutors encourage them to continue their studies, offer advice, contact the families, and resolve any issues that arise. They dedicate a continuous effort both to encourage greater academic performance and to promote student participation in the school's extracurricular activities. When the last year approaches, they carry out work orientation activities, to facilitate the incorporation into the labor market at the end of the studies. This is one of the activities best valued by students.

Participants have access to clinical care and mental health services as part of the program. The most common activity is to provide counseling and personal advice. To evaluate the program, attendance and performance data were collected from participants and their peers. The psychologist measured their skills and subjective well-being at the beginning and end of each school year.

In the six schools where the FUTURES program was implemented, dropout rates remained 5–6% points below the Baltimore average during the years when the preventive intervention was implemented. One year after completing the program, 85% of the participants were either in an occupational training course or a job. In addition, high-risk students experienced improved psychological well-being throughout their participation in the program.

It is worth noting that such positive results were obtained with a group exposed to multiple social problems. In fact, the dropout rates of at-risk children were even below the rest of the students in the school. The intervention also had an impact on the transition to the labor market.

One of the most significant aspects of the intervention was the development of positive relationships with adults in the educational context. In practice, the tutors accompanied the program participants for 4 or 5 years, so they developed a relationship of trust and became a figure with prescriptive power over the children's behavior.

At the end of the program, the school board decided to repeat it with a new class of students starting the following year. As a novelty in the development of the intervention, they decided to establish an alliance with the local chamber of commerce. With this, they wanted to strengthen the component of labor preparation during the last year of secondary education. Employers can indicate what their labor needs are and thus guide the type of occupational training that students receive.

The importance of receiving training in job skills may seem paradoxical. On the one hand, it is necessary to prevent children from working before their time. However, in order to retain adolescents in school, it may be important to incorporate content that prepares them for their imminent entry into the job market.

The development of pre-employment skills is important for minors who perceive the need to work to help the family. Occupational training offers them an incentive to complete their compulsory studies, while slightly delaying their entry into the job market. Besides, when they join, they have already developed a series of skills that improve both their employability and expectations about their professional career (Fig. A.2).

Fig. A.2 Mothers accompany their children to celebrate "Mother's Day" at a school on the outskirts of Lima. In low-income districts, the participation of families plays a fundamental role in structuring the neighborhood and in keeping their children in school. A good relationship between the family and the school prevents early school abandonment. Photo: José Orihuela, Laboratory of Personal Networks and Communities®

Commentary on the Case

Tutors and mentors offer the possibility to act in a personalized and intensive way with children at risk. In this case we have seen a program that uses the figure of adult tutors to establish relationships of trust with the target population and act as positive role models. Although for parents and other external observers this type of program can be understood fundamentally as a supplementary academic support, as we have just shown, the intervention covers motivational factors, study techniques, development of competencies and, in general, the social-academic integration of the minors into the life of the educational center.

1. Describe the community's needs and resources prior to intervention.

    The intervention takes as a reference the poorest districts of Baltimore and justifies the need to intervene in (a) the characteristics of the context, (b) the prevalence of the problem and (c) the serious consequences associated with it:

    - In disadvantaged neighborhoods there is a high concentration of social problems that are antecedents to academic failure, absenteeism, and school dropout.
    - In the United States, the prevalence of the problem of dropping out of compulsory education is above 10%.
    - Finally, it is known that dropping out of school has a negative impact on job opportunities and average wages.

2. Identify the objectives and target population.

    The program aims to prevent dropouts among at-risk Baltimore high school students. In selecting participants, it was taken into account that during the previous school year they showed poor academic performance and frequent absences. To delimit the target population, a defined academic risk profile was established, based on (a) repeating a year, (b) having low grades and/or (c) skipping class regularly.

3. Describe the theoretical analysis on which the intervention is based, indicating where appropriate the theoretical models, evidence-based practices, functional analysis of the problem, good practices, or implicit assumptions of the program.

    The central elements of preventive action consist of (a) adapting educational conditions to the special needs of minors at high risk of dropping out of school, (b) promoting personal experiences that link minors to the educational context, and (c) facilitating the skills needed to cope with personal normative transitions.

    - First, the intervention reduces the ratio of classes in which participants are served and completes the training hours with extracurricular sessions of academic reinforcement. Tutors stimulate the motivation of the participants.
    - Second, the FUTURES program offers higher risk students the opportunity to develop positive personal experiences at school, strengthening the bond with peers and teachers. The tutors also offer personalized accompaniment and

develop a relationship of trust with the students they serve. Overall, a positive climate is promoted in the school.

- Third, participants receive life skills training before starting secondary school and job preparation training before entering the job market. Job readiness gives students a reason to complete their studies and allows them to anticipate the long-term consequences of everyday learning activities.

The summer course before starting high school allows two distinct groups to be distinguished: (a) students at higher risk, with whom personalized accompaniment is reinforced; and (b) students who are motivated but also at some risk of not completing their studies, with whom academic reinforcement could be sufficient to obtain the desired results.

Therefore, the program offers personalized attention, opportunities to develop positive experiences in school, and specialized training in the type of job skills in which adolescents are interested.

4. Identify the elements of community adjustment in the intervention.

All the changes introduced in the program are aimed at facilitating a personalized performance with high-risk minors. Therefore, this allows adapting the contents of the intervention to the specific needs of each participant.

The teachers who teach the academic reinforcement sessions were selected for their motivation to work with high-risk minors. This can also improve the program's appropriateness to the characteristics of the population.

The collaboration of the community environment with the school can be a decisive factor in the implementation of educational improvements. In particular, the involvement of families has a direct influence on reducing absenteeism and school dropout. Complementarily, service-learning strategies could be implemented so that children acquire a sense of community responsibility and develop skills that can be used in their professional careers in the future.

5. Describe the organizational context in which the program is implemented.

The six Baltimore high schools are the immediate organizational context in which the program is implemented. The educational centers are a privileged context to carry out prevention, since they allow to reach the whole population, including the groups of higher risk. As the program improves relationships with teachers and peers, participants feel more connected to their school and are less likely to drop out prematurely. Having highly cohesive schools, with a positive learning climate and clear behavioral norms, is critical to making dropout prevention programs work well.

The involvement of parents is used to create a pleasant atmosphere and learning environment while emphasizing the value of education and the importance of completing the academic grade. The organization of extracurricular activities and meetings with families also serve to create a more friendly environment.

6. Outline the action plan and sequence of activities in a structured manner.

The program has academic and behavioral components, with a special emphasis on the transitional stages, before and after compulsory secondary education:

- Academic reinforcement sessions are provided, and motivation is encouraged.
- Life skills training is provided, and a positive school climate is promoted.
- Personalized psychological care is provided.
- Students are prepared for entry into compulsory secondary education.
- Students are prepared for entry into the job market.

  Before entering high school, students receive specialized training to improve their ability to adapt to the new educational context. In addition, a part of the group is detected with which it is necessary to act more intensively.

  During high school, they receive personalized psychological counseling and support. Before leaving the institute, they receive job orientation and specific training to plan their professional career and manage adequately in the labor market.

  Therefore, it is a multi-component intervention, which affects several risk factors simultaneously. For the mentoring actions to work, it is essential that participants develop a relationship of trust with adults.

7. Summarize how the evaluation of the intervention was done.

Two types of data were used for the program evaluation. On the one hand, the indicators of attendance and academic performance that each educational center regularly generates. On the other hand, the psychometric evaluation of the participants in the program and the rest of their peers (non-participants) was carried out by the psychologist in the development of their usual clinical activity. Both allow the comparison of participants with a group outside the program and explore the possible impact of the intervention.

Although it is not an experimental design, the data provided interesting information about the results of the intervention. Specifically, it served to verify the improvements experienced by the participants both in the psychological and academic fields. It also showed the potential of the program to influence work aspects during the adult life of the participants.

8. Analyze the results of the intervention.

The evaluation provided three basic pieces of information about the results of the intervention:

- *Efficacy.* There was a reduction in the dropout rate among program participants, with a significantly greater improvement than for the school as a whole.

- *Effectiveness*. Participants in the program found jobs or accessed occupational training courses at a very high rate.
- *Effectiveness*. Program participants experienced an improvement in subjective psychological well-being throughout the intervention.

    It is a program with good indicators of efficacy and effectiveness, especially considering that it is a group of high-risk students. It should be noted that the dropout data was even below the school average.

9. Suggests improvements in the intervention from the experience of implementing the program.

    An alternative to adult mentors is the implementation of mentoring programs in which academic support is exchanged between peers. Mentoring students improves the community fit of the intervention, while contributing to the medium-term sustainability of the program. On the other hand, those who act as mentors can improve their self-esteem and personal skills, so they are indirect beneficiaries of the intervention.

    Second, there are programs that provide scholarships to low-income students. The use of economic incentives is particularly relevant to students from the most vulnerable families and could help reduce the risk of child labor. Also in this case, one way to increase the impact on retention in compulsory education could be to provide financial incentives to students.

10. Assess the sustainability of the intervention.

    The school board is committed to the continuity of the intervention and plans to strengthen the labor preparation component in the last year of secondary education. The duration of the program, which was extended by 4–5 years, is one of the strengths of the intervention. Not only is it a relevant factor in obtaining results, but it also contributes to the sustainability of the intervention. After the program has been implemented for several years there is some inertia for the intervention to continue developing with a new class of students (Fig. A.3).

- It is a program that provides personalized tutoring and accompaniment to children at high risk of dropping out of school.
- It is a multi-component intervention in which academic reinforcement is complemented by behavioral training and job preparation.
- The development of positive relationships with peers and with adults of reference in the school has a preventive value in itself.

Fig. A.3 A group of children participate in extracurricular activities in a school in the outskirts of Lima, Peru. The playful activities, with the involvement of the families, foster a sense of belonging to the school and reduce the risk of absenteeism and dropout. The development of a positive school climate has preventive value. Photo: José Orihuela, Laboratory of Personal Networks and Communities®

Bibliography

Fashola, O. S., & Slavin, R. E. (1997). Promising programs for elementary and middle schools: Evidence of effectiveness and replicability. *Journal of Education for Students Placed at Risk, 2*(3), 251–307.

Fashola, O. S., & Slavin, R. E. (1998). Effective dropout prevention and college attendance programs for students placed at risk. *Journal of Education for Students Placed at Risk, 3*(2), 159–183.

Freeman, J., & Simonsen, B. (2015). Examining the impact of policy and practice interventions on high school dropout and school completion rates: A systematic review of the literature. *Review of Educational Research, 85*(2), 205–248.

Lever, N., Sander, M. A., Lombardo, S., Randall, C., Axelrod, J., Rubenstein, M., & Weist, M. D. (2004). A drop-out prevention program for high-risk inner-city youth. *Behavior Modification, 28*(4), 513–527.

Annex B: Protection, Rehabilitation, and Reintegration of Street Children

Programs that recruit minors with street educators and develop personalized educational itineraries in residential contexts.

Several systematic reviews agree that there is insufficient evidence of the effectiveness of residential services for street children. Despite being the predominant intervention strategy with this group, rigorous evaluation of impact has been relatively rare, and programs sometimes define their objectives imprecisely. Nevertheless, assistance and housing needs can be used as an incentive to improve the coverage of educational activities, whether formal or focused on structured behavioral training. Likewise, street educators have a contrasting impact on improving the accessibility of this type of program. Therefore, residential units are necessary but not sufficient for the community reintegration of street children: to be effective they have to be used as a context that facilitates personal rehabilitation along with intensive psychological preparation to start a new life after leaving the center.

The term "street children" is often used to refer to children who have made the street their home or source of livelihood. This category overlaps in part with working children, children who have dropped out of school, or homeless children. However, not all street children work, not all have left school, and not all lack a reference home. Although there is a common element of living on the street without adult supervision, there is also great variability among the children who are assigned to this category, along with varying degrees of intensity in the personal disruption that living on the street brings (Lieten & Strehl, 2014). Children living in these conditions are generally more vulnerable to violence, sexual abuse, drug abuse, and involvement in criminal activities. They are also more often victims of labor exploitation or engage in subsistence activities that condition their personal development and future opportunities.

Both early detection and primary prevention strategies are particularly relevant in this area: as far as possible, it is important to avoid the serious psychological

© The Author(s), under exclusive license to Springer Nature Switzerland AG 2021
I. Maya Jariego, *Community Prevention of Child Labor*, Human Well-Being
Research and Policy Making, https://doi.org/10.1007/978-3-030-70810-8

Table B.1 Risk factors that lead minors to live on the street

- Low-income families
- Homelessness
- Family conflicts, abuse, and neglect
- Armed conflicts, natural disasters, and epidemics
- Alcohol and other drug abuse
- Urbanization and growth of marginal settlements

consequences associated with life on the streets. However, in this chapter we will focus on programs for the protection, rehabilitation, and reintegration of children who, to varying degrees, may already be living on the streets. Many of these programs are developed in shelters, while others are implemented directly on the street. They generally consist of educational, psychological support, and occupational training activities aimed at reintegrating them into the family, school, or community.

Risk and Protective Factors

Living on the streets normally entails the rupture of relationships, either temporary or definitive, with the family or with the community of reference. The incidence of this problem is greater in vulnerable families in disadvantaged neighborhoods. Among the factors that lead to this situation are family conflicts, child abuse, sexual abuse, and school abandonment. However, the conditions can be very variable. Sometimes children start to do some activity in the street to earn income to help the family. Other times the trigger is forced displacement or the loss of parents in armed conflict. It can also be linked to the abuse of alcohol and other drugs by parents, or to child exploitation by adults.

The combination of the above factors produces very diverse cases of street life, so it is advisable to take into consideration some of the key dimensions of inter-individual variability:

- While in some cases there has been a breakdown in family relationships, in other cases children spend discontinuous periods of their life in the family home. That is why it is important to distinguish between children who live on the street intermittently and those who live permanently.
- Similarly, UNICEF introduced a distinction between children *in the street* and children *of the street*. The former can work, beg, or socialize on the streets during the day, but go home at night, while the latter live and sleep on the streets. Children in the street maintain some relationship with the family, while children of the street have little or no contact with family members.

In the street, children are also more exposed to the influence of adults who take advantage of them or are exploited by organized crime groups. Many children earn their living through begging, drug dealing, theft, and prostitution. Sometimes they form street gangs or are instrumentalized by criminal groups to carry weapons, collect extortion money, or, in the most extreme cases, commit contract killings (Atkinson-Sheppard, 2016). The sexual exploitation of children by organized crime networks can also occur (Estes & Weiner, 2001).

The most significant risk factors are summarized in Table B.1. In contrast, this is a group of children who soon gain independence and see their maturation process accelerated, so that they can react assertively to opportunities for participation and in unique cases deploy their personal skills for community leadership. Both an adequate family climate and the educational level of the parents can act as protective factors. At the macro-social level, having a quality education system and adequate child protection services contribute in a general way to improving the quality of life of the child population.

Exemplary Programs

The two most frequent components in the strategies of community reinsertion of street children are residential resources and street educators. With younger children, interventions are often carried out that combine welfare services with educational activities aimed at school and family reintegration. With adolescents, occupational training and sexual education modules are also implemented. In this way, the aim is to facilitate social and labor insertion in the medium term and to prevent risk behaviors, unwanted pregnancies, and sexually transmitted diseases.

When used, residential programs have an immediate impact on housing needs. However, many times the challenge lies precisely in getting minors to agree to stay in temporary shelters or reception centers. That is why it is frequent to resort to street educators to improve accessibility. Subsequently, once the minors come into contact with the residential units, educational activities aimed at personal rehabilitation and community reintegration are implemented. Some residential interventions have been shown to be effective in reducing psychological stress, drug use and reintegration into their families. However, this is an area where there have been few rigorous evaluations of effectiveness and which requires more systematization (Watters & O'Callaghan, 2016).

Residential programs with good results are those that, along with housing, provide structured behavioral training or that combine welfare benefits with access to formal education and job placement workshops. They work best when they adopt a multidisciplinary approach, which meets the diverse needs of the minors, and when they provide for a more autonomous and demanding itinerary in the different phases of the rehabilitation process. The educational components, which train reading and writing skills, are more effective when the minors perceive that their survival needs are adequately covered by the program.

On the other hand, street educators play a decisive role in convincing the minors that their participation in existing programs can help them get out of poverty, solve their problems with drugs or prevent criminal behavior. The educators' job is to provide information and motivate children to use residential and educational services. They can also provide training. Educators are most effective in influencing children to leave the streets when they show empathy, establish a positive relationship, and take the time to make the children feel understood. Peer education has also been used for high-risk behavior related to HIV/AIDS transmission. This can be done with young people who were once street children and who have experienced a positive evolution, so they can serve as mentors or peer educators.

Table B.2 Some promising programs in the community reinsertion of street children

"Associãcao Promocional Oracão e Trabalho" (Association for the promotion of spirituality and work)	It is a residential program located in Campinas (Brazil), which carries out educational and professional training activities with street children. It has three shelters through which the minors pass along their personal rehabilitation itinerary. First of all, the "open house" is available for any child who wants to use accommodation, food or health care services. It works in direct coordination with the street educators to maximize the program's coverage. Second, the other two homes require the prior commitment of the children to the rehabilitation process and require them to give up drug use in order to participate. In each of these two shelters there is a group of professionals who train social skills and socio-emotional competencies. The program prepares for access to formal education and has achieved a family reintegration rate of over 50%
Casa Alianza (Covenant House)	*Casa Alianza* is a non-governmental organization that defends the rights of street children in Central America and provides rehabilitation services to the collective. The community reintegration program starts by contacting the parents (or guardians) and identifying a support network in the community. The intervention is focused on the families, with whom the educators meet periodically. In addition to providing them with advice and guidance, the conditions for possible reunification are studied. It is important to ensure that children are well cared for and to reduce the risk of relapse as much as possible. Families receive material support for participating in the program and support groups are organized with the participation of parents. There are also specific activities for minors who have practiced prostitution or are mothers, as well as for minors with drug problems. The family reintegration rate is above 80%

A special case in the implementation of this type of program is that of unaccompanied minors. These are children who migrate without the company of an adult and, consequently, are in a situation of high vulnerability. They may also be separated from their parents as a result of armed conflict or natural disasters. Many of them are street children before or after displacement. In the case of foreign unaccompanied minors (UNAM), they are often placed in residential centers, where they receive education and specialized psychological care. Along with the need to adapt services to the cultural characteristics of the population, one of the main difficulties is in locating family members (Evans etal., 2018).

When family reintegration is not possible, there is a high risk of community integration problems at the end of their stay in the center for minors. Cases have been documented where the problems of living on the street or forming criminal gangs arise precisely at the end of the child protection services these minors have been receiving. Therefore, it has been recommended to integrate the residential units into community coalitions that provide for the follow-up of cases once the minors have finished their involvement with the assistance services. A key element is to make educational interventions compatible with the personal projects and motivations of the minors (Table B.2).

Don Bosco City The Salesian priests have a residence for children under 18 years of age, which offers accommodation and educational opportunities for street children in Medellín (Colombia). Access to the program is through the recruitment activities of the street educators, who encourage the minors to spend the night in the shelter.

Once the children enter the shelter, in order to obtain room and board, they participate in educational activities focused, among other aspects, on building self-esteem, training in social skills, and workshops to prevent disruptive behavior. In a second phase, when their presence in the center has been consolidated, they resume schooling at the primary or secondary school level. In the case of adolescents, they also receive social and occupational training.

All participants receive medical and psychological care, and in each case a personalized reintegration plan is prepared. The program has wide coverage, with several hundred students in each school year, and has shown positive impact indicators with high academic graduation rates. Therefore, it can be stated that it is very effective in terms of school reinsertion.

[Colombia]

Principles of Effective Prevention

From the above review, we can deduce some of the characteristics of programs that are effective with street children. Among other ingredients with which to improve the life opportunities of children, we can mention the following:

- Every time a child of the street stays in a shelter or uses the care services of an assistance center, an opportunity is opened to deploy the educational components of rehabilitation programs. This is why the staff of such devices must have specialized training to involve and train the minors who come into contact with the residential units. In addition to being motivated staff, they must be properly trained professionals. The fact that the staff working in some residences for street children have no specialized training has sometimes been criticized. To participate in this type of rehabilitation and social reintegration programs, it may be useful to have specialized training to work with the child population, have good communication skills or even have some knowledge about psychological processes and the stages of personal development.
- Accommodation is necessary, but not sufficient. Rehabilitation programs are effective when they focus on reintegration into the family and school, while preparing for access to the labor market when they are at the minimum age required. As we have noted, residential services can be managed as an incentive to provide the education or training that juveniles need.

Fig. B.1 Two children play with garbage bags and plastic containers on the streets of Barranquilla, Colombia. Forced internal displacement is one of the antecedents of the existence of street children in Colombia. When they lose contact with their parents, children are more vulnerable and may end up working in agriculture or domestic service, or even being victims of human trafficking. Photo: Laboratory of Personal Networks and Communities®

- In fact, the mere provision of accommodation can break the incentive for behavior change, as children can have their needs met without having to leave the streets. It is important to examine the impact that care services have on minors and on their possibilities of rehabilitation to get off the streets.
- The participation of children and families improves the functioning of the program. Not surprisingly, children have life experiences that can be an asset to the intervention, while strengthening families and the community can make it easier for them to take charge of the children's needs.
- Programs targeting this population need to be flexible, providing proximity services, tailored to individual needs. Customized rehabilitation programs have been shown to work more effectively. The program has to be adapted to each local context and to the peculiarities of the population in each case.
- Finally, as elements of community preparedness, cooperation between institutions, comprehensive service planning, and community development initiatives, along with community awareness and child rights advocacy, are relevant. More generic policies, such as the availability of quality childcare or the existence of aids for the care of young children, together with policies for the promotion of affordable housing, have an impact on the problem in question Fig. B.1.

Case Study: A Therapeutic Community for the Rehabilitation of Children and Adolescents in Lima (Peru)

The *Instituto Mundo Libre* (IML) was started as a program for high-risk children living on the streets of Lima who had problems with drug use[2]. In the district of Pachacámac it has a residential unit where "preventive programs of psychoactive substance abuse" are applied to minors. Training is also provided to parents and community leaders in psychosocial rehabilitation. In addition, street educators regularly visit the different settlements located in the area of influence and work with the children living on the streets.

The district of Pachacámac has been formed by settlements in the south of Lima, with a marked predominance of self-built houses and little urban infrastructure. Many houses are located on steep slopes and spaces not suitable for habitation. A large part of the district is occupied by low-income families.

In surveys of the population, neighbors are concerned about violence and public safety problems. Petty theft, drug sales, street gangs, land invasions, and family violence are frequent. A part of the child population spends most of its time in the streets. Some children have dropped out of school and beg or do small jobs on the street to earn an income for the family. Instead of compulsory schooling, they spend their time with other children their age, with whom they have learned basic survival skills. Some of them are also looking to find money for their expenses on tobacco, alcohol and nights out.

The *Casa Hogar* functions as a referral center for the children in the area, where they cover their immediate needs: "At first, the children come to us for food, clothing, or temporary shelter. This first contact serves to provide medical and psychological care, and to inform the children about the opportunities for training and psychosocial rehabilitation offered by the center". Over time, the *Casa Hogar* has also become a place where street children seek refuge and protection, when they are persecuted by their parents, other minors, drug dealers or the police.

Secondly, the *Casa Hogar* functions as a semi-open therapeutic community for minors, where users enter voluntarily to initiate a process of behavior change. The purpose of the program combines both risk criteria, so that it is aimed specifically at "rehabilitating and training abandoned street children and adolescents who are habitual consumers of psychoactive substances". The actions also include the rehabilitation of drug addictions with family and community reinsertion.

Once their food and shelter needs are met, program facilitators work intensively with the children to develop the skills necessary for their social reintegration. To this end, they conduct training sessions individually and in groups. The children are also incorporated into formal education at the appropriate level.

While at the center, the minors attend primary or secondary school classes, participate in sports activities, take part in training workshops, and receive individualized psychological counseling. Throughout their stay, they are always accompanied by adults who try to develop a relationship of trust with the children in the

---

[2]The program description is based, with minor adaptations, on the article by Harris et al. (2011).

program. The institution offers a context that allows you to isolate yourself from the outside and focus on training, learning and personal rehabilitation.

The therapeutic community is a drug-free residential unit in which users go through different stages in the rehabilitation process, as they gain personal autonomy. Training is intensive. In the psychosocial workshops, participants receive specific training on personal hygiene, self-esteem, health education, and balanced personal development. Educators explain the long-term consequences of living on the streets, how to build positive interpersonal relationships, and the importance of early cessation of psychoactive substance use and involvement in criminal activities. Individual sessions are usually combined with group sessions. Residential staff use religion to teach "life lessons".

The program follows four successive stages, with the ultimate goal of integration into the community with an independent lifestyle:

1. The first months begin with the activity of the street educators who contact the street children in their usual contexts of interaction, provide them with information about the home and encourage them to participate in the program. This phase provides a basic orientation to the potential users and, besides expanding the coverage, is very important for the good use of the program.
2. Once they join the center, there is a first stage in which the minors adapt to life in the residence and go through the detoxification process. It consists of overcoming the physical addiction, breaking up the dependence on the drugs or any substances they used before entering the program. It is essential to pass this phase so that they can then focus on more ambitious goals. As a consequence, participants increase their confidence in the ability to achieve behavior change. Then, over the course of a year, the children participate in behavioral-based sessions to develop skills and promote positive values. They are usually done in a small group. These activities are implemented by psychologists who use a guide to monitor personal development, compliance, and interpersonal skills. Social skills training is one of the activities with the best results.
3. When conditions are right, educators work with the families of the children and prepare them for family reintegration, whenever possible. Although they give special importance to the development of adequate intra-family communication skills, it is also necessary to identify in each case what are the problems that led to their children living on the streets, and to face them specifically. Alternatives are sought when there is a history of child abuse or when parents abuse alcohol and other drugs.
4. Once their stay in the *Casa Hogar* is over, the children and their families are followed on a monthly basis for 1 year. It is checked that the children attend school regularly and that they remain drug-free. Relapses or recidivism are a permanent threat in rehabilitation programs. The climate and coexistence in the family group are also monitored.

While the rehabilitation program was being consolidated, the IML established partnerships with social services, police, and juvenile courts in surrounding districts for the referral of street children with drug abuse problems. Although these types of

Fig. B.2 Empty classroom in a school in Barranquilla, Colombia. Reintegration into academic life is a particularly complex challenge for street children. It is common for adaptation problems to occur, to remain isolated or to come into conflict with other students. For this reason, specialized programs with intensive training have been used. Photo: Laboratory of Personal Networks and Communities®

alliances were mainly carried out to expand coverage, they have also slightly diversified the psychosocial profile of program participants.

Many children who only stay for a short time to use the center's services usually live in the residence with a comparatively small group that participates in the long-term rehabilitation program. Of the latter, 48% successfully entered the community upon leaving home. This group, in turn, is almost equally divided between those who returned to their families and those who began a period of independent living. The likelihood of community reintegration was significantly higher among those who made longer stays in the residence. In contrast, juveniles who had been referred to the program from a correctional facility were less likely to succeed.

The success of the program led to the location of other similar residential units in other areas of Lima and Peru. The IML has incorporated innovations to meet the needs of girls. Some exclusively female residences have been launched. The *Instituto* also develops activities so that children who have completed their treatment program maintain some type of contact with the *Casa Hogar,* so that they serve as a model and encouragement for other minors. Having positive role models improves perceived self-efficacy among children undergoing rehabilitation (Fig. B.2).

Commentary on the Case

Interveners who take a strong community-based approach often maintain some misgivings about residential programs. Some of the earliest community intervention initiatives emerged precisely as a reaction to psychiatric hospitalization, promoting the re-entry of patients into standardized community settings. As part of the deinstitutionalization movement, residential units were attributed a number of iatrogenic effects, which were counterproductive to the rehabilitation process of people with mental problems. Among other possible consequences, institutional settings often generate dependency relationships, so that they interfere with the autonomous functioning of individuals when faced with independent living situations. There are also a number of studies with elderly people, psychiatric patients and refugees in which community-based alternatives show a more positive impact on psychological well-being and quality of life than residential care facilities.

This same type of effect has been observed with institutionalized children (Lieten & Strehl, 2014). However, on occasion, as we have illustrated with the case of IML, residential units can function as a safe space in which children develop the skills to resume community life. These are temporary stays, under controlled training conditions, in which a combination of formal education and individualized accompaniment can facilitate family reintegration.

In these cases, the residential units are used, paradoxically, as instruments of community integration.

1. Describe the community's needs and resources prior to intervention.

   The existence of street gangs is one of the problems perceived by the residents of Pachacámac. The residents of the district associate street children with the problems of citizen insecurity, petty theft, and drug trafficking. From the point of view of the neighbors, it is therefore a problem that must be faced for the benefit of the community. This can be the trigger for a psychosocial intervention.

   Although not explicitly mentioned in the case, it can be expected that street children in the periphery of Lima suffer from the same type of problems that have been identified in similar groups in Latin America, such as school dropout, low educational level, poorly developed social-emotional skills and low self-esteem. This is a high-risk group with a high incidence of sexually transmitted diseases, unwanted pregnancies, and drug abuse. They are also exposed to violence on the streets and exploitation by adults.

2. Identify the objectives and target population.

   The purpose of the program is to "rehabilitate and train street children and adolescents in a state of abandonment who are habitual consumers of psychoactive substances". The target population is children on the street who have problems with drugs, especially in the periphery of Lima. One of the singularities of this intervention is in combining the rehabilitation of drug dependencies with the community reinsertion of minors living on the street. Detoxification and personal training take place in a protected residential environment, from which tertiary prevention strategies are implemented. Overcoming dependence on psychoactive substances is a step prior to psychosocial rehabilitation, and this in turn is a step prior to academic, family and community reintegration.

3. Describe the theoretical analysis on which the intervention is based, indicating where appropriate the theoretical models, evidence-based practices, functional analysis of the problem, good practices, or implicit assumptions of the program.

The program uses evidence-based practices for the treatment of drug abuse. Therapeutic communities provide a residential environment for voluntary behavior change, with elements of self-help and social learning. In addition, the intervention context facilitates the establishment of clear norms of behavior and intensive intervention in the rehabilitation process. Program psychologists work with each user to motivate behavior change and develop an individualized treatment to maintain abstinence.

On the other hand, in the context of providing care services, the community reintegration component is based on compulsory education and structured training of personal skills. The intervention is developed for a sufficient time to consolidate the behavioral changes, both in the consumption of psychoactive substances and in the reorganization of personal time. In the case of the IML, it seems that the effectiveness observed is also partly attributable to the preparation, training, and follow-up activities with the families. Family reintegration is a complex process, in which the mistreatment or abuse circumstances that caused the problems may recur, or where there may be relapses due to abandonment of the home.

Residential settings appear to provide a safe environment in which to resume compulsory education under controlled circumstances, offering stability to participants. The residence offers a parenthesis between life on the street and normalized incorporation into the community, in which individuals can focus on their psychological recovery and learning the skills that allow them to integrate socially.

4. Identify the elements of community adjustment in the intervention.

The accessibility of the program is based on (a) the location of the center in one of the disadvantaged settlements on the outskirts of Lima, (b) the participation of street educators, and (c) the semi-open nature of the therapeutic community. It is therefore a center of proximity, which reduces access barriers and adapts the program to the characteristics of the target population.

In the intervention with street children, shelters and semi-open shelters have been subject to controversy. On the one hand, they encourage greater coverage of the program by eliminating access requirements. However, they also make it easier for minors to access welfare services without having to leave the streets. In the case of the MFI, they are asked, prior to entering the program, to make an explicit commitment to behavior change and a desire to leave drugs and return to the community.

5. Describe the organizational context in which the program is implemented.

The IML is a non-profit association that has been financed by international cooperation projects and donations from private companies. Since its foundation in 1984, it has established institutional contacts with the United Nations, the

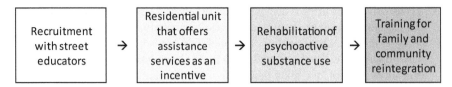

Fig. B.3 A strategic sequence of the therapeutic community

Peruvian government, and the Pan American Health Organization. The Lima home has psychologists, educators, and social workers. It is a consolidated organization, with solid alliances and with sufficient resources for the development of effective interventions.

The center also relies on the participation of volunteers who collaborate with the educators, with occupational workshops and literacy courses. They are also particularly active in organizing sports and recreational activities. It offers volunteers the opportunity to learn about the problems of the most disadvantaged groups, contributing to community awareness. It puts minors in contact with members of the community, which allows them to develop skills for life in the community.

6. Outline the action plan and sequence of activities in a structured manner.

The therapeutic community of Pachacámac simultaneously develops several actions of psychosocial rehabilitation with the children of higher risk:

- It is a residential facility that provides assistance services such as housing, food, and basic health care.
- It has street educators who provide information, carry out educational activities and carry out the recruitment of minors living on the streets in the settlements on the outskirts of Lima.
- It provides training courses to parents, guardians, and community leaders in the area. In this way, they acquire knowledge about psychosocial rehabilitation strategies and can collaborate in preventive activities.
- The therapeutic community promotes the inhabitation and rehabilitation of psychoactive substance use.
- Children are also trained (individually and in groups) to reintegrate into their families and return to the community.
- One of the actions best valued by the adolescents is the pre-labor courses, to facilitate their subsequent incorporation into the labor market.

The central component of the rehabilitation/reinsertion program is the training sessions that the minors receive. As a preparatory action, it is expected that the first step will be to get rid of the psychoactive substances. The assistance services of the "Casa Hogar" work as an incentive for participation in the program, while the street educators act as intermediaries to improve the coverage of the intervention with a high-risk group and difficult to access. We have illustrated the intervention logic model in Fig. B.3.

7. Summarize how the evaluation of the intervention was done.

   The impact of programs with street children has rarely been evaluated. The case of the IML is an exception, since (a) a continuous psychological and educational monitoring of the participation of the minors in the program was carried out, (b) the impact of the program on the family and community reinsertion of the minors was quantitatively evaluated, and (c) the children were followed up when they were already reintegrated into their family or some form of independent living. To complete the evaluation, a discriminating analysis of the predictors of social and community reinsertion was carried out. The program also has data on coverage and implementation of activities.

   In evaluating these types of programs, indicators of detoxification, rehabilitation and reintegration could be taken into consideration, as different but related processes. It is important to know what competencies the minors have developed throughout their participation in the program. It is also necessary to assess how the situation evolves when they have rejoined family life.

8. Analyze the results of the intervention.

   Residential programs tend to have poor results in terms of reintegration, on the few occasions in which they have been systematically evaluated. In the case of IML, however, almost half of the users were effectively reintegrated into the community upon leaving the residence. Although we do not have many elements of comparison, it seems a fairly positive result in a high-risk group, with multiple associated problems.

   On the other hand, along with the impact of the community reintegration measures, the participants regularly attended classes corresponding to their level of compulsory schooling and participated in psychosocial workshops, where they had the opportunity to develop their socio-emotional skills. Both the level of education achieved and the development of personal skills are results that can be associated with participation in the program.

   Ensuring compulsory schooling, as well as removing children from work activities while they are at home, are two outcomes that in themselves are of great value when it comes to working children. In this case, through rehabilitative actions, it is a question of going in the opposite direction to school dropout, which always carries a risk of relapse and recidivism.

9. Suggests improvements in the intervention from the experience of implementing the program.

   It may be of interest to design specific rehabilitation and reintegration itineraries for children who, before living on the streets, were subjected to situations of child abuse, sexual abuse, or violence by parents and other significant adults. This is a group with special needs, in which not only is family reintegration complex (or sometimes simply impossible) but independent living becomes a challenge in itself. On the other hand, as some of these children have been victims of criminal groups and organized crime networks, it may be necessary to design guidelines for comprehensive intervention, with police actions or collaboration with the judicial system.

10. Assess the sustainability of the intervention.

Fig. B.4 Two minors accompany an adult during the workday in Barranquilla, Colombia. For street children, the most common activities to earn income are selling water, juice and sweets, cleaning cars or doing shoeshine. Many of them belong to families displaced by political violence. Photo: Laboratory of Personal Networks and Communities®

The IML home is a consolidated service, with a long history, so we can expect its continuity in the medium term. Both drug abuse rehabilitation and family reintegration are unstable achievements, in which relapses are frequent. It is important to be vigilant in the follow-up of the participants, when they have left the residence, to prevent them from ending up abandoned again on the street.

However, both personal skills and contact with preventive services are protective resources that can contribute to the maintenance of the results. It would be of interest to evaluate in this type of services what is the time necessary to be effective in the rehabilitation process. The recovery process can take several years, when children have experienced serious personal difficulties.

- Although residential services have little evidence of effectiveness, this case illustrates that there are promising experiences, where welfare benefits can serve as an incentive for children to access compulsory education and prepare for community reintegration (Fig. B.4).
- The temporary withdrawal of children from the streets reduces, at least temporarily, the risks to which they are exposed when they live without the protection of trusted adults.

(continued)

- The preparation of families to receive the minors reduces the risk of relapses.
- The isolation characteristic of therapeutic communities during the detoxification process becomes an opportunity to intervene intensively with the children and prepare them to reintegrate into the community.

Bibliography

Atkinson-Sheppard, S. (2016). The gangs of Bangladesh: Exploring organized crime, street gangs and 'illicit child labourers' in Dhaka. *Criminology & Criminal Justice, 16*(2), 233-249.

Watters, C., & O'Callaghan, P. (2016). Mental health and psychosocial interventions for children and adolescents in street situations in low-and middle-income countries: A systematic review. *Child Abuse & Neglect, 60*, 18-26.

Berckmans, I., Velasco, M. L., Tapia, B. P., & Loots, G. (2012). A systematic review: A quest for effective interventions for children and adolescents in street situation. *Children and Youth Services Review, 34*(7), 1259-1272.

Estes, R. J., & Weiner, N. A. (2001). *The commercial sexual exploitation of children in the US, Canada and Mexico*. Philadelphia: University of Pennsylvania, School of Social Work, Center for the Study of Youth Policy.

Evans, K., Diebold, K., & Calvo, R. (2018). A call to action: Re-imagining social work practice with unaccompanied minors. *Advances in Social Work, 18*(3), 788-807.

Harris, M. S., Johnson, K., Young, L., & Edwards, J. (2011). Community reinsertion success of street children programs in Brazil and Peru. *Children and Youth Services Review, 33*(5), 723-731.

Lieten, G. K., & Strehl, T. (2014). *Child Street Life: an inside view of hazards and expectations of street children in Peru*. New York: Springer.

Volpi, E. (2002). *Street children: Promising practices and approaches. WBI Working Papers*. Washington, World Bank.

Annex C: C182 Worst Forms of Child Labor Convention, 1999. Convention concerning the Prohibition and Immediate Action for the Elimination of the Worst Forms of Child Labor

The *General Conference of the International Labour Organization,*

- Having been convened at Geneva by the Governing Body of the International Labour Office, and having met in its 87th Session on 1 June 1999, and
- Considering the need to adopt new instruments for the prohibition and elimination of the worst forms of child labour, as the main priority for national and international action, including international cooperation and assistance, to complement the Convention and the Recommendation concerning Minimum Age for Admission to Employment, 1973, which remain fundamental instruments on child labour, and
- Considering that the effective elimination of the worst forms of child labour requires immediate and comprehensive action, taking into account the importance of free basic education and the need to remove the children concerned from all such work and to provide for their rehabilitation and social integration while addressing the needs of their families, and
- Recalling the resolution concerning the elimination of child labour adopted by the International Labour Conference at its 83rd Session in 1996, and
- Recognizing that child labour is to a great extent caused by poverty and that the long-term solution lies in sustained economic growth leading to social progress, in particular poverty alleviation and universal education, and
- Recalling the Convention on the Rights of the Child adopted by the United Nations General Assembly on 20 November 1989, and
- Recalling the ILO Declaration on Fundamental Principles and Rights at Work and its Follow-up, adopted by the International Labour Conference at its 86th Session in 1998, and
- Recalling that some of the worst forms of child labour are covered by other international instruments, in particular the Forced Labour Convention, 1930, and the United Nations Supplementary Convention on the Abolition of Slavery, the Slave Trade, and Institutions and Practices Similar to Slavery, 1956, and

© The Author(s), under exclusive license to Springer Nature Switzerland AG 2021
I. Maya Jariego, *Community Prevention of Child Labor*, Human Well-Being
Research and Policy Making, https://doi.org/10.1007/978-3-030-70810-8

- Having decided upon the adoption of certain proposals with regard to child labour, which is the fourth item on the agenda of the session, and
- Having determined that these proposals shall take the form of an international Convention;

ADOPTS this seventeenth day of June of the year one thousand nine hundred and ninety-nine the following Convention, which may be cited as the Worst Forms of Child Labour Convention, 1999.

Article 1. Each Member which ratifies this Convention shall take immediate and effective measures to secure the prohibition and elimination of the worst forms of child labour as a matter of urgency.

Article 2. For the purposes of this Convention, the term child shall apply to all persons under the age of 18.

Article 3. For the purposes of this Convention, the term the worst forms of child labour comprises:

(a) All forms of slavery or practices similar to slavery, such as the sale and trafficking of children, debt bondage and serfdom and forced or compulsory labour, including forced or compulsory recruitment of children for use in armed conflict;
(b) The use, procuring or offering of a child for prostitution, for the production of pornography or for pornographic performances;
(c) The use, procuring or offering of a child for illicit activities, in particular for the production and trafficking of drugs as defined in the relevant international treaties;
(d) Work which, by its nature or the circumstances in which it is carried out, is likely to harm the health, safety or morals of children.

Article 4

1. The types of work referred to under Article 3(d) shall be determined by national laws or regulations or by the competent authority, after consultation with the organizations of employers and workers concerned, taking into consideration relevant international standards, in particular Paragraphs 3 and 4 of the Worst Forms of Child Labour Recommendation, 1999.
2. The competent authority, after consultation with the organizations of employers and workers concerned, shall identify where the types of work so determined exist.
3. The list of the types of work determined under paragraph 1 of this Article shall be periodically examined and revised as necessary, in consultation with the organizations of employers and workers concerned.

Article 5. Each Member shall, after consultation with employers' and workers' organizations, establish or designate appropriate mechanisms to monitor the implementation of the provisions giving effect to this Convention.

Article 6

1. Each Member shall design and implement programmes of action to eliminate as a priority the worst forms of child labour.
2. Such programmes of action shall be designed and implemented in consultation with relevant government institutions and employers' and workers' organizations, taking into consideration the views of other concerned groups as appropriate.

Article 7

1. Each Member shall take all necessary measures to ensure the effective implementation and enforcement of the provisions giving effect to this Convention including the provision and application of penal sanctions or, as appropriate, other sanctions.
2. Each Member shall, taking into account the importance of education in eliminating child labour, take effective and time-bound measures to:

   (a) Prevent the engagement of children in the worst forms of child labour;
   (b) Provide the necessary and appropriate direct assistance for the removal of children from the worst forms of child labour and for their rehabilitation and social integration;
   (c) Ensure access to free basic education, and, wherever possible and appropriate, vocational training, for all children removed from the worst forms of child labour;
   (d) Identify and reach out to children at special risk; and
   (e) Take account of the special situation of girls.

3. Each Member shall designate the competent authority responsible for the implementation of the provisions giving effect to this Convention.

Article 8. Members shall take appropriate steps to assist one another in giving effect to the provisions of this Convention through enhanced international cooperation and/or assistance including support for social and economic development, poverty eradication programmes and universal education.

Article 9. The formal ratifications of this Convention shall be communicated to the Director-General of the International Labour Office for registration.

Article 10

1. This Convention shall be binding only upon those Members of the International Labour Organization whose ratifications have been registered with the Director-General of the International Labour Office.
2. It shall come into force 12 months after the date on which the ratifications of two Members have been registered with the Director-General.
3. Thereafter, this Convention shall come into force for any Member 12 months after the date on which its ratification has been registered.

Article 11

1. A Member which has ratified this Convention may denounce it after the expiration of 10 years from the date on which the Convention first comes into force, by an act communicated to the Director-General of the International Labour Office for registration. Such denunciation shall not take effect until 1 year after the date on which it is registered.
2. Each Member which has ratified this Convention and which does not, within the year following the expiration of the period of 10 years mentioned in the preceding paragraph, exercise the right of denunciation provided for in this Article, will be bound for another period of 10 years and, thereafter, may denounce this Convention at the expiration of each period of 10 years under the terms provided for in this Article.

Article 12

1. The Director-General of the International Labour Office shall notify all Members of the International Labour Organization of the registration of all ratifications and acts of denunciation communicated by the Members of the Organization.
2. When notifying the Members of the Organization of the registration of the second ratification, the Director-General shall draw the attention of the Members of the Organization to the date upon which the Convention shall come into force.

Article 13. The Director-General of the International Labour Office shall communicate to the Secretary- General of the United Nations, for registration in accordance with article 102 of the Charter of the United Nations, full particulars of all ratifications and acts of denunciation registered by the Director-General in accordance with the provisions of the preceding Articles.

Article 14. At such times as it may consider necessary, the Governing Body of the International Labour Office shall present to the General Conference a report on the working of this Convention and shall examine the desirability of placing on the agenda of the Conference the question of its revision in whole or in part.

Article 15

1. Should the Conference adopt a new Convention revising this Convention in whole or in part, then, unless the new Convention otherwise provides—

    (a) The ratification by a Member of the new revising Convention shall ipso jure involve the immediate denunciation of this Convention, notwithstanding the provisions of Article 11 above, if and when the new revising Convention shall have come into force;
    (b) As from the date when the new revising Convention comes into force, this Convention shall cease to be open to ratification by the Members.

2. This Convention shall in any case remain in force in its actual form and content for those Members which have ratified it but have not ratified the revising Convention.

Article 16. The English and French versions of the text of this Convention are equally authoritative.

Annex D: C138—Minimum Age Convention, 1973

The *General Conference of the International Labour Organization,*

- Having been convened at Geneva by the Governing Body of the International Labour Office, and having met in its Fifty-eighth Session on 6 June 1973, and
- Having decided upon the adoption of certain proposals with regard to minimum age for admission to employment, which is the fourth item on the agenda of the session, and
- Noting the terms of the Minimum Age (Industry) Convention, 1919, the Minimum Age (Sea) Convention, 1920, the Minimum Age (Agriculture) Convention, 1921, the Minimum Age (Trimmers and Stokers) Convention, 1921, the Minimum Age (Non-Industrial Employment) Convention, 1932, the Minimum Age (Sea) Convention (Revised), 1936, the Minimum Age (Industry) Convention (Revised), 1937, the Minimum Age (Non-Industrial Employment) Convention (Revised), 1937, the Minimum Age (Fishermen) Convention, 1959, and the Minimum Age (Underground Work) Convention, 1965, and
- Considering that the time has come to establish a general instrument on the subject, which would gradually replace the existing ones applicable to limited economic sectors, with a view to achieving the total abolition of child labour, and
- Having determined that these proposals shall take the form of an international Convention,

ADOPTS this twenty-sixth day of June of the year one thousand nine hundred and seventy-three the following Convention, which may be cited as the Minimum Age Convention, 1973:

Article 1. Each Member for which this Convention is in force undertakes to pursue a national policy designed to ensure the effective abolition of child labour and to raise progressively the minimum age for admission to employment or work to a level consistent with the fullest physical and mental development of young persons.

© The Author(s), under exclusive license to Springer Nature Switzerland AG 2021   185
I. Maya Jariego, *Community Prevention of Child Labor*, Human Well-Being
Research and Policy Making, https://doi.org/10.1007/978-3-030-70810-8

Article 2

1. Each Member which ratifies this Convention shall specify, in a declaration appended to its ratification, a minimum age for admission to employment or work within its territory and on means of transport registered in its territory; subject to Articles 4 to 8 of this Convention, no one under that age shall be admitted to employment or work in any occupation.
2. Each Member which has ratified this Convention may subsequently notify the Director-General of the International Labour Office, by further declarations, that it specifies a minimum age higher than that previously specified.
3. The minimum age specified in pursuance of paragraph 1 of this Article shall not be less than the age of completion of compulsory schooling and, in any case, shall not be less than 15 years.
4. Notwithstanding the provisions of paragraph 3 of this Article, a Member whose economy and educational facilities are insufficiently developed may, after consultation with the organisations of employers and workers concerned, where such exist, initially specify a minimum age of 14 years.
5. Each Member which has specified a minimum age of 14 years in pursuance of the provisions of the preceding paragraph shall include in its reports on the application of this Convention submitted under article 22 of the Constitution of the International Labour Organisation a statement—

    (a) That its reason for doing so subsists; or
    (b) That it renounces its right to avail itself of the provisions in question as from a stated date.

Article 3

1. The minimum age for admission to any type of employment or work which by its nature or the circumstances in which it is carried out is likely to jeopardise the health, safety or morals of young persons shall not be less than 18 years.
2. The types of employment or work to which paragraph 1 of this Article applies shall be determined by national laws or regulations or by the competent authority, after consultation with the organisations of employers and workers concerned, where such exist.
3. Notwithstanding the provisions of paragraph 1 of this Article, national laws or regulations or the competent authority may, after consultation with the organisations of employers and workers concerned, where such exist, authorise employment or work as from the age of 16 years on condition that the health, safety and morals of the young persons concerned are fully protected and that the young persons have received adequate specific instruction or vocational training in the relevant branch of activity.

Article 4

1. In so far as necessary, the competent authority, after consultation with the organisations of employers and workers concerned, where such exist, may exclude from the application of this Convention limited categories of

employment or work in respect of which special and substantial problems of application arise.

2. Each Member which ratifies this Convention shall list in its first report on the application of the Convention submitted under article 22 of the Constitution of the International Labour Organisation any categories which may have been excluded in pursuance of paragraph 1 of this Article, giving the reasons for such exclusion, and shall state in subsequent reports the position of its law and practice in respect of the categories excluded and the extent to which effect has been given or is proposed to be given to the Convention in respect of such categories.

3. Employment or work covered by Article 3 of this Convention shall not be excluded from the application of the Convention in pursuance of this Article.

Article 5

1. A Member whose economy and administrative facilities are insufficiently developed may, after consultation with the organisations of employers and workers concerned, where such exist, initially limit the scope of application of this Convention.

2. Each Member which avails itself of the provisions of paragraph 1 of this Article shall specify, in a declaration appended to its ratification, the branches of economic activity or types of undertakings to which it will apply the provisions of the Convention.

3. The provisions of the Convention shall be applicable as a minimum to the following: mining and quarrying; manufacturing; construction; electricity, gas and water; sanitary services; transport, storage and communication; and plantations and other agricultural undertakings mainly producing for commercial purposes, but excluding family and small-scale holdings producing for local consumption and not regularly employing hired workers.

4. Any Member which has limited the scope of application of this Convention in pursuance of this Article—

    (a) Shall indicate in its reports under Article 22 of the Constitution of the International Labour Organisation the general position as regards the employment or work of young persons and children in the branches of activity which are excluded from the scope of application of this Convention and any progress which may have been made towards wider application of the provisions of the Convention;

    (b) May at any time formally extend the scope of application by a declaration addressed to the Director-General of the International Labour Office.

Article 6. This Convention does not apply to work done by children and young persons in schools for general, vocational or technical education or in other training institutions, or to work done by persons at least 14 years of age in undertakings, where such work is carried out in accordance with conditions prescribed by the competent authority, after consultation with the organisations of employers and workers concerned, where such exist, and is an integral part of—

(a) A course of education or training for which a school or training institution is primarily responsible;
(b) A programme of training mainly or entirely in an undertaking, which programme has been approved by the competent authority; or
(c) A programme of guidance or orientation designed to facilitate the choice of an occupation or of a line of training.

Article 7

1. National laws or regulations may permit the employment or work of persons 13–15 years of age on light work which is—

    (a) Not likely to be harmful to their health or development; and
    (b) Not such as to prejudice their attendance at school, their participation in vocational orientation or training programmes approved by the competent authority or their capacity to benefit from the instruction received.

2. National laws or regulations may also permit the employment or work of persons who are at least 15 years of age but have not yet completed their compulsory schooling on work which meets the requirements set forth in sub-paragraphs (a) and (b) of paragraph 1 of this Article.
3. The competent authority shall determine the activities in which employment or work may be permitted under paragraphs 1 and 2 of this Article and shall prescribe the number of hours during which and the conditions in which such employment or work may be undertaken.
4. Notwithstanding the provisions of paragraphs 1 and 2 of this Article, a Member which has availed itself of the provisions of paragraph 4 of Article 2 may, for as long as it continues to do so, substitute the ages 12 and 14 for the ages 13 and 15 in paragraph 1 and the age 14 for the age 15 in paragraph 2 of this Article.

Article 8

1. After consultation with the organisations of employers and workers concerned, where such exist, the competent authority may, by permits granted in individual cases, allow exceptions to the prohibition of employment or work provided for in Article 2 of this Convention, for such purposes as participation in artistic performances.
2. Permits so granted shall limit the number of hours during which and prescribe the conditions in which employment or work is allowed.

Article 9

1. All necessary measures, including the provision of appropriate penalties, shall be taken by the competent authority to ensure the effective enforcement of the provisions of this Convention.
2. National laws or regulations or the competent authority shall define the persons responsible for compliance with the provisions giving effect to the Convention.
3. National laws or regulations or the competent authority shall prescribe the registers or other documents which shall be kept and made available by the

employer; such registers or documents shall contain the names and ages or dates of birth, duly certified wherever possible, of persons whom he employs or who work for him and who are less than 18 years of age.

Article 10

1. This Convention revises, on the terms set forth in this Article, the Minimum Age (Industry) Convention, 1919, the Minimum Age (Sea) Convention, 1920, the Minimum Age (Agriculture) Convention, 1921, the Minimum Age (Trimmers and Stokers) Convention, 1921, the Minimum Age (Non-Industrial Employment) Convention, 1932, the Minimum Age (Sea) Convention (Revised), 1936, the Minimum Age (Industry) Convention (Revised), 1937, the Minimum Age (Non-Industrial Employment) Convention (Revised), 1937, the Minimum Age (Fishermen) Convention, 1959, and the Minimum Age (Underground Work) Convention, 1965.

2. The coming into force of this Convention shall not close the Minimum Age (Sea) Convention (Revised), 1936, the Minimum Age (Industry) Convention (Revised), 1937, the Minimum Age (Non-Industrial Employment) Convention (Revised), 1937, the Minimum Age (Fishermen) Convention, 1959, or the Minimum Age (Underground Work) Convention, 1965, to further ratification.

3. The Minimum Age (Industry) Convention, 1919, the Minimum Age (Sea) Convention, 1920, the Minimum Age (Agriculture) Convention, 1921, and the Minimum Age (Trimmers and Stokers) Convention, 1921, shall be closed to further ratification when all the parties thereto have consented to such closing by ratification of this Convention or by a declaration communicated to the Director-General of the International Labour Office.

4. When the obligations of this Convention are accepted—

    (a) By a Member which is a party to the Minimum Age (Industry) Convention (Revised), 1937, and a minimum age of not less than 15 years is specified in pursuance of Article 2 of this Convention, this shall ipso jure involve the immediate denunciation of that Convention,

    (b) In respect of non-industrial employment as defined in the Minimum Age (Non-Industrial Employment) Convention, 1932, by a Member which is a party to that Convention, this shall ipso jure involve the immediate denunciation of that Convention,

    (c) In respect of non-industrial employment as defined in the Minimum Age (Non-Industrial Employment) Convention (Revised), 1937, by a Member which is a party to that Convention, and a minimum age of not less than 15 years is specified in pursuance of Article 2 of this Convention, this shall ipso jure involve the immediate denunciation of that Convention,

    (d) In respect of maritime employment, by a Member which is a party to the Minimum Age (Sea) Convention (Revised), 1936, and a minimum age of not less than 15 years is specified in pursuance of Article 2 of this Convention or the Member specifies that Article 3 of this Convention applies to maritime employment, this shall ipso jure involve the immediate denunciation of that Convention,

(e) In respect of employment in maritime fishing, by a Member which is a party to the Minimum Age (Fishermen) Convention, 1959, and a minimum age of not less than 15 years is specified in pursuance of Article 2 of this Convention or the Member specifies that Article 3 of this Convention applies to employment in maritime fishing, this shall ipso jure involve the immediate denunciation of that Convention,

(f) By a Member which is a party to the Minimum Age (Underground Work) Convention, 1965, and a minimum age of not less than the age specified in pursuance of that Convention is specified in pursuance of Article 2 of this Convention or the Member specifies that such an age applies to employment underground in mines in virtue of Article 3 of this Convention, this shall ipso jure involve the immediate denunciation of that Convention,

if and when this Convention shall have come into force.

5. Acceptance of the obligations of this Convention—

(a) Shall involve the denunciation of the Minimum Age (Industry) Convention, 1919, in accordance with Article 12 thereof,

(b) In respect of agriculture shall involve the denunciation of the Minimum Age (Agriculture) Convention, 1921, in accordance with Article 9 thereof,

(c) In respect of maritime employment shall involve the denunciation of the Minimum Age (Sea) Convention, 1920, in accordance with Article 10 thereof, and of the Minimum Age (Trimmers and Stokers) Convention, 1921, in accordance with Article 12 thereof,

if and when this Convention shall have come into force.

Article 11. The formal ratifications of this Convention shall be communicated to the Director-General of the International Labour Office for registration.

Article 12

1. This Convention shall be binding only upon those Members of the International Labour Organisation whose ratifications have been registered with the Director-General.

2. It shall come into force 12 months after the date on which the ratifications of two Members have been registered with the Director-General.

3. Thereafter, this Convention shall come into force for any Member 12 months after the date on which its ratifications has been registered.

Article 13

1. A Member which has ratified this Convention may denounce it after the expiration of 10 years from the date on which the Convention first comes into force, by an act communicated to the Director-General of the International Labour Office for registration. Such denunciation shall not take effect until 1 year after the date on which it is registered.

2. Each Member which has ratified this Convention and which does not, within the year following the expiration of the period of 10 years mentioned in the preceding paragraph, exercise the right of denunciation provided for in this Article, will be bound for another period of 10 years and, thereafter, may denounce this Convention at the expiration of each period of 10 years under the terms provided for in this Article.

Article 14

1. The Director-General of the International Labour Office shall notify all Members of the International Labour Organisation of the registration of all ratifications and denunciations communicated to him by the Members of the Organisation.
2. When notifying the Members of the Organisation of the registration of the second ratification communicated to him, the Director-General shall draw the attention of the Members of the Organisation to the date upon which the Convention will come into force.

Article 15. The Director-General of the International Labour Office shall communicate to the Secretary-General of the United Nations for registration in accordance with Article 102 of the Charter of the United Nations full particulars of all ratifications and acts of denunciation registered by him in accordance with the provisions of the preceding Articles.

Article 16. At such times as it may consider necessary the Governing Body of the International Labour Office shall present to the General Conference a report on the working of this Convention and shall examine the desirability of placing on the agenda of the Conference the question of its revision in whole or in part.

Article 17

1. Should the Conference adopt a new Convention revising this Convention in whole or in part, then, unless the new Convention otherwise provides:

   (a) The ratification by a Member of the new revising Convention shall ipso jure involve the immediate denunciation of this Convention, notwithstanding the provisions of Article 13 above, if and when the new revising Convention shall have come into force;
   (b) As from the date when the new revising Convention comes into force this Convention shall cease to be open to ratification by the Members.

2. This Convention shall in any case remain in force in its actual form and content for those Members which have ratified it but have not ratified the revising Convention.

Article 18. The English and French versions of the text of this Convention are equally authoritative.

Lightning Source UK Ltd.
Milton Keynes UK
UKHW022211270622
405042UK00002B/10